23

# THE

# WORLD
# TODAY

## ITS PEOPLE AND PLACES

# THE
# WORLD
# TODAY
## ITS PEOPLE AND PLACES

**William Norton**

**Michele Visser-Wikkerink**

**Linda Connor**

PORTAGE & MAIN PRESS

Portage & Main Press acknowledges the financial support of the Government of Canada through the Book Publishing Industry Development Program (BPIDP) for our activities.

**Library and Archives Canada Cataloguing in Publication**

Norton, William, 1944-
    The world today: its people and places/William Norton, Michele Visser-Wikkerink, Linda Connor.

ISBN 1-55379-082-0

1. Human geography-Textbooks.   I. Connor, Linda   II. Visser-Wikkerink, Michele   III. Title.

GF41.N673 2006        304.2        C2006-901925-8

Project Coordinator: William Norton
Project Development: Renée Gillis
Editor: Carol Dahlstrom
Proofreader: Leigh Hambly
Production: Marcela Mangarelli
Book and cover design: Relish Design Studio Ltd.
Cartographer: Douglas Fast
Photo Editors: Karen Press and Pat Paige

Printed and bound in Canada by Friesens.

ISBN-13: 978-1-55379-082-2
ISBN-10: 1-55379-082-0

**Acknowledgments**

The publisher would like to thank the following individuals who reviewed the text and illustrations for accuracy and suitability:

David McDowell, University of Winnipeg; Richard Harbeck, University of Manitoba; Christopher Torrance, Grant Park High School; Lorelei Steffler, St. James-Assiniboia School Division.

PORTAGE & MAIN PRESS

100-318 McDermot Ave.
Winnpeg, MB, Canada  R3A 0A2
Tel: 204-987-3500
Toll free: 1-800-667-9673
Toll free fax: 1-866-734-8477
Email: books@portageandmainpress.com

Printed on 30% PCW paper.

# CONTENTS

# THINKING GEOGRAPHICALLY

Have you ever heard of the "six degrees of separation"? This idea claims that everyone in the world knows everyone else within six separate connections: the six degrees of separation. What an intriguing idea! You do the six degrees when you tell people, for example, that you have an uncle who has a friend whose brother's girlfriend is a close personal friend of a famous movie star. (See figure 0.1)

Six degrees of separation becomes an even more interesting idea when it is applied to the **human geography** of our world, and it is an idea that we will enjoy exploring throughout this book: Can you travel around the world with only six connections? Where would those connections be? What are your six degrees of separation? We will encourage you to learn more about some of the interesting places you might visit one day. By developing a travel portfolio, you will be able to imagine what your world trip could look like.

Every life and every place is connected to other lives and other places. Human geographers look for links among people, their environment, and their ways of living and being; they look for links among past, present, and future, and they look for links among countries, continents, and the world. Perhaps you often ask human geographic questions in your everyday life. You might, for example, find yourself asking who made the shirt you are wearing or grew the vegetables you are eating. Asking these

FIGURE 0.1. Chelsea knows Tom, who is friends with Rob. Rob is a cousin to Alisha, who is friends with Amanda. Amanda lives in Los Angeles working as a chef in Kevin Bacon's favourite restaurant.

questions might also make you wonder where those people live, what their world is like, and how they are treated by others.

Human geography and history together make up **social studies**. Social studies looks at humans in their physical, social, and cultural worlds, and examines the past and present while looking to the future. Social studies helps you acquire the skills, knowledge, and values necessary to become an active citizen and a contributing and responsible member of your local, national, and global communities.

**human geography** The study of peoples and places on the surface of the earth

**social studies** The study of people in relation to each other and to the world in which they live.

## How to Use this Book

Besides the introduction and conclusion, there are 20 chapters in this textbook, which are organized into four sections.

Section I describes the earth as a very special planet. If space engineers ever did come up with affordable civilian space travel, what would a trip around the world be like, from a perspective beyond the atmosphere? What would you notice? What would the important characteristics of the earth be, and how would we describe them?

FIGURE 0.2. "It suddenly struck me that that tiny pea, pretty and blue, was the Earth. I put up my thumb and shut one eye, and my thumb blotted out the planet Earth. I didn't feel like a giant. I felt very, very small" (Neil Armstrong, United States astronaut and the first person to walk on the moon, in July 1969).

Section II describes the earth as a village. Because all peoples and places are connected, living on earth is like living in a village. In different parts of this village, people experience life differently. Some people are rich, while others are poor. Some come from homes where they are safe and well-treated. Others experience hurt and abuse. We will investigate reasons for and details of these inequalities, and also discuss what it might mean for our world, our village, to function fairly.

Section III describes the earth as a home. How do people live? What do people look like? What do they eat and drink? What clothing do they wear? What do they appreciate as art? How and what do they celebrate? What do they care about? Who are their neighbours? These questions are considered in this section, with a particular focus on Africa, Asia, and Australasia.

FIGURE 0.3. One world: many people and many places. Left: a Maori man in New Zealand with traditional face painting. Right: a Padaung woman in Myanmar wearing traditional dress.

Section IV describes the earth as potential. We change our environments so that we can live our lives. Some of the changes are needed; for example, we grow crops for food, develop machines that make our work easier, and build shelters so that we have shade in the summer and can keep warm in the winter. Some of these changes damage the environment, and future generations—the children and the grandchildren that you may have some day—will not have the same potential (raw ingredients) for crops, machinery, and shelter as you do. What would it mean for you to be a good global citizen? In this section, these issues are considered with a focus on Europe and the Americas.

FIGURE 0.4. One world: many activities. Top: an oil refinery in North Carolina, U.S.A. Bottom: an open-pit copper mine in Nevada, U.S.A.

## Features of this Book

Let us imagine for a moment that we could get around the world in just a few steps, or that hopping on a plane would be inexpensive, easy, and quick. What would be your choice of destinations, and what would you hope to learn in each place?

 Without the country names included, what does the map in figure 0.5 mean to you? How many countries of the world are you able to identify?

Are you able to locate the four countries shown in the photographs on this page? Don't worry. By the time you and your teacher have completed work with this textbook, you will know not only the names of many of these countries but also quite a lot about the people and places in them.

FIGURE 0.6. Clockwise from top left: Taj Mahal, Agra, India; Sydney Harbour Bridge and Sydney Opera House, Sydney, Australia; Statue of Christ, Rio de Janeiro, Brazil; Eiffel Tower, Paris, France

### Countries of the World

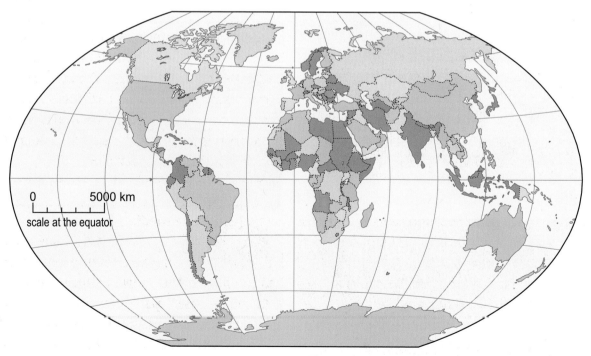

FIGURE 0.5. This map, showing the political boundaries of the countries of the world, is the one that most of us picture in our minds when we think about the world. This is the first of many maps in this book that show the whole world, and you will note that none of them includes a north arrow and some do not include a key. The reasons for not including these features are explained toward the end of chapter 1.

As you read through this book, look for five icons. They guide you to further learning adventures, discussion topics, media investigations, opportunities for development of skills, informative Internet sites, and more.

**The World Traveller icon** appears when selected countries or regions are mentioned. You might choose to include some of these locations in your travel portfolio.

**The Speaker's Corner icon** appears when there is a question for group or class discussion and/or debate.

**The Social Studies Skills icon** highlights tools and strategies used by geographers and other social scientists to help them understand people and places around the world.

**The Internet Site icon** points to the website that accompanies this book. The site includes updates on topics and interesting links to Internet sources. This icon draws your attention to web-based research. The address is <www.theworldtoday.ca>.

**The Media Literacy icon** appears along with a suggestion to analyze current events. What's in the news? What's in the newspaper? Why do sources use a particular vocabulary to describe various people, places, and events? This icon will remind you that it's important to think about your sources and the way they report the news.

# What in the World?

When you hear the word *geography*, what do you think about? Globes, maps, textbooks, quizzes maybe, might come to mind. But geography is much more than any one of these. Geographers describe and analyze the world, and to do this they ask and answer three questions. Reflect on these three questions throughout this book.

1. What is where?—the basic task: Geographers ask the basic question Where? Obviously, our world is different from country to country and region to region. Learning geography means learning about the physical world: the natural features. The physical world includes the distribution of land and water, climate and weather characteristics, and different landforms. Learning geography also means learning about the human world: the people and the places they live. A study of the human world includes a consideration of how we adapt to and change the physical world, how we make our living, how we communicate with other people, what we eat and drink, how we spend our leisure time, and what we believe.

2. Why there?—seeking explanations: Geographers explain the basic facts of geography—for example, why rivers, farms, and cities are where they are. This often means connecting one part of geography to another. For instance, understanding differences between soils on the Canadian prairie and soils in tropical Africa requires that a person know about temperature and precipitation (rain and snow). Understanding the **location** of a shopping mall requires that a person know about road networks and where people live in relation to them.

> "There are no passengers on spaceship earth. We are all crew" (Marshall McLuhan, 1911–1980, Canadian scholar).

3. Why care?—a practical subject: Why should you care about geography? Geography matters when you need to get to school from home, when you decide where to shop, and when you decide whether to spend an afternoon in February skiing or surfing. Many of our daily decisions are based on the geography of where we live. Did you wear a parka or a tee-shirt to school this morning? Did you wear a parka six months ago?

**Geography Defined** Greek scholars were the first to use the word *geography*, about 2 200 years ago. *Geo* refers to the earth, while *graphy* means writing about or drawing. Very simply, then, *geography* means "writing about the earth." One of the easiest ways of writing about the earth is to use maps, and maps are geographers' favourite tools. For a geographer, a good map is worth a thousand words. Maps provide facts and help answer the question Where? Geography deals with not just one kind of subject matter but, rather, with two different, but closely related, types of subject matter: physical geography and human geography. This textbook is about human geography: the human world. However, as you study human geography, you will see that human and physical worlds are closely related; therefore, the physical world is a very important part of our study. A glacier and a shopping centre are two entirely different things, but we can use the same three questions to study them: What is where? Why there? Why care?

**location** A specific position on the surface of the earth.

## Growing Season and Population Density in Canada

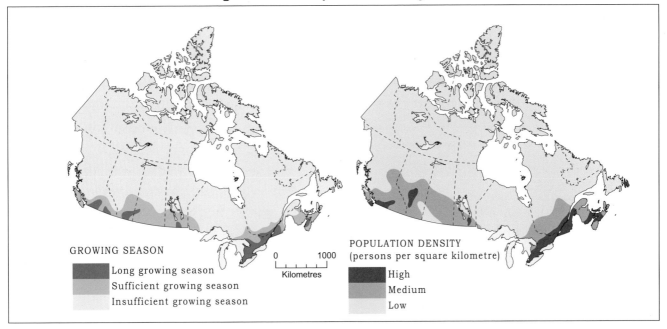

GROWING SEASON

- ■ Long growing season
- ■ Sufficient growing season
- ■ Insufficient growing season

POPULATION DENSITY
(persons per square kilometre)

- ■ High
- ■ Medium
- ■ Low

0   1000
Kilometres

**FIGURE 0.7. Left: where we are able to farm in Canada. Right: where we live in Canada.**

Figure 0.7 helps highlight our three questions:

1. The map on the left shows differences in the length of the **growing season** (crops do not usually grow when the temperature falls below 5°C). The map on the right shows the population **distribution** and **density** (where people live and how many people live there). Together, these two maps answer the question What is where? Where is it warmer? Where is it colder? Where is it easiest to grow food? Where are the people living?

2. When we look at the two maps, we can answer the question Why there? They show that the two distribution patterns are closely related and, specifically, that the longer the growing season, the more people will live there.

3. The two distribution patterns shown on the maps really do matter. They show us why we should care. Understanding climate helps a farmer decide when to plant a crop, what to plant, and when to harvest, for example.

Understanding population distribution and density helps governments, city planners, and businesses decide where to build roads, what

services to offer, and where to establish new industries. It is why you often notice fast-food outlets close to high schools and convenience stores close to bus stops.

**density** Refers generally to the frequency of a geographic fact within a unit of area—how many cases there are (e.g., a house, a farm, or a factory).

**distribution** Refers generally to the spatial pattern or spread of a geographic fact—where things are.

**growing season** That part of the year when temperatures are hot enough to allow plants to grow (for most plants this is about 5°C).

 Think about the best possible places in Canada to establish the following activities: grain farming, making wine, starting a remote-adventure-travel company, building a mega-mall, skiing, starting a fishing camp. Discuss your responses with classmates.

## Space and Time in Geography

Geographers often say that their approach to studying physical and human facts is **spatial**—that is, they look at how space is occupied. For example, there is a spatial distribution of furniture in a classroom (each piece of furniture is located in a particular place). In geography, the spatial viewpoint refers to the location of all things on the surface of the earth, whether they occur naturally (such as mountains) or are made by humans (such as houses). History uses a **temporal**, or time-related, approach. Historians look at people, events, and places in the past and study how these have changed through time.

Although human geography is mostly concerned with the spatial viewpoint, the temporal viewpoint is also used because the facts of human geography change constantly. For example:

- Political boundaries are adjusted. In 1991, the Soviet Union was divided into several new countries. In 1999, the eastern boundary of the Northwest Territories was changed to create Nunavut.

- People move from one house, neighbourhood, region, province, or country to another.

- Cities change. Downtown areas are rebuilt, farmland is replaced by suburbs, bridges are built to connect parts of the city that were separated by rivers or rail yards.

- Rural areas and small towns may lose people as cities expand. The town of Lynn Lake lost much population when the mine—the primary employer in the remote northern Manitoba town—closed. If a new precious metal were discovered there, the population would probably grow again.

**spatial** Refers to space on the surface of the earth.

**temporal** Refers to time.

 Look at figure 0.9 and notice what kinds of changes have occurred between 1965 and 2006. List three reasons showing how the changes may have occurred. Why might these changes matter to people? Discuss your thoughts with classmates. Will there be changes in the future? Why or why not? Are there any examples of cities that had NHL teams after 1965 but lost them before 2006?

FIGURE 0.8. An abandoned mining town in the mountain region of the American West. Often known as ghost towns, such places reflect the fact that the human geography of the world is always changing.

**Spatial and Temporal** The term *spatial* describes the arrangement of things—for example, in your bedroom there may be a bed in one place and a bookshelf in another. The term *temporal* describes the changes that have occurred over time—for example, you may not want to wear the jeans you wore last summer. A spatial viewpoint describes a space; a temporal viewpoint describes changes over time.

Human geographers use maps like the one shown in figure 0.9 to explain what changes occur and why they occurred. This map shows the location of National Hockey League (NHL) teams in 1965 and 2006. The two patterns are very different. Geographers use the spatial viewpoint to explain where the hockey teams are located in 1965 and in 2006. They use the temporal viewpoint to explain the change.

Do you agree that places and the people who live there are always changing? Get your geographic imagination going! Reading this textbook will help you discover how you can use geography to understand the changing peoples and places of the world. Look outside your classroom window and imagine how the spot you are looking at may have changed over the past 200 years. Could the area have been forested? Then could it have been farmed? Then could it have been subdivided into residential lots? What might it look like next year or in 50 years' time? What were the people who lived here in the past like, and who might live here in the future?

## The Changing Location of NHL Teams in North America

FIGURE 0.9. Cities with NHL teams in 1965 and in 2006. Note that the 1965 teams are all present also in 2006.

# The Five Themes of Geography

As you develop your geographic imagination, you will discover more about the following five geographic themes: location, place, humans and environments, movement and globalization, and region.

## Theme 1: Location

Where is it? Geographers answer this question in four ways:

1. Absolute location: Your house has an address: a number, a street name, a town, a province, and a country. This does not change, and neither does **absolute location**. Geographers use a method that allows them to give each place on earth an address. Latitude and longitude refer to a grid system, or system of intersecting lines, created to help us map absolute locations. This system, and how to use it, is explained in chapter 1.

2. Relative location: If someone needed to find your house, you might tell that person your address, but to further explain how to find the house, you might say that it is close to the hospital, or the library, or the church with the tall spire on the corner of your street. This is its **relative location**.

3. Site: The **site** characteristics of your school grounds might include flat and poorly drained land. Winnipeg's site characteristics

### Selected Geographic Features of Africa

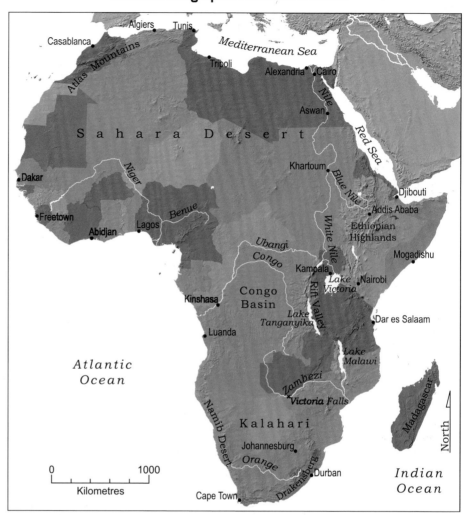

FIGURE 0.10. This map shows political boundaries and identifies some of the principal rivers, mountains, towns, and other geographic features of Africa.

include the confluence, or meeting (the Forks), of the Red and Assiniboine rivers.

4. Situation: The **situation** characteristics of your school grounds might include being close to a major highway, a convenience store, and a public park. Winnipeg's situational characteristics include the Red River flood plain, which is suitable for farming.

 Look at figure 0.10 and write one or two sentences about the relative location of five of the named geographic features. For instance, you could say that Cape Town is at the very southwestern tip of the continent of Africa.

**Absolute and Relative Locations** Look around your classroom. Your absolute location in the class might be first row, fourth from the front, while your relative location is close to the window and beside your best friend. The absolute location of your school might be 25 Scholar Drive, while the relative location might be close to the sewage treatment plant. The absolute location of Manitoba can be described in latitude and longitude, but you might say it is east of Saskatchewan and north of North Dakota.

**absolute location** Refers to precisely where a place is on the surface of the earth.

**relative location** Describes a place in relation to other places.

**site** Refers to the ground the location occupies—for example, to the relationship between a building or activity and the immediate physical and human environment. Site is "vertical."

**situation** Refers to regional interdependencies —for example, to the relationship between a building or activity and the surrounding physical and human environment. Situation is "horizontal."

## Theme 2: Place

What is it like there? When geographers describe a part of the surface of the earth, they are describing a place. The difference between *location* and *place* is that *location* refers to where something is, and *place* describes that location. Geographic descriptions of places may focus on physical characteristics, human characteristics, or both. What are some of these physical and human characteristics?

1. Physical characteristics include geographic facts like temperature, precipitation, landforms, drainage, soil type, plants, and animals. Few, if any, places on earth

This is the church where my parents got married. They tell the story that it was a really hot summer day and all the doors were left open to let in the breeze. It didn't help much— my dad passed out in the heat and they had to stop the service until he felt better.

We've fished at this lake since I was little. It used to be really remote—no campsites, no bathrooms . . . we'd put all our gear in a canoe and not see anyone else for a week. It's more popular there now, and last time we went, there was another family on the other side of the inlet. We'll probably paddle further next year.

**FIGURE 0.11. The power of place.**

consist of only physical characteristics, because humans affect most places around the world either directly (because they live there) or indirectly (because air pollution might drift to a sparsely inhabited place such as the Arctic, for example).

2. Human characteristics include geographic facts like population distribution and density, settlement of rural and urban areas, economic activities (like agriculture and industry), and communication lines (such as roads and railways). These human characteristics are all geographic facts of a place that have been added to the physical characteristics already there naturally. Geographers study the people who live in places and include language, religion, and ethnic identity as part of their study.

Geographers are not the only people who describe places. Novelists, poets, artists, and even dancers can describe places. They often highlight what makes a place distinctive.

Places mean something to us. Houses are not just buildings; they are also homes. Mosques, churches, temples, and shrines mean something to the people who worship in them. For some people, a shopping mall, restaurant, or park may have significant meaning, perhaps because of something that happened there. Places are much more than just their human and physical characteristics.

 Many of us use the word *place* on a regular basis. Consider the following phrases and reflect with classmates on how each of them could show whether the word *place* is or is not being used in a geographical sense. Do you sometimes use these phrases? List three other everyday phrases that use the word *place*.

- I put her in her place.

- I feel out of place.

- A place for everything, and everything in its place.

- This is my kind of place.

## Theme 3: Humans and Environments

How do humans and their environments relate? Geography deals with both the physical and human characteristics of places, and the two are often studied together. People are both adapting to and changing their environments all the time.

Here are five questions that geographers use to help focus on human and environment relationships—that is, how people interact with their physical surroundings.

1. Why do humans live where they do? Why do they grow crops, raise animals, or build cities where they do? How is it that some places are well-suited for one activity or lifestyle and others are more suitable for another?

2. How do people affect their physical environment? Is their effect positive or negative? Are some changes positive in one respect and negative in another?

3. In what ways do humans change their environments to make them easier to live in? Do humans change their environments to "suit themselves"?

4. In what ways do humans depend on physical environments? What do we mean when we talk about **natural resources**?

5. Does the environment influence humans? People who live in different environments live different lifestyles. Does this mean that environments influence our lives and characters? Or is it better to think of humans as choosing to adapt to environments?

 Write a paragraph or a poem about a place that has meaning to you. Bring to class a photograph, or draw a picture of the place you are describing.

FIGURE 0.12. Left: a pleasant and well-maintained residential neighbourhood typical of a Canadian suburban area. Right: a barely livable Brazilian slum typical of the outskirts of urban areas in the less-developed world.

These questions are discussed throughout this book, but it is a good idea to start thinking about them now. Let us simplify and rewrite the five questions for your local circumstances.

1. Why is your city, town, or farm located where it is? Why is the area that you live in urban or agricultural?

2. What do you and your neighbours do that affects the physical environment? Are your effects positive or negative?

3. In what ways do you and your neighbours change the local environment to make it easier to live in?

4. In what ways do you and your neighbours depend on the physical environment, locally and elsewhere?

5. Are you influenced by the environment (it is minus 40°C, therefore you *have* to wear a winter coat), or do you choose to adapt to the environment (it is minus 40°C, therefore you *choose* to wear a winter coat)?

 Write down possible answers to the five questions listed above. Discuss your answers with classmates. Is everyone in agreement?

**natural resources** All the resources of use to humans that are produced by the earth's natural processes. Includes air, soil, fossil fuels, minerals, plants, and animals.

 Look at the two pictures on this page and consider possible answers to the following seven questions. Present your answers in two columns: one for the Canadian location and one for the Brazilian location. Discuss your answers with classmates.

1. What aspects of the physical environment—such as climate, vegetation, slopes, and drainage—are evident in the photos?

2. Why might these areas be suitable for building homes? Do the homes look permanent or temporary?

3. Look at the building materials used. Do you think that these have been locally obtained, or might they have come from far away?

4. What might be some negative effects from building homes in these areas?

5. How have residents changed their environments? What do you think might have been here before homes were built?

6. Will people living in these areas be able to cope with extreme weather, such as unusual heat or cold, heavy rain, or snowfall?

7. Make a list of the kinds of waste materials that people living in these areas might produce. How will the waste material be disposed of?

## Theme 4: Movement and Globalization

How do geographic facts interact? Places and the people who live in these places do not exist in separate, unrelated worlds. They interact in many different ways; they connect and cross. A fundamental geographic fact is that all of us are affected by the lives and actions of others— we are part of the global village. Here are three examples of geographic movement:

1. People move from place to place as part of their everyday lives. In some cases, people even move from one country to another. Approximately 3 percent of the people in the world do not live in the country of their birth.

2. The goods that people produce move from place to place. Next time you go to the grocery store, ask yourself where some of the foods and other products came from and how they might have arrived on those shelves. Because we are now able to move goods quickly and efficiently, items that were impossible to get 50 years ago are now part of our daily lives. If you enjoy strawberries in a Manitoba winter, consider what technology is needed to make it possible to import them.

3. Ideas move from place to place. Several of the major world religions had their origin in a particular place but are now dispersed throughout the world. Consider the effect of technological changes on the movement of ideas, from the printing press through to the development of the Internet.

Movement requires a means and a system of transportation. *Means* refers to the actual manner of movement: walking, for example, or using animals, boats, trains, automobiles, trucks, and planes. *System* refers to what these conveyances travel on: paths, rivers and seas, rail lines, roads, and air routes.

FIGURE 0.13. These two photographs are early examples of developments in communication technologies. Left: an early-16th-century printing press. Right: a late-19th-century desk telephone.

One word captures the role played by movement in our present-day world: *globalization*. We see the consequences of **globalization** in two general ways. Together, they further develop the concept of the *global village*.

1. Parts of the world that used to be completely separate are increasingly connected because of ease of travel, the Internet, and freer trade among countries. As we will explore in later chapters, however, the economic, cultural, and political consequences of this trend are not yet fully understood.

2. Many differences from place to place are being erased, especially because of the expansion of what might be called the *Western influence*, which includes the spread of the English language and some American cultural preferences, such as fast food, for example. Again, the implications of this are still not yet fully understood.

One result of globalization is very clear: we are more aware than ever that we all live in one shared place: our home, the earth.

**globalization** Changes in global economy, culture, and politics brought about mainly by new communication technologies.

**global village** Term coined by Canadian scholar Marshall McLuhan (1911–1980). Refers to the ever-increasing links between people and places that are, perhaps, resulting in the replacement of many local cultures by a single global culture.

### Global Village Fusion Noodles

(Warning: contains nuts)

**In large frying pan or wok, sauté:**

30 ml oil

1 onion, finely chopped or
    crushed in food processor

1 clove garlic, crushed

15 ml fresh ginger, finely chopped

5 ml hot pepper flakes (more if you like it hot)

**Add:**

120 ml peanut butter

30 ml brown sugar

45 ml lemon juice

5 ml coriander and one sprinkle of cinnamon

1 can coconut milk

Remove from heat. Add water if too thick, or add peanut butter if too thin. Boil 450 grams of your favourite pasta according to package directions. Steam 700 to 950 ml of your favourite vegetables until tender crisp. Toss pasta, sauce, and vegetables together. Sprinkle with peanuts and raisins.

FIGURE 0.14. Top: a refugee camp on the border of Kenya and Somalia in East Africa. Bottom: a Kentucky Fried Chicken restaurant in Nanking, China.

 See if you can find out how many countries are represented in the ingredients of the recipe for global village fusion noodles.

 Using the two photographs in figure 0.14 to assist your thinking, list three reasons showing that the idea of the global village is meaningful. List three reasons showing that the idea of the global village might be misleading. For instance, do you think the people living in a refugee camp are aware of the *global village* concept?

## Theme 5: Region

To make sense of a world that is made up of many different peoples and places, with different physical and human geographies, geographers often choose to divide the world into smaller, more manageable, units for study. But how is this done? Often, the closer locations are to each other, the more similar they are. Because of this, geographers are able to impose some order on our world by classifying locations that are close to each other and similar to each other as **regions**.

**The Six Regions of Canada**

FIGURE 0.15. This map shows one generally accepted regionalization of Canada.

---

**region** An area on the surface of the earth distinguished from other areas by some physical and/or human characteristic(s). Regions are parts of the surface of the earth defined by one or more unifying characteristics.

---

Just as oranges are packaged with oranges or apples with apples, like locations are "packaged" together by geographers. This is known as *regionalizing*. For example, we might identify or package regions according to average winter temperatures, amount of rainfall, what kinds of plants are grown there, what language is spoken by the people living there, or what religion is practised.

Remember that identifying regions is just a tool to help us do geography and not an end in itself. There is no one correct set of regions, and the boundaries and characteristics of a region that a geographer identifies may change from time to time.

 Figure 0.15 uses provincial and territorial boundaries to divide Canada into regions. Does the division of the six regions make sense to you? Suggest some other ways of regionalizing Canada (e.g., French/ English, urban/rural).

"A journey of a thousand miles begins with a single step" (Confucius, 551–479 BCE, Chinese philosopher).

Identify the photo in figure 0.16 that shows the physical or human geography found in each of the six regions of Canada.

d.

a.

e.

b.

f.

FIGURE 0.16. Images of the six geographic regions of Canada.

c.

ANSWERS

a) Atlantic Canada
b) Quebec
c) Ontario
d) Western Canada
e) Territorial North
f) British Columbia

# The Tools of the Geographer

## Tools for Collecting, Organizing, and Displaying

Geographers must be able to collect, organize, and display facts in order to answer the question Where? Travel and fieldwork are often basic to a geographer's work. For much of history, the only way for geographers to discover the world was to travel the world, and many explorers, such as Samuel de Champlain (1567–1635) and James Cook (1728–1779), were geographers as well. They observed and recorded a lot of information about the places and peoples they visited. Geographers are explorers today, travelling locally and globally.

Geographers also acquire facts using censuses and other statistical information. They sometimes distribute questionnaires and interview people, study maps that others have prepared, or study photographs taken by others.

Increasingly common are **remote sensing** technologies: aerial photography and satellite imagery, for example. Aerial photography uses film to record parts of the earth's surface, while satellites orbit the earth and use sensors to scan the earth's surface and transmit data back to computers. Both technologies are helpful for displaying geographic changes through time, such as crop growth, forest removal, and urban expansion.

Once geographic facts have been acquired, they can be organized and displayed in a number of ways: by writing, by using tables and graphs, and especially by mapping. While maps cannot provide the whole picture, they are useful for showing us part of the picture.

> **remote sensing** Observation and measurement of the surface of the earth through use of aircraft and satellites. Sensors include photographic and radar images.

In the Cree language, *Win* means dirty, *Nipi* means water

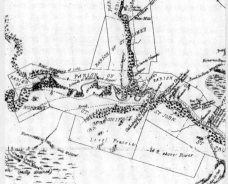

| Winnipeg: | |
|---|---|
| Population in 2001 | 619 544 |
| Population in 1996 | 618 477 |
| 1996 to 2001 population change | 0.2 % |
| Land area | 465.16 sq km |

**FIGURE 0.17.** Six examples of geographic data that provide information about Winnipeg. Top left: an 1881 bird's-eye-view sketch. Bottom left: part of an 1858 map. Centre (from top to bottom): reference to the meaning of the place name Winnipeg, a current photograph, and some data from the 2001 census. Top right: part of a 1963 aerial photograph.

The word *cartography* comes from the French word *carte,* which means "card" or "map," and the Greek word *graphy,* which means "to draw" or "write." Therefore, a cartographer is one who draws maps. When a cartographer sets out to make a map, she needs to decide many things. What is the map supposed to tell the reader? Is it supposed to display regional boundaries, political boundaries, climate distinctions, population distribution and density? It is also necessary to make a decision about **scale**.

**cartography** The art and science of map-making.

**scale** Refers to the ratio between actual kilometres and what you see on the map.

For a map to be useful, the scale must be noted. When a map needs to represent a small area, the scale might be 1 centimetre to 1 kilometre. This is known as a large scale. When a map needs to represent a large area, such as the entire world, the scale might be 1 centimetre to 100 000 kilometres. This is known as a small scale, because, in order to fit all the information on the map, it needs to be drawn much smaller. In other words, when the space represented on a map is small, the scale is large. When the space represented on a map is large, the scale is small. There is no right or wrong scale, only a most useful scale for the subject matter referred to in the map.

 The two maps shown in figure 0.18 are drawn at different scales, but the centre point of each map shows the same place in the Red River Valley of Manitoba. What are the advantages and disadvantages of each particular scale chosen? How would you use each map?

**Mapping Morris, Manitoba**

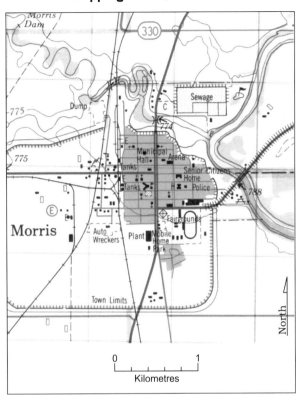

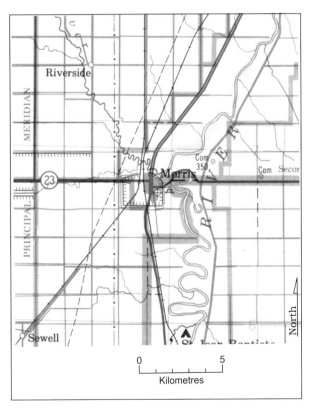

FIGURE 0.18. Mapping Morris, Manitoba, at two different scales. Top is at a scale of 1:50 000 and bottom is at a scale of 1:250 000.

## Tools for Analyzing

In order to answer the questions Why there? and Why care?, geographers need to analyze and discover the importance of the facts that are collected, organized, and displayed. Two things are clear:

1. The facts that interest geographers usually form some sort of pattern. They are not random. And they usually make sense. Geographers describe these as **spatial patterns**. A spatial pattern might show a connection between bodies of water (lakes and seas) and temperature, or between temperature and where people choose to live.

## Communication Lines and Landforms

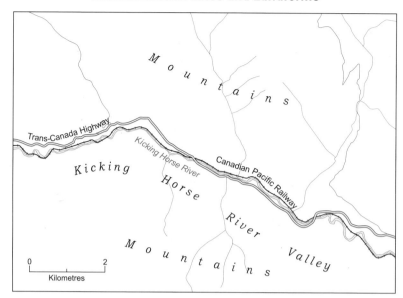

FIGURE 0.19. Communication lines and landforms in the Kicking Horse River Valley east of Golden, British Columbia. Note that the railway and road follow the same route through the mountains as does the river.

2. The patterns noted are caused by something, and geographers want to find out that cause. They want to understand why things are the way they are. Why is winter rainy and warmer in Vancouver and sunny and colder in Winnipeg?

When we analyze geographic facts, we uncover spatial patterns and determine relationships between two or more patterns. One popular way of comparing spatial patterns is to place one map on top of another and then observe the similarities and differences in patterns between the two. For instance, if you place a map of landforms over a map of communication lines, you can learn about where people build communication lines and how this relates to landforms.

A newer way of finding spatial patterns is through use of a **geographic information system**, or GIS. Geographers use the GIS to answer the question Why there? As spatial relationships among patterns are uncovered, geographers can ask why the relationship matters, or Why care? For instance, if a relationship is discovered among economic status, vehicle use, and air pollution, a geographer can ask Why is it happening there? Why should we care?

**geographic information system** Computer software used to capture, store, transform, analyze, and display geographic facts.

**spatial patterns** The distribution of a geographic fact or facts in an area. Spatial patterns usually are either (1) uniform, with facts spaced out evenly throughout an area, or (2) clustered, with facts located as close together as is possible within an area.

 Give one example of a geographic fact that might be located in an area in a uniform pattern, and suggest why. Give one example of a geographic fact that might be located in an area in a clustered pattern, and suggest why.

 List some television shows that use a GIS. Compare your list to those prepared by classmates.

## Using a GIS

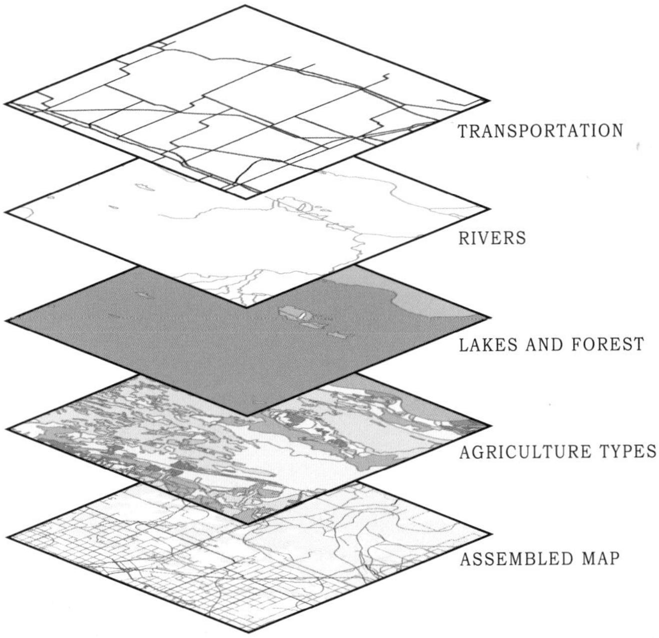

TRANSPORTATION

RIVERS

LAKES AND FOREST

AGRICULTURE TYPES

ASSEMBLED MAP

FIGURE 0.20. This simplified diagram suggests how different layers of geographic data are added together in a GIS to produce a finished map that includes all of the layers of data.

### Some Uses for a GIS

- monitoring and managing agricultural activities
- monitoring and managing climate change, air quality, and water quality
- identifying environmental hazards
- helping emergency-service vehicles use the best route
- planning, locating, and managing utilities like water, sewer lines, and electricity
- mapping property values

 Look at figure 0.20, which shows how several different patterns, or layers, of geographic facts can be superimposed. With reference to any one of the applications listed above, or any other possible application of your choosing, draw a similar diagram that includes the relevant layers of geographic data.

## Enriching Our Lives

Geography is, quite literally, all around us. In our 21st-century world, many of us have access to faraway places through television, the Internet, and travel. But geography is, of course, also right outside our doors. When we hear about a disaster such as an earthquake or flood in another part of the world, a geographic awareness helps us understand the people and places in the news, and can even help us contribute to solving problems. Studying geography helps us live better lives. It teaches us how to respect and value human diversity, take care of the environment, and understand connections between people and the physical world. Having a good geographic imagination helps us be better citizens and global neighbours.

 By yourself, finish the following sentence in five ways:
Geography is the study of . . .
Discuss your five responses with a small group or with the class. Remember, the best way to define geography is to answer these three questions:

1. What is where?

2. Why there?

3. Why care?

By asking and answering What is where? Why there? and Why care? you gain a better understanding of the world around you and your place within it. Thinking geographically really does make a difference; it helps you become a better citizen, locally, nationally, and globally. When you recognize that everyone else living in the world is a neighbour to whom you are connected, perhaps very closely, you will be able to care for your global village and its inhabitants responsibly and reliably. Geography helps you become an informed and responsible citizen.

# DESCRIBING THIS PLANET

It really is quite remarkable that we live on a planet that is, as far as we know, unlike any other, in that it is able to support life. Knowing some facts about the physical and human geography of the planet we live on is essential to understanding the detailed discussions of peoples and places that are included in this book. Section I provides those physical and human geographic facts. Here we show the big picture, and the details will follow later.

Chapter 1 lays out the basic facts about the shape of the earth, how to determine direction and location, measure time, and represent the earth on globes and maps. Together, these facts introduce the language used by geographers as they write about the world.

Chapter 2 focusses on global physical geography as it relates to human activities.

There are accounts of the distribution of land and water, the identification of continents, surface shapes and landforms, rivers and lakes, and climate and weather. The chapter concludes with a general description of places that have similar environments. We call these places *physical geographic regions,* or *global environmental regions*.

In chapter 3 you discover key facts about the number of people living on earth, in the past, present, and possible future. There is a description of the parts of the earth where many people choose to live and of the parts of the earth where few people choose to live. We introduce the complex relationships between people and their environments and explore the very important human geographic fact that our world is divided into more- and less-developed regions.

"Touch the earth, love the earth, honour the earth, her plains, her valleys, her hills, and her seas; rest your spirit in her solitary places" (Plato, ca. 427–347 BCE, Greek philosopher).

"Keep your eyes on the stars, and your feet on the ground" (Alfred North Whitehead, 1861–1947, British mathematician and philosopher).

"I'm grateful for the opportunity to live on this beautiful and astonishing planet Earth. In the morning, I wake up with a sense of gratitude" (Earl Nightingale, 1921–1989, American philosopher).

 Use the Internet to learn more about the authors of the three quotes included on this page.

# WHERE IN THE WORLD

## Guiding Questions

1. What shape is the earth, and how are geographers able to determine direction on the surface of the earth?

2. How do geographers determine location on the surface of the earth?

3. What system has been developed to enable us to know what time it is regardless of where we are on the surface of the earth?

4. What methods are used to allow us to represent the earth at a smaller, more manageable scale?

5. What are some of the advantages and disadvantages of globes and of maps of the world?

**Middle Ages** Lasted about 1 000 years from the fall of Rome in the 5th century CE to the Renaissance, in the 15th century CE. The middle period in a division of European history into Classical, Middle Ages, and Modern.

**Eratosthenes** (pronounced Air-a-*toss*-thin-ees, 276–194 BCE) was smart enough to figure out the circumference of the earth in about 200 BCE (2 200 years ago). He also catalogued over 600 stars, figured out why the Nile flooded, and made advances in mathematics theory that are still in use today. Too bad he was under-appreciated and thought of as second best. His nickname was *Beta*, which means "second," because, while he did well in many fields, he never took top prize. (*Beta* is the second letter in the Greek alphabet.) He went blind in his old age, and some say he ended his life by starving himself.

## A Spherical Earth

Although some ancient Greek scholars believed that the earth was a sphere, in the **Middle Ages** most people believed that the earth was flat and that the stars and sun revolved around the earth. During the Middle Ages, the round-earth theory began to catch on, accompanied by a new belief that the earth was not the centre of the universe. This theory was scandalous at first, but it became widely acknowledged and is now acknowledged as scientific fact.

### Dimensions of the Earth

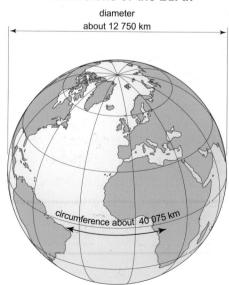

diameter about 12 750 km

circumference about 40 075 km

FIGURE 1.1. The earth is a medium-sized planet with a diameter of about 12 750 km and a circumference of about 40 075 km.

Interestingly, while the earth is a sphere, it is not perfectly round. Because the earth spins on its axis (around and around like a basketball spinning on a finger), it is slightly flattened at the top and the bottom. This happens to any sphere that spins, and the shape is called an *oblate ellipsoid*.

### The Shape of the Earth

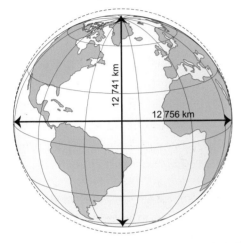

FIGURE 1.2. Our planet departs from a perfect spherical shape, as is shown in this diagram. Note that the distance from top to bottom is about 15 km less than the distance from side to side.

Another fact that makes the earth interesting is that its surface is not perfectly flat. The vertical distance between the peak of the highest mountain (Mt. Everest, at 8 847 metres above sea level) and the deepest ocean location (Challenger Deep in the Pacific Ocean, at 11 033 metres below sea level) is 19 880 metres—almost 20 kilometres. If the earth were the size of a basketball, this difference would translate into a little less than half a millimetre.

 List three things that would be very different in our world if the earth were perfectly smooth. Discuss your list with classmates. Don't forget to consider climate and wind patterns as well as landforms.

FIGURE 1.3. Left: On top of the world—Mt. Everest in the Himalaya Mountain Range. Right: The depths—the land surface of the earth is more than 11 000 m below the waves in the part of the Pacific Ocean known as Challenger Deep.

### Oblate Ellipsoid Chocolate Chip Cookies

Stir together:

| 120 ml shortening |
| 120 ml brown sugar |
| 50 ml white sugar |
| 5 ml vanilla extract |
| 1 egg |

Mix together:

| 240 ml flour |
| 5 ml baking soda |
| 2.5 ml salt |

Stir flour and shortening mixtures together, then add 120 ml plus 30 ml chocolate chips. Chill dough for a while. Use approximately 30ml dough per cookie, and shape into perfect spheres. Place on lightly greased cookie sheet. Flatten gently until they resemble oblate ellipsoids. Bake at 160°C for 10 minutes or until they have spread and are lightly browned. Cool on cookie sheet. Enjoy!

**Planetary Personals** Medium-sized planet seeks sun for warm relationship. If you are flaming hot with a good gravitational pull, this attractive, water-loving, almost perfectly round sphere just may be for you. Write via the Milky Way.

## Direction

Let us say that your family has chosen somewhere to spend your vacation, and you are about to leave from your home. Everyone is excited because you are going somewhere interesting. And then you realize that the driver does not know how to get there. Anyone who has ever been a passenger in a car with a driver who is lost and does not want to ask directions knows how important direction is. *Location* and *direction* are important geographical concepts.

FIGURE 1.4. Where in the world are we?

Because the earth spins on its axis, geographers can establish two key locations, known as **poles**: the North Pole and the South Pole. These two points are **antipodes**. Geographers also divide the earth halfway between the two poles, at the **equator**. North as a direction always faces the North Pole and south as a direction always faces the South Pole. East and west are the perpendicular directions to north and south.

**antipodes** A pair of points that are on opposite sides of a planet.

**equator** The line of fastest rotation on the earth. It is a full circumference, located midway between the poles.

**poles** The two ends of the axis around which the earth rotates (North Pole and South Pole).

### Direction on the Surface of the Earth

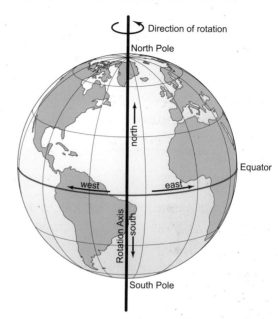

FIGURE 1.5. This diagram identifies directions (north, south, east, and west) on the surface of the earth as they relate to the axis of rotation of the earth and to the direction of rotation.

### A Compass Rose

FIGURE 1.6. The compass rose has been included on maps since at least the 1300s. The term *rose* comes from the compass points, which resemble the petals of the flower. This compass rose shows 16 directions.

## Rotation

What is the earth's axis? It is an imaginary line that goes through the centre of the earth between the North Pole and the South Pole. The earth always spins the same way, in an eastward direction. This is why the sun always "rises" in the east. Here is another way to think about axial rotation: if you were able to float above the North Pole, you would see the earth spinning counter-clockwise. Would it look the same over the South Pole?

## Night and Day

One full rotation of the earth on its axis defines one of the most basic measures of time: the 24-hour day. This axial rotation results in a dark phase and a light phase: night and day. Virtually every living thing has adapted to this cycle, including humans, and it is difficult to imagine life without night and day.

## Up and Down

North is often thought of as up, while south is thought of as down. But the terms *up* and *down* are simply how we choose to think about our world. Just as correct, although less usual, would be a map that places south at the top and north at the bottom.

## So What?

Imagine that, after you met someone, all you said was, "We'll meet again." You gave no hint of the time or place. You might bump into each other some time in the future, but if you really

had wanted to get together, you would have arranged a time and a place.

All of these—north/south, east/west, night/day, up/down—give us reference points for place and time. We can more easily figure out where we need to go and how we need to get there when we understand direction and location.

 Discuss how your world is connected to the rhythms of night and day. What would it be like to be in a place that lacked night and day? Do you know anyone who regularly works night shifts? What is this schedule like for them?

**Night and Day** Maybe having night and day is a good thing. Statistics Canada has reported that men who worked an evening or a rotating shift were more likely to report stress, relationship problems, and feelings that they lacked control over their lives. As well, 45 percent of men working an evening shift were daily smokers, compared with 27 percent of daytime workers.

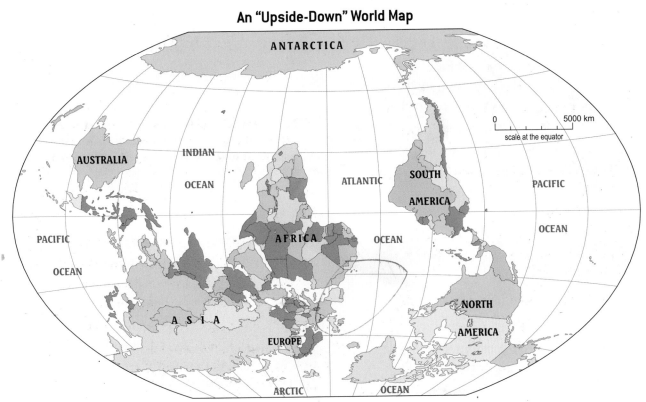

FIGURE 1.7. This map is not wrong, just different. Notice that Australia—often called the land "down under"—has become the land "up above."

# Latitude and Longitude

One of the simplest ways to describe location on the earth's surface is to use two sets of lines that intersect. After they understood *north*, *south*, *east*, and *west*, geographers chose to use intersecting north-south and east-west lines. The points where these lines intersect are called *coordinates*. Think of coordinates as a kind of global house address, or an absolute location that never changes.

## Latitude

Lines that encircle the earth from east to west are called lines of **latitude**. Notice that these lines are parallel to each other, so they are also known as **parallels**.

The equator is the longest line of latitude and is known as zero degrees latitude. As the lines of latitude approach the poles, they necessarily become shorter and shorter. At the poles, the lines are so short that they really are just points of latitude. The North Pole is 90 degrees north, the South Pole is 90 degrees south.

A line of latitude tells you if you are north or south of the equator as well as your distance from the equator. The distance from one line of latitude to the next is represented by one degree and is about 111 kilometres.

**latitude** The distance of a place north or south of the equator measured in degrees.

**parallels** Imaginary lines on the surface of the earth drawn parallel to the equator.

## The Earth with Selected Lines of Latitude and Longitude

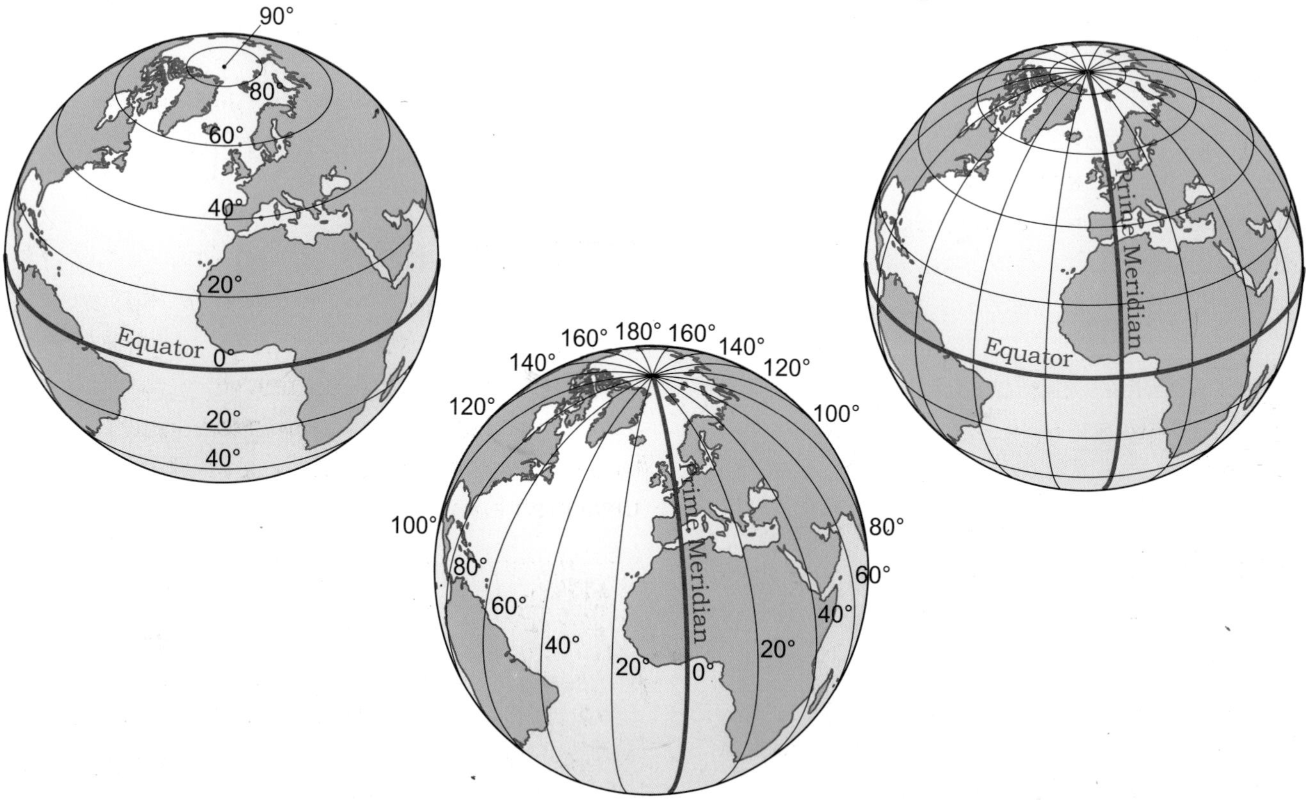

FIGURE 1.8. Left: the lines of latitude take the form of concentric circles numbered from the equator. Centre: the lines of longitude are half circles with end points at the poles and are spaced farthest apart at the equator and numbered from the prime meridian. Right: the two sets of lines intersecting.

## Longitude

The lines that run north to south are called lines of **longitude** and stretch from one pole to the other. They are also known as **meridians**, because they are the basis for our time system (*meridian* is a Latin word meaning "midday"). Meridians are not parallel to each other. Rather, they meet at the poles and are farthest apart at the equator. Look at a chocolate orange and you will see these lines. There are 360 degrees of longitude around the earth, and they are approximately 111 kilometres apart at their widest point of separation, which is at the equator.

The equator is an obvious choice for zero degrees latitude, but there is no obvious choice for zero degrees longitude. Because longitude is used to determine time zones, shipping and railroad requirements made people want a more uniform time system. It was decided, in 1884, that the Greenwich Observatory in London, England, would become zero degrees longitude, or the **prime meridian**. Why was Greenwich chosen? In 1884, Britain was the major world power and could influence others. It also helped that the Greenwich Observatory was one of the most accurate timekeepers of its day.

**longitude** The distance of a place east or west of the prime meridian measured in degrees.

**meridians** Imaginary half-circles around the earth that pass through a given location and terminate at the North Pole and the South Pole.

**prime meridian** The baseline used to measure east-west location on the surface of the earth in terms of lines of longitude.

 Imagine that you have pitched a tent with a friend precisely at the North Pole or South Pole. You tell your friend that you are just popping out for a stroll around the world. Where do you walk?

**Longitudinal Lines** Draw some longitudinal lines around your orange at lunchtime, and you'll notice that, if you flatten out your meridians, they are elliptical, or eye-shaped—slender at the top and bottom, widest at the middle. Find a friend and draw latitudinal lines around her or his orange. Notice that no matter where you draw them—close to the top or right in the middle—the lines will always be parallel.

**Latitude and Longitude** Latitude runs east to west, so it can tell you how far north or south you are. Longitude runs north to south, so it can tell you how far east or west you are. Latitude comes from the Latin word *latus,* which means "width," or "wide." Longitude comes from the Latin word *longus*, which means "long."

## Minutes and Seconds

In the same way that an hour is divided up into minutes and seconds, degrees of latitude and longitude are divided into 60 portions. Minute measurements allow geographers to be more specific about location than hour measurements do.

 Visit a site that will help you discover more about longitude: <www.theworldtoday.ca> and follow "Links" to <www.pbs.org/wgbh/noval/longitude/find.html>, for example.

## More about Time

We have always wanted to know what time it is. Early humans likely counted their days by the the progress of the sun, their months by the stages of the moon. Although we are not certain about how a place like Stonehenge in Britain worked, it is clear that its purpose had to do with marking time. Ancient civilizations attempted to increase their time-telling accuracy by inventing timekeepers like sundials and water clocks.

Figure 1.9. This sundial is in the Forbidden City in Beijing, China. Sundials have been found in many ancient civilizations, such as China, Egypt, Greece, and Rome. Although there are many different kinds of sundials, all were used to tell time by the position of the sun on the dial. In North America today, most sundials are for decorative reasons.

### Sundials

One of the earliest tools for measuring time was a sundial, used in the Middle East at least 4 000 years ago. A sundial is a circular disk that is divided into 12 equal "pie-shaped" parts and has a base plate and a stick. In some sundials, the base plate is angled upwards. It is situated so that it faces east to west. The stick casts a shadow on the 12 markers so that you can tell the time of day—on a sunny day, that is.

### Water Clocks

A water clock is basically a bowl with a small hole in the bottom and rings marked around the inside, indicating the "hours" that pass as the water slowly drips out.

 Imagine using a water clock or a sundial to regulate your daily life. List three challenges you would face. How would you "synchronize your watches"?

**Primary Timekeeper** Since the the 1600s, when the first pendulum clocks became widely used, people set their clocks based on the sun's highest point, at noon. Each town had a primary timekeeper, whose job it was to set the town clock and let the villagers know the time. With the beginning of railroads in the early 19th century, there was a lot of difficulty scheduling trains when "noon" in one town might have been 25 minutes earlier than "noon" in another. This became a primary push for standardizing time around the world. This was done by establishing a set of time zones that remove local time variations. Time at each and all locations inside the zone is always the same. Many people resisted this idea. Can you imagine why?

**Duodecimal System** As you can see, both the way we identify locations and the way we measure time involve a system of arithmetic notation that has 12 as a base; this is known as the duodecimal system. Why use the number 12? In the past, 12 was considered better than 10 because 12 has more factors (2, 3, 4, 6) than 10 has (2, 5).

## How We Keep Time

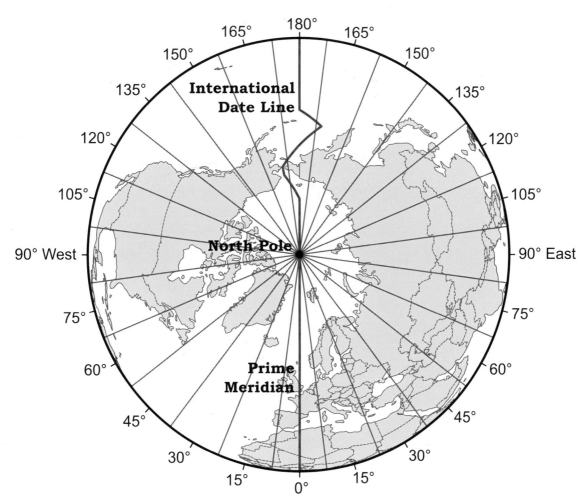

FIGURE 1.10. Our system of keeping time uses 24 time zones evenly placed around the globe (one every 15°, for a total of 24 x 15 = 360°). The series of points that make up the International Date Line are generally the antipodes of the series of points that make up the prime meridian.

## Time Zones and the International Date Line

The diagram in figure 1.10 assumes that the observer is looking down on the earth from above the North Pole. Note that the earth can be divided into 360 degrees. Now imagine that you are walking around the world eastwards. You add an hour every time you cross a time zone, until you eventually have added a full day. However, you cannot just keep adding days. What if you walked around two or three times? This is the reason for the International Date Line. When you cross the International Date Line moving west to east (and you might

not do this too often in your life), you do not add an hour; rather, you lose a day. Similarly, when you cross the International Date Line moving east to west, you do not lose an hour, you add a day.

**Crossing the International Date Line** Magellan completed his three-year westward voyage around the world in 1522. According to his meticulously kept log, the day of return was Wednesday, 7 September. Imagine how shocked he was when he was told it was Thursday, 8 September!

## World Map of Time Zones

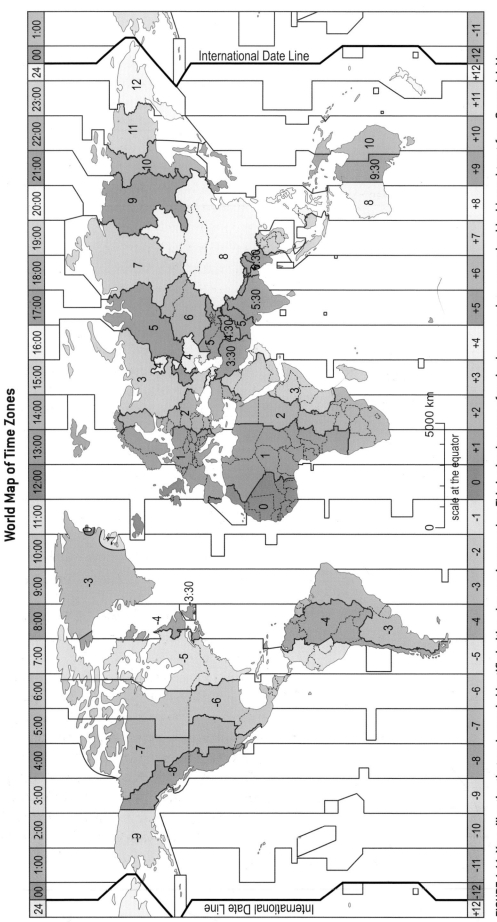

FIGURE 1.11. You will notice that each zone is identified with a plus or minus number. This is simply a way of saying how many hours you should add or subtract from Greenwich Mean Time. (Greenwich is the point that was chosen to represent 0 degrees longitude.) Greenwich Mean Time is also known as Universal Time Coordinated, and most people now use the abbreviation UTC to refer to time rather than Greenwich Mean Time.

## More about Time Zones

Have you ever crossed a time zone? Time zones change in order to keep "12 noon" somewhat close to midday wherever you are located. Sometimes towns or islands that are located close to a time-zone boundary choose to modify their zone so that it is in keeping with the nearest large city, or perhaps their primary trading partner. For this reason, when you look at the time-zone map, you will see that not all the lines are perfectly straight. Some time zones are much larger than 15 degrees. All of China, which extends a great distance from east to west, is in a single time zone. In Canada, Newfoundland is in a little time-zone bubble all to itself.

While many countries are small enough to be located in just one time zone, countries like Canada and the United States stretch many thousands of kilometres from east to west and need to include several time zones.

 Use an atlas to find the answers to the following questions: In which time zone is Beijing located? In which time zone is Canberra located? In which time zone is Nairobi located? In which time zone is Buenos Aries located?

 Look at an atlas and answer the following questions: If you are travelling from Toronto, Ontario, to Orlando, Florida, how many time zones do you cross? If you travel from Winnipeg, Manitoba, to Vancouver, British Columbia, how many time zones do you cross? Do you gain time or lose time? If it is 12 noon in Saskatoon, Saskatchewan, what time is it in Charlottetown, Prince Edward Island? If it is 4:00 p.m. in San Antonio, Texas, what time is it in Gander, Newfoundland and Labrador?

### Time Zones in North America

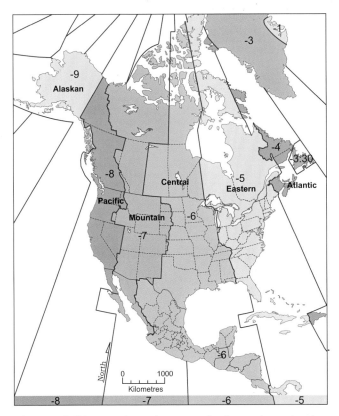

FIGURE 1.12. This map shows time zones for the continental region of North America.

**The Beginning of the Long Dash . . .** On 5 November 1939, CBC Radio began network broadcasting of the Dominion Observatory official time signal. Generations of CBC Radio listeners have set their watches and clocks to the familiar daily announcement, aired at exactly 11:59 a.m. Central Standard Time. Early mariners and surveyors relied on an accurate time signal to calibrate their instruments for navigation and mapping. More recently, precise timekeeping is essential for the coordination of communications, transportation, and power distribution networks. You can still hear the time signal today—just turn on CBC Radio a minute before noon.

## The Global Positioning System

Today, thanks to the development of the global positioning system (GPS), it is easier than ever for someone to determine location in terms of latitude and longitude. The GPS uses 24 satellites that orbit the earth every 12 hours and provides data that can be picked up by hand-held receivers. The receiver shows your exact latitude and longitude coordinates, and, while this might not be of much use to you when you are looking for the nearest convenience store, it is useful if you are lost in the middle of a forest hoping that the search-and-rescue people will spot you. Using a GPS transmitter-receiver, you can send your coordinates to rescuers, who will then be able to find you. Virtually every new plane, ship, train, truck, and some cars and cell phones around the world are made with a built-in GPS receiver.

FIGURE 1.14. A hand-held GPS transmitter-receiver.

There are more uses for a GPS than just helping locate a person lost in a forest. In the event of a fire or natural disaster, the location of all emergency vehicles can be established quickly so that those nearest to the emergency are able to provide assistance. Most trucking companies equip their long-distance trucks with a GPS so that they can easily find out where their trucks are at any given time.

 How is a GPS good and helpful? Can you see some ways that it could cause privacy problems? How would you feel if your parents or teachers attached a GPS to your coat? What if a GPS chip were placed in your cell phone?

FIGURE 1.13. A GPS satellite.

FIGURE 1.15. The parents of this very active child would know where he was playing every minute of every day if he carried a GPS everywhere he went.

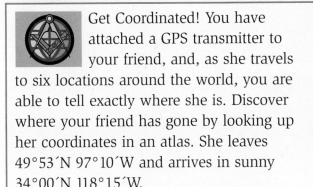

 Get Coordinated! You have attached a GPS transmitter to your friend, and, as she travels to six locations around the world, you are able to tell exactly where she is. Discover where your friend has gone by looking up her coordinates in an atlas. She leaves 49°53′N 97°10′W and arrives in sunny 34°00′N 118°15′W.

After a short layover, her plane takes off again. She waves as she crosses the International Date Line. She lands in 33°55′S 151°10′E for a few weeks of backpacking. At 8°0′N 72°51′E she is incredibly hot and buys some inexpensive cotton shirts for only a few rupees.

After that, she is off to see the pyramids in 30°00′N 31°15′E. Her world tour ends in 52°22′N 04°54′E, and she spends a few weeks there travelling canals and biking before heading home again.

FIGURE 1.16. Clockwise from bottom left: Sydney, Winnipeg, Los Angeles, Mumbai (Bombay), Cairo, Amsterdam.

Mark the locations that your friend has visited on a map provided by your teacher. We'll visit some of the countries where these places are located later in the book, discovering more about their culture, their landscapes, and their people. Begin to collect newspaper or magazine articles about these places, and put them in your travel portfolio.

## Mapping the World

### Globes

The best way to represent our spherical earth at a reduced scale is to use a globe. This is because a globe is the same shape as the earth. Just as a model car is a miniature replica of a full-sized car, a globe is a model of the earth.

FIGURE 1.17. A globe.

*Advantages*

A globe is a true representation of four important properties of the earth's surface: (1) Size: The relative size of land masses and water bodies is reflected accurately because the globe is the same shape as the earth. (2) Shape: Because the shape of the globe is the same as the earth, the shape of the land masses is accurate.

(3) Distance: Distance is reflected accurately because the globe models the true shape of the earth. (4) Direction: North, south, east, and west are reflected accurately.

*Disadvantages*

Because globes are small and need to represent the entire earth, they can give only a general representation, and details are lost. You cannot see the entire globe all at once; half of it is always hidden from view. Globes are not easily portable. While you can buy them with floor stands, there are no "glove-compartment" models. You would never pull out a globe to help you find a street in your city, and you cannot carry one in your back pocket if you are touring a new country.

### Maps

Cartographers (or map-makers) face a huge challenge to minimize distortion when they try to represent our spherical earth on a flat piece of paper. Imagine drawing a detailed picture on an orange, and then peeling the orange and laying it out on your desk so that it looks the same as it did when it was still round. Map-makers have tackled this problem by developing various **map projections**, that is, various ways of projecting a three-dimensional surface onto a two-dimensional surface.

Because map-makers take the three-dimensional globe and try to flatten it onto a two-dimensional piece of paper, they can never make perfect representations of the earth. This imperfection is called *distortion*. Distortion on a map is at a minimum when the area mapped is small: perhaps only your street or your town. The larger the area that needs to be mapped, the greater the distortion.

FIGURE 1.18. An equivalent map (left) chats with a conformal map (right).

## World Map Projections

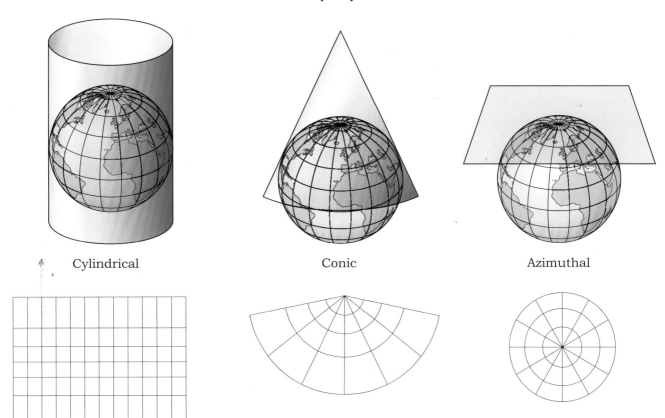

Cylindrical  Conic  Azimuthal

**FIGURE 1.19.** Map-makers have used several different techniques to project the surface of the earth onto a flat map. The cylinder, cone, and plane are three geometric shapes. The figure on the left shows the popular cylindrical technique, which involves wrapping a cylinder around a sphere (the globe) and projecting the details of the globe onto the cylindrical surface. The cylinder is then unwrapped to create a rectangular-shaped map. The figure second from the left shows the conical technique, which involves placing a cone on either the North Pole or South Pole. This is unsuited to a map of the world; its use is limited to high-latitude areas, such as Canada. The figure at the right shows the plane, or azimuthal, technique, which is also especially suited to the polar regions.

No matter what map projection is used, something will always be wrong with at least one of the four important properties that globes represent correctly: size, shape, distance, and direction. Generally, size and shape are the most important characteristics, and, since no map is able to represent both of them correctly, cartographers need to choose which is more important for the information they need to display at the time. A map that represents size correctly is called an **equivalent map projection**, while a map that represents the shape of areas correctly is called a **conformal map projection**.

**conformal map projection** One that retains the proper shape of surface features. All conformal projections have meridians and parallels crossing each other at right angles

**equivalent map projection** One that shows the relative sizes of places correctly in all areas of the map. An equivalent world map will have disfigured shapes; it is sometimes more simply known as an equal-area map.

**map projection** The representation on a flat surface of part or all of the surface of the earth.

## Examples of Map Projections

There are several map projections that are generally used by cartographers: the Mercator, the Goode Homolosine, and the Winkel-Tripel.

### The Mercator Projection

The Mercator projection is the most popular and one of the oldest. Gerardus Mercator (1512–1594) was a great map-maker. His map projection, which he devised in 1569, is still well-known.

The Mercator projection solved the problem, at least in part, of how to flatten the globe into a two-dimensional map and keep the lines of latitude and longitude accurate. Mercator realized that sailors had trouble staying on-course on long ocean voyages, and so his goal was to help them navigate in straight lines.

The Mercator projection uses the cylindrical technique. The map is conformal, meaning that shapes are correctly shown with the parallels and meridians intersecting at right angles. However, the size of land masses is wrong —Antarctica looks huge, and Greenland looks larger than South America, even though it is only one-ninth the size. The biggest problem with the Mercator projection is that users obtain an incorrect impression of the relative sizes of land masses.

### The Mercator Projection

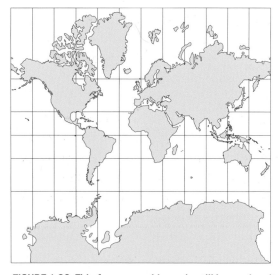

FIGURE 1.20. This famous world map is still in use despite the obvious problems noted in the text description.

### The Goode Homolosine Projection

In 1923, geographer J. Paul Goode (1862–1932) developed a map based on a pseudo-cylindrical technique. Shapes are distorted, but sizes are correct, so it is an equivalent map projection. It is usually presented in an interrupted format to minimize the distortion of the shapes of major land masses.

### The Interrupted Goode Homolosine Projection

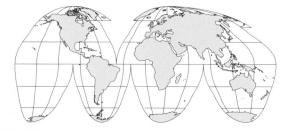

FIGURE 1.21. Many geographers use interrupted projections in order to minimize distortion of the shape of land masses.

### The Winkel-Tripel Projection

The Winkel-Tripel projection is used for world maps throughout this book. Developed in 1921 by Dutch Cartographer Oswald Winkel (1873–1953), this projection is based on a modified azimuthal technique and is neither equivalent nor conformal. Instead, it tries to combine the best of both models to produce a map that "feels" right (*tripel* means "a combination of three elements": area, direction, and distance). In 1998, the National Geographic Society adopted the Winkel-Tripel projection for all its world maps.

### The Winkel-Tripel Projection

FIGURE 1.22. This is a compromise world map and is the one used for the majority of world maps in this textbook.

## Wrapping It Up

Many geographers, including many explorers who were also good geographers, have contributed to what we know about the world today. Because of the pioneering work of people who dared to chart unknown territories and develop new theories, we have found out more about our planet Earth than ancient peoples would ever have dreamed possible.

Today, we are used to the idea of a rotating spherical earth. It is hard to imagine what a radical idea it was at the time that mediaeval astronomers began to believe that the earth was round. The round-earth idea angered many people, and some astronomers were punished for this belief and also for suggesting that the earth was not the centre of the universe.

Our identification of direction, and our nights and days, all depend upon the fact that the earth rotates 360 degrees on its axis every 24 hours. Because of the earth's rotation, a different portion of the earth is always experiencing sunrise, sunset, high noon, and night. It is because of this that the lines of longitude are used to determine time zones.

Development and use of an arbitrary mathematical grid (the lines of latitude and longitude) was an important advance. Figuring out how to plot latitude and longitude in the middle of the ocean, where there are no physical land masses to use as guides, was a very important challenge.

 The earth has been plotted and charted for many years. Do you think there are still new places to discover? Where are they? Look for magazine and newspaper articles that cover uncharted territories, and find out about places where people are still making geographic discoveries.

Globes and maps are commonplace to us now, but they were difficult for people long ago to plot. They were also difficult to replace, because each map was an original that was carefully drawn by a cartographer. It was not until the introduction of printing that maps could be mass-produced. While modern maps do not represent the earth perfectly, they are an excellent guide for getting around your neighbourhood, your city, or the world. When a map's scale is large, the area it plots is usually quite small, perhaps a park or a neighbourhood. When a map's scale is small, it plots large areas, perhaps the entire world. While globes can offer a better representation of the world than maps do, they are not portable and therefore not usually preferred.

**Amazing Canadian** George Dawson was born in Montreal in 1849 (d. 1901). At the age of 11 he almost died from tuberculosis of the spine. His spine was permanently deformed, and he never grew beyond his 11-year-old size. During and for a time after his illness, he was unable to go to school, so he had tutors and his father to teach him at home. He was very intelligent and studied geology and palaeontology at McGill University in Montreal and at the Royal School of Mines in London, England, earning the highest marks possible. This is not what made him amazing, however.

Some of his greatest and longest-lasting contributions to Canada were made when he was working as a surveyor, determining the correct boundary line between Canada and the United States from Lake of the Woods, Ontario, to the Rocky Mountains, British Columbia. He did more, however, than just determine the boundary lines. He reported back on many other matters, including such aspects of physical geography as landforms and wildlife, and prepared many maps of the boundary areas. He loved climbing and the outdoors, and, despite his crooked back and small size, he never avoided the challenge of a new mountain to climb or a new area to discover.

# OUR PHYSICAL WORLD

**2**

## Guiding Questions

1. Why are human and physical geographies often closely related?

2. Does the physical environment influence human activities, or do humans adapt to physical environments?

3. What are the four interacting and overlapping spheres that make up our earth system?

4. What are the names of the six continents?

5. How does the land surface of the earth vary in terms of topography, climate, and location of water bodies?

6. What are the 10 basic physical geographic (environmental) regions of the world?

## Human and Physical Worlds

Human geographers always need to consider physical geography. Physical and human worlds are closely related, especially when we look at the big picture: the entire world. This chapter describes the global physical environment and explores some ways in which we relate to our physical environment.

**Prairie Town** by Randy Bachman
(Winnipeg-born singer and songwriter, b. 1943)

Born and raised in a prairie town
Just a kid full of dreams
We didn't have much but an old radio
Music came from places we'd never been
Growing up in a prairie town
Learning to drive in the snow
Not much to do so you start a band
And soon you've gone as far as you can go
(chorus)
Winter nights are long, summer days are gone
Portage and Main fifty below
Springtime melts the snow, rivers overflow
Portage and Main fifty below
Portage and Main fifty below
All the bands in a prairie town
Try to outdo the next in line
Learning records out of Liverpool
Dreams of England on their minds
On the other side of Winnipeg
Neil and The Squires played the Zone
But then he went to play
For awhile in Thunder Bay
He never looked back and he's never coming home
Just a band from a prairie town
Sometimes we'd drive from coast to coast
One call from LA and we'd pack and fly away
But in our hearts we're always prairie folk
Looking back at a prairie town
People ask me why I went away
To fly with the best, sometimes you have to leave the nest
But the prairies made me what I am today

We are not "slaves" to our physical geography. But we do usually take physical geography into consideration when making decisions.

We try to choose the best places according to such characteristics as landforms, climate, soil, vegetation, and wildlife. For instance, the fur trade would not have been established in the Canadian Shield if it had not been for the many fur-bearing animals found there. You would not plant potatoes in a field full of hard, rocky soil; it simply would not make sense.

What we do in a particular place, therefore, depends to some extent on physical geography. But physical geography also reflects who we are, especially our ability to modify environments —for example, whether we know about agricultural technologies or about industrial technologies. Consider how life on the prairies has changed through time:

- One thousand years ago, Aboriginal peoples hunted, fished, and used native grasses and plants for their food, shelter, and clothing.

- Three hundred years ago, travelling mostly by water, European fur traders came to the region and altered a way of life that had been relatively stable for many centuries.

- Just over one hundred years ago, there was a huge influx of European settlers who adjusted to a challenging but promising agricultural environment and established towns and cities.

- Today, life on the prairies is different again from the kinds of lives people lived one hundred years ago; most people now live in large cities.

**Adapting to Our Physical Geography** The mountains (or cold weather, full moon) made me do it! If we were totally bound to our physical geography, we could blame it for our bad behaviour, our poor choices, and the mistakes we've made. Of course we adapt to our physical geography, but we do not have to behave in a certain way because of the particular physical geography we find ourselves in.

 Consider the relationship between physical geography and the words of Randy Bachman's "Prairie Town." What might someone from the Maritimes have written? How about someone from northern British Columbia?

 The physical geography of the prairies has remained largely unchanged, but the technologies of the people living in the region have changed. Discuss what differences new technologies have made for people (such as the steel plough, railways, cars, telephones).

## Spheres

Our planet is a sphere (slightly flattened at the top and bottom), but there are several additional spheres in and on this planetary sphere to think about. First, the earth can be divided into four hemispheres, or half-spheres. Geographers refer to northern, southern, western, and eastern hemispheres when they want to identify some large area of the earth:

- The northern hemisphere is the area from the equator to the North Pole.

- The southern hemisphere is the area from the equator to the South Pole.

- The western hemisphere extends from the prime meridian west to the International Date Line.

- The eastern hemisphere extends from the prime meridian east to the International Date Line.

Second, there are four interacting and overlapping spheres into which the earth is organized. The boundaries among these four spheres are transition zones and cannot be precisely identified. The spheres are closely connected, and geographers often study the spheres as they relate to each other.

### The Atomosphere

The atmosphere is a gaseous layer, a blanket of air that surrounds the earth. Critical for all life, earth is the only planet in our solar system that has a lower atmosphere made up of nitrogen (78 percent) and oxygen (21 percent). This is the air that we breathe.

### The Lithosphere

The lithosphere is the outer rocky shell of the earth. In some areas this surface is exposed; in others it is under water. Some parts of the exposed lithosphere have a shallow layer of soil. We live on the exposed lithosphere, especially in areas covered by soil; this is where we farm and build our cities and towns.

### The Hydrosphere

The hydrosphere is the water surface of the earth; most of this water is in oceans and seas. Of the planets in our solar system, only earth has large quantities of water. The cryosphere is the area of the hydrosphere that is frozen and includes ice fields, frozen seas, and glaciers.

**Division of the Earth into Hemispheres**

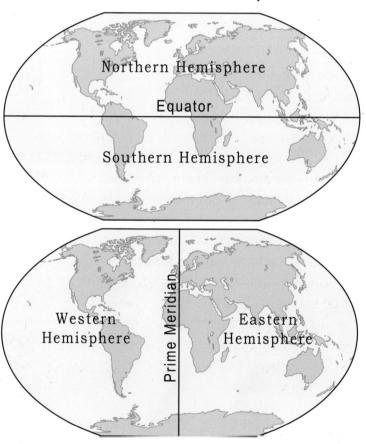

FIGURE 2.1. These two small world maps locate the four hemispheres (northern, southern, eastern, western) that are sometimes referred to by geographers when discussing aspects of world geography.

*The Biosphere*

The biosphere is the thin layer of the earth containing all living organisms and the environment that supports them. It includes plants, animals, and humans. These life forms are dependent on the other spheres: the gases of the atmosphere, the water of hydrosphere, and the nutrients of the lithosphere. The biosphere is located on the lithosphere and in about the upper 100 metres of the hydrosphere.

**The Spheres**

*atmos* means "air"

*litho* means "rock"

*hydro* means "water"

*cryo* means "frozen"

*bio* means "life"

## The Natural Environment

Geographers often talk about the *natural environment*. This refers to all four spheres, except for the human part of the biosphere. The natural environment is made up of land surface, soils, atmosphere, oceans, plants, and animals; it is also often called *nature*. Nature provides us with a wide range of natural resources needed to support our lives and activities.

The natural environment is different from place to place, and the history of humans on earth is one of adaptation to these differences. Also, the history of humans on earth shows how we interfere in and even change some of the details of the natural environment. Human interactions with environment are one component of **ecology**.

**ecology** The study of interactions of living organisms with each other and with their environment.

**The Four Interacting Spheres**

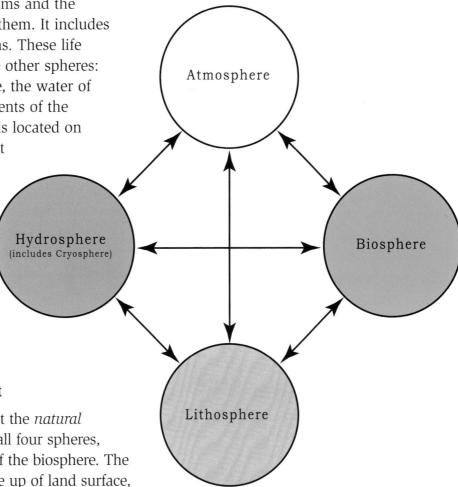

FIGURE 2.2. This diagram suggests the complex interacting links among the four interacting spheres.

 Think of examples of ecological interactions. Compare your suggestions with those of your classmates.

 Think about the Canadian prairies. Talk about three ways that people—past and present—have adapted to the natural environment of the prairies. Also talk about three ways that people have changed the natural environment of the prairies.

# Land and Water

If you had a chance to make oblate ellipsoid chocolate chip cookies (recipe on page 25), you may have wondered about the odd amounts of chocolate chips called for in the recipe. The amount was chosen for a reason. If the cookie dough represents water, and the chocolate chips represent land, then the proportions are just about right: about 71 percent of the earth is covered with water, and about 29 percent is covered with land. If you take a look at a globe, you see that the land and water are not distributed evenly—most land is in the northern hemisphere, and most water is in the southern hemisphere.

## The Oceans

Most of the water area of the earth is found in the four oceans. Of course there are no clear dividing lines separating oceans where they meet.

The Pacific Ocean is the largest ocean, covering 31 percent of the world's surface. It is divided into the North Pacific and the South Pacific. There are three main island regions:

1. Polynesia (many islands), a triangle-shaped region with Hawaii, Easter Island, and New Zealand at the corners.

2. Micronesia (small islands), the island region west of Polynesia.

3. Melanesia (black islands), located between Micronesia and Australia-New Zealand. Traditionally, people who lived in Melanesia had darker skin than those in the other two regions, which is how it got its name.

The Atlantic Ocean is the next largest (about 15 percent of the earth's surface) and is divided into the North Atlantic and the South Atlantic. There are far fewer islands in the Atlantic than in the Pacific.

The Indian Ocean is slightly smaller than the Atlantic and covers about 13 percent of the earth's surface. It includes two large islands—Madagascar and Sri Lanka—and a number of smaller islands.

The Arctic Ocean is much smaller than any of the other oceans and includes some large islands belonging to Norway, Russia, and Canada. It is harder to mark this ocean on a map than the other oceans because so much of the Arctic Ocean is covered with a frozen surface, and it shows as ice and not as the deep water that is below the ice.

 In addition to the oceans, there are many large bodies of water that are identified as seas (e.g., the North Sea and the South China Sea), which are usually located close to land. Seas are smaller than oceans. There are no precise boundaries between one ocean and another, or between an ocean and a sea. There are yet other large bodies of water—these surrounded by land—that are identified as lakes (for example, Lake Michigan and Lake Victoria). Some lakes (that is, large bodies of water surrounded by land) are called seas. Check your atlas and locate the Black Sea, the Caspian Sea, and the Aral Sea.

**Blue Sky** Why is the ocean blue? It really isn't blue; it only mirrors the sky. On blue-sky, sunny days, the ocean looks blue. On grey, cloudy days, the ocean looks grey. Of course, this answer raises another question—Why is the sky blue? The short answer is that the sun's blue light is scattered by the nitrogen and oxygen in the atmosphere, meaning that we see the entire sky as blue.

The ocean area south of the Cape of Good Hope, at the southern tip of Africa, is where the icy Benguela ocean current and the warm Agulhas ocean current mix. This makes not only for a bountiful marine **ecosystem** but also for a greater than usual number of storms. Cape Agulhas, located to the east of the Cape of Good Hope, is farther south and is more correctly the meeting place of the two oceans. However, the Cape of Good Hope is still often viewed as the meeting point.

 Take the Cape of Good Hope tour and learn about its history. Visit <www.theworldtoday.ca> and follow "Links" to <www.capepoint.co.za>.

**ecosystem** The total environment of a community of plants and animals.

FIGURE 2.4. The Cape of Good Hope. Early seafarers had for a long time wanted to find a way to get from the Atlantic Ocean to the Indian Ocean. Bartolomeu Dias (ca. 1450–1500) was the first European to sail around the bottom of Africa (in 1488). He named the tip of Africa the Cape of Storms. It was renamed by his king, John II of Portugal (who didn't himself sail around the cape). He named it Cape of Good Hope because it opened up a previously undiscovered route to the east. Some people believe that he renamed the cape so that the sailors he wanted to send that way wouldn't worry about coming to the Cape of Storms (the Cape of Good Hope sounded a lot more promising and safer).

## Distribution of Land and Water

FIGURE 2.3. Notice that there is no Antarctic Ocean. This is because an ocean must occupy a basin—a large area of the earth's surface that lies below sea level—and Antarctica is a continent, not a basin. Despite this, some world maps do label the ocean area around Antarctica as the *Southern Ocean*.

## The Polar Regions

You may have heard the riddle about polar bears and penguins. When do polar bears eat penguins? The answer is that polar bears never eat penguins. They have never had the chance, because polar bears live in the Arctic and penguins live in the Antarctic.

Fauna is not the only difference between the two polar regions. The Arctic region in the northern hemisphere is not a land mass. It is a number of islands that are covered by thick layers of ice and includes a mass of sea ice that floats on the Arctic Ocean around the North Pole.

The Antarctic region in the southern hemisphere is a large land mass covered with ice. Beneath the ice sheet, Antarctica has mountains, lowlands, and valleys. Antarctica has an average height of about 2 500 metres, not because there are high mountains but because the ice cap has an average thickness of 2 000 metres and even reaches 4 500 metres in some places.

Both polar regions have been the site of expeditions and voyages of discovery. Both have claimed the lives of people who have set out to explore them. Both spend part of the year in darkness and part of the year in continuous daylight. Both are sparsely

FIGURE 2.5. Above: a polar bear climbs onto an ice floe in the Arctic. Below: penguins dive into the ocean in the Antarctic.

populated but closely watched by scientists who believe that the health of the poles is a good indicator of the overall health of our planet. In particular, the effects of global warming, such as melting ice and rising sea levels, are especially evident in the polar regions (see chapter 20 for a discussion of global warming that is caused by humans).

World maps centred on the poles show the distribution of land and water in these regions. The maps in figures 2.6 and 2.7 are equivalent (equal area) projections. This means that they distort shape with increasing distance from the map centre. Compare these maps to the true representation provided by a globe. Notice how the South Pole is located on a land mass and the North Pole is in the frozen Arctic Ocean.

 For more about the Arctic (North Pole), visit <www.theworldtoday.ca> and follow "Links" to <www.athropolis.com>. For more information about Antarctica (South Pole), visit <www.theworldtoday.ca> and follow "Links" to <www.south-pole.com>.

"Life is everywhere. The earth is throbbing with it, it's like music. The plants, the creatures, the ones we see, the ones we don't see, it's like one, big, pulsating symphony" (Pablo Picasso, 1881–1973, Spanish painter).

**The Two Polar Regions**

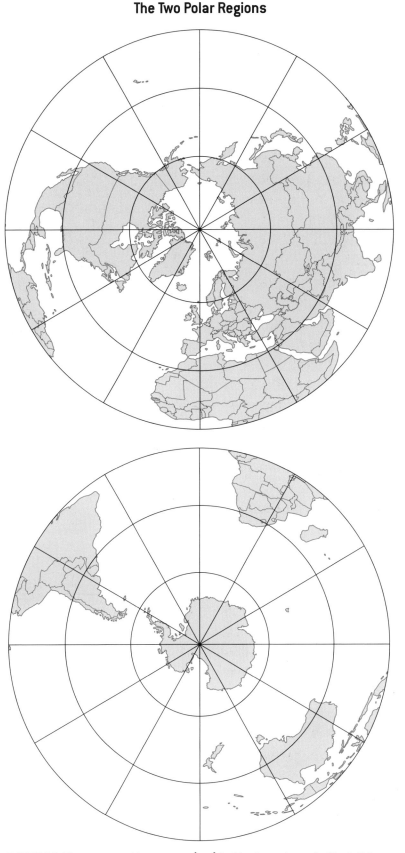

FIGURE 2.6. These two world maps, one (top) looking from above the North Pole and the other from above the South Pole, provide different and very interesting perspectives on the earth.

## The Six Continents

FIGURE 2.7. Geologically, there are six continents, as shown on this map. A continent is a major land mass on the surface of the earth. All the other land masses, including Greenland, are considered islands, as they are too small to be continents.

## Continents

Continents are large land masses with geologically meaningful boundaries. Geographers recognize six continents. From largest to smallest, they are:

1. Eurasia, which is made up of Asia and Europe: It covers 36 percent of the land surface of the earth. The dividing line between Asia and Europe is uncertain, because the division is based more on human histories than on physical geographies, although the Ural Mountains provide a basic dividing line.

2. Africa, which takes up 20 percent of the earth's land surface: It straddles the equator and includes large areas in both hemispheres. Africa is linked to Eurasia at the northeastern corner where the Suez Canal is located.

3. North America, which extends from polar regions in the north to subtropical regions in the south: It covers 17 percent of the land surface of the earth. Greenland and Iceland are part of North America.

4. South America, which covers 12 percent of the land surface of the earth: It is mostly in the southern hemisphere. The boundary with North America is generally considered to be the Panama Canal.

5. Antarctica, which is a continent (unlike the Arctic) because it is a large land mass: It is circular in shape and is almost completely covered by an ice cap. It includes 9 percent of the earth's land mass.

6. Australia, which covers 6 percent of the earth's land mass: Along with Antarctica, it is located entirely in the southern hemisphere.

Look at figure 2.7 and consider the following four questions about the way geographers identify continents:

1. Is it appropriate to regard Asia, Africa, and Europe as one single continent because they represent a single, linked land mass? Are you able to make a case for a specific boundary between Asia and Europe?

2. Is it appropriate to regard North America and South America as one single continent because they represent a single, linked land mass?

3. Australia is a continent, so why is Greenland not a continent? List three reasons showing that Greenland should be regarded as a continent.

4. The five Olympic rings represent the bringing together of people from five different areas (continents) of the world. Name these five areas. Why are there not six areas?

 Use an atlas to locate the ten largest countries in terms of area and then state on which continent each is located. The 10 largest countries are:

| | |
|---|---|
| Russia | 17 million km² |
| Canada | 9.9 million km² |
| United States | 9.8 million km² |
| China | 9.6 million km² |
| Brazil | 8.5 million km² |
| Australia | 7.6 million km² |
| India | 3.0 million km² |
| Argentina | 2.7 million km² |
| Kazakhstan | 2.7 million km² |
| Sudan | 2.4 million km² |

## Where Did They Get that Name?

- *Continent* comes from the Latin word *continere*, which means "to hold together."

- *Africa* comes from Roman times, possibly from the Phoenician term *Afryqah*, which means "colony."

- *America* was first used in 1507 by the cartographer Martin Waldseemuller, who named America after Amerigo Vespucci, an Italian navigator who was the first to recognize that America was a new continent, not part of Asia, as had been thought.

- *Asia* is of Latin and Greek origin. It comes from the word *asu*, which means "to rise," making Asia the land of the sunrise.

- *Australia* comes from the Latin *Terra Australis incognita*, which means "unknown southern land." Before Australia was "discovered" by Europeans, they speculated that there was a large continent in the southern hemisphere.

- *Europe* comes from Latin and Greek: from *eurys* meaning "wide," and from *ops* meaning "face."

- *Antarctic* comes from Old French, Latin, and Greek. *Anti* means "opposite," and *arktikos* means "of the north."

 Test your geography knowledge. Visit < www.theworldtoday.ca > and follow "Links" to < www.lizardpoint.com/fun > .

## Topography and Landforms

Over geologic time, which is measured in millions of years, **topography** changes dramatically. For example, continents move and mountains are created and worn down. **Landforms**, therefore, are considered to be temporary, not permanent, features of the earth's surface.

For geographic purposes, however, landforms are considered permanent because they do not change much over shorter time periods, such as a human lifespan, or even over several human life spans. Sometimes an **earthquake** or a **volcano** will change the land, but these are usually local in effect.

> **earthquake**  A brief period of groundshaking associated with a volcano or a sudden movement along a rock fracture (fault) below the surface of the earth. Earthquakes are often a serious hazard. The intensity of an earthquake is measured with a seismograph.
>
> **landform**  A particular land surface feature, such as a mountain, hill, plateau, or plain.
>
> **topography**  The shape of the land surface of the earth.
>
> **volcano**  A conical hill that has been built up as a result of the ejection of rock materials through a vent.

There are four major types of landform:

1. Mountains, which are irregular surfaces at high elevations: Mountains in humid regions are usually rounded; those in more arid (dry) climates are more angular (sharp).

2. Hills, which are similar to, but lower than, mountains, although the distinction between mountains and hills varies from place to place: Riding Mountain in Manitoba would be considered only a small hill in the Rockies, but, relative to the land around it, it has become known as a mountain.

3. Plateaus, which are large, flat areas at higher elevations than the surrounding land: They are also called *tablelands*. Plateaus are usually located within mountainous or hilly regions and are often drained by rivers that run through deep canyons (in arid areas) or gorges (in more humid areas).

4. Plains, which are extensive regions that are relatively flat and often treeless: Unlike plateaus, they are drained by rivers that run through shallow valleys.

> **Topography and Landforms**  If your face were the surface of the earth, the topography might be described as somewhat irregular, with higher elevations giving way to flatter, low-lying areas. Your nose, cheeks, and eye sockets would be landforms.

**FIGURE 2.8. Left: Mt. St. Helens in Washington State, U.S.A., as photographed in the 1970s. Right: the barren landscape surrounding Mt. St. Helens following the explosive eruption that occurred in 1980.**

In which of the four major landform types would you like to live, and why? In which would you like to vacation, and why? Which landform type would you least favour for living, working, and vacationing? Why? Would it make a difference where in the world your chosen landform is located?

FIGURE 2.9. Top left: aerial view of mountains in Alberta. Top right: rolling hills in California. Bottom left: plains grasslands near Val Marie, Saskatchewan. Bottom right: plateau landscape in the province of Cotopaxi, Mexico.

## Continental Landform Features

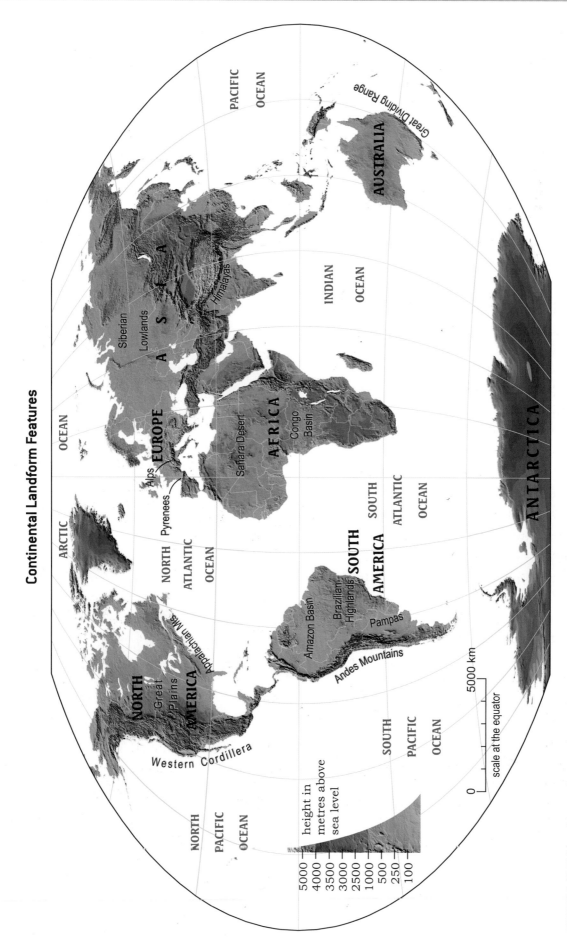

FIGURE 2.10. This world map shows major continental landform features. As shown in the key, the colours used on the map reflect different elevations. To enhance the appearance of the map, a 3-dimensional shading has been applied. This shading helps highlight areas of high elevation.

## Continental Landform Features

Eurasia has several east-west-trending mountain ranges, including the Himalayas, Alps, and Pyrenees. Northern Eurasia has the largest continuous lowland region in the world, which includes the Siberian Lowland. Look at an atlas and locate important rivers, such as the Danube, Ganges, and Huang He.

Much of Africa is a plateau at more than 1 000 metres above sea level; the coastal lowland areas are usually narrow. The principal mountain range trends north-south on the eastern side of the continent. Principal physical regions include the Sahara Desert and the Congo Basin. Look at an atlas and locate important rivers, such as the Nile and the Congo.

In North America, the Western Cordillera is a series of mountain ranges, including the Rocky Mountains, that trend north-south along the western side of the continent. The older and lower Appalachian system trends north-south on the eastern side of the continent. Between these two mountain ranges is an extensive lowland region that includes the Great Plains. The south and east are mainly coastal lowlands. Look at an atlas and locate important rivers, such as the St. Lawrence, the Mississippi, and the Missouri.

In South America, the basic pattern is similar to that in North America. The Andes mountains extend down the western edge. Older and lower mountain ranges, such as the Brazilian Highlands, are located in the east. Most of the rest of South America is a series of plateaus, plains, and river valleys. Major regions include the Amazon River Basin and the Pampas.

Note that the western mountain systems of North and South America are one continuous feature that extends from the Aleutian Islands in the far northwest to the tip of South America.

Although completely covered with ice, Antarctica is a land mass with varied topography, including mountain ranges.

The major mountain range in Australia, the Great Dividing Range, runs north-south on the eastern side of the continent. Most of the rest of the continent is a series of extremely dry plains and plateaus.

Except for New Zealand and Iceland, many of the world's large islands are located close to continents. Many islands, such as the Hawaiian Islands, are mountainous because they have volcanic origins. Look at an atlas and locate these islands.

 To say "close to" is to speak in relative terms. How close are the New Zealand islands to the continent of Australia?

 Use an atlas to locate the highest points on each continent. Name the mountain group to which each belongs (where applicable).

| | |
|---|---|
| Eurasia | Mt. Everest, 8 850 metres above sea level |
| South America | Mt. Aconcagua 6 960 metres above sea level |
| North America | Mt. McKinley 6 194 metres above sea level |
| Africa | Mt. Kilimanjaro 5 895 metres above sea level |
| Antarctica | Vinson Massif 4 895 metres above sea level |
| Australia | Mt. Kosciuszko 2 228 metres above sea level |

# Rivers and Lakes

A **drainage basin** often integrates a variety of physical environments. Most rivers begin in humid, mountainous areas or flow out of lakes that are at higher elevations. From these higher elevations, most rivers flow into an ocean or sea.

> **drainage basin** An area of land drained by a river and its tributaries. Also known as a catchment area. The boundary of a drainage basin is known as a watershed.

Have you ever noticed that people like to live close to water, sometimes in a coastal location and sometimes next to a river? Rivers attract people for six reasons:

1. In many areas, rivers provide a protein-rich food source (fish).

2. River valleys and river flood plains often provide soils suitable for farming, which allows for villages and eventually large towns. Some rivers that flow through dry areas, like the Nile River in Egypt, also provide water for irrigating crops.

3. Rivers provide relatively easy movement of people and goods (except where they may take meandering routes or have rapids and falls).

4. Rivers provide opportunities to generate power from hydroelectric dams.

5. Rivers are often favoured as locations for recreational activities.

6. Rivers and their valleys often provide the best routes through difficult hilly or wooded terrain.

 Use an atlas to locate and name the countries that border on the Caspian Sea.

**Save the Sturgeon!** Some lakes are so large that they can be regarded as inland seas. The Caspian Sea, which is by far the largest lake in the world, is a landlocked salt-water lake bordered by four countries. The Caspian Sea is the primary source of the world's supply of beluga sturgeon caviar, but illegal fishing and the destruction of spawning grounds have threatened the sturgeon, the source of beluga sturgeon caviar. One kilogram of the rare beluga caviar costs several thousand dollars. Further threatening to the Caspian Sea area are the large oil and gas deposits in the region. Great care must be taken in any further development of the area to preserve it and the people and wildlife living there.

 Check the newspaper or the Internet over the next few weeks to find examples of disputes involving bodies of water: rivers, lakes, and dams. Research the history of a dispute and report your findings to the class.

**Salty Water** How does water become salty? Rivers provide most of the water that flows into lakes and oceans. As the river flows, it picks up minerals and salts from the land it runs through. When a lake or ocean does not have an outlet, the only way for the amount of water to diminish is through evaporation. Since the minerals and salts cannot leave through evaporation, the water gradually gets saltier and saltier.

 Many rivers, such as the Nile and the Ganges, are as spiritually important to the people living close by as they are physically important. Discuss why people might worship a river.

Use an atlas or do Internet research to answer the following four questions:

1. Which is the largest drainage basin in the world?

2. Which is the largest drainage basin in North America?

3. Which is the longest river in the world?

4. Which is the largest lake in North America?

FIGURE 2.11. Top left: water rushes over the Horseshoe Falls, Niagara Falls, Ontario. Top right: the meandering Mississippi River as it approaches the Gulf of Mexico. Bottom left: the Nile River passing through Egypt. Bottom right: the Elburz Mountains and the Caspian Sea coast in Iran.

# Climate and Weather

Climate is the long-term balance of temperature, precipitation, wind, and cloud cover. It describes the average atmospheric conditions over a long period of time. Weather is the short-term condition of the atmosphere and can change in a few minutes and from one day to the next.

## The Climate of an Area

There are three main factors that combine to determine the climate of an area: latitude, air masses, and global low- and high-pressure zones.

### Latitude

Low latitudes (close to the equator; the equator is zero) receive more heat from the sun than high latitudes do, which are close to the poles. Of course, the more heat received from the sun, the warmer will be the land surface.

### Air Masses

Air masses are large bodies of air covering several thousand square kilometres that have

## Heating Power of the Sun on the Surface of the Earth

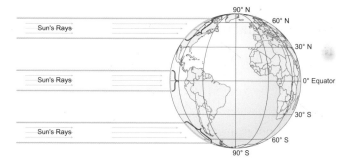

FIGURE 2.13. The sun's rays have to heat more of the earth's surface close to the poles than they do close to the equator. This is because the earth is a sphere, not a flat surface.

relatively uniform temperature and humidity characteristics. Air masses form, move, and gradually change in character.

### Global Low- and High-Pressure Zones

In general, air that is warmer than the surrounding air is lighter and rises, which creates a low-pressure area at the earth's surface. Cold air is denser and sinks, which creates high-pressure areas. Winds usually blow from high- to low-pressure areas.

## Climate Regions of the World

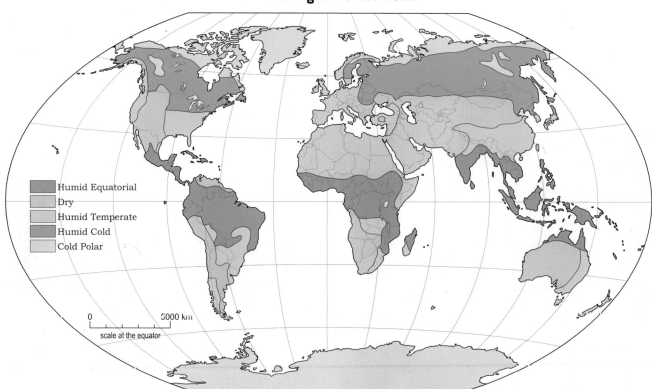

Humid Equatorial
Dry
Humid Temperate
Humid Cold
Cold Polar

FIGURE 2.12. This is a very general map. The names of the five types of climate provide only a basic description of the climate.

## Climate on a Local Scale

The three main factors—latitude, air masses, and pressure zones—result in a global pattern of five general types of climate. They are called humid-equatorial, dry, humid-temperate, humid-cold, and cold-polar. In addition to the three principal factors that affect the climate of a large area, there are five factors that have a local or regional effect.

### Ocean Currents

Ocean currents distribute heat energy in certain patterns throughout the earth. The Netherlands, with a latitude similar to that of Winnipeg, has a much warmer winter temperature partly because it is warmed by an ocean current called the Gulf Stream.

### Prevailing Winds

Wind (air in motion) moves moisture and temperature from one place to another. Prevailing winds are the general wind patterns, much the same as ocean currents. In Manitoba, we experience dry, cold weather when the wind blows from the Arctic and lots of precipitation when a Colorado low sets in from the south.

### Mountain Barriers

Mountains block prevailing winds. Moisture-laden air hits the mountain slope (the windward side), and, because cool air cannot hold as much water as warm air, the moisture in the air falls as precipitation. This leaves the leeward side—that is, the side that does not face the prevailing winds—very dry.

**Global Surface Ocean Currents**

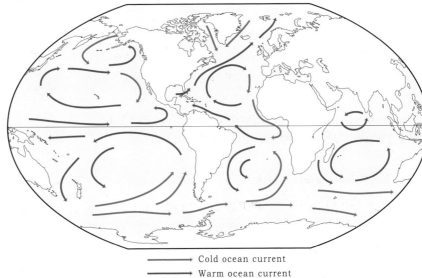

→ Cold ocean current
→ Warm ocean current

FIGURE 2.14. This figure shows why cold currents are cold and warm currents are warm: cold ocean currents typically begin close to one of the polar regions, where the water is cold; warm ocean currents typically begin close to the equator, where the water is warm.

**Global Surface Wind-Belt Pattern**

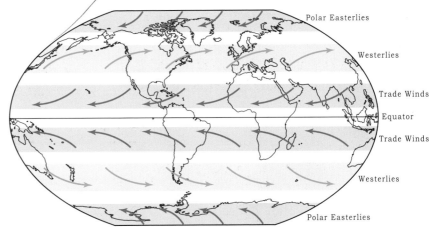

Polar Easterlies
Westerlies
Trade Winds
Equator
Trade Winds
Westerlies
Polar Easterlies

FIGURE 2.15. Most of Canada is in a zone of westerly winds.

### Altitude

The altitude of mountains has an effect on climate because air high up is cooler and dryer than air that is closer to sea level.

### Distribution of Land and Sea

Water absorbs heat much more slowly than land, so the climate of land close to water is moderated by the water; the water keeps the land warmer during the winter and cooler during the summer. This is why the Netherlands has a warmer winter than Winnipeg (and also why it has a cooler summer).

# World Environmental Regions

To a large extent, climate determines soils and vegetation. Geographers combine climate, soils, and vegetation physical characteristics, and also topography, to identify natural global environmental regions. Humans have changed many of these environmental regions through agriculture and the building of settlements.

## The Ten Regions

### Temperate Forests
Temperate Forests are located in much of Europe and eastern North America. They are naturally forested and have fertile soil and obvious seasons. Today these regions tend to be agricultural or urban, with high population density.

### Temperate Grasslands
Temperate grasslands are located in a continental interior. Examples include the Canadian prairies, the Russian steppes, and the Argentinean pampas. There is too little precipitation for trees, but the soil is good for growing grain, and there are clearly defined seasons. These regions have a medium population density.

### Mediterranean Forests
Mediterranean forests are usually located on the western side of a continent in a temperate latitude. Summers are hot and dry, and winters are warm and moist. Naturally forested, these areas are usually agricultural or left as scrubland today with medium population density.

### Tropical Rainforests
Tropical rainforests are close to the equator. They have high rainfall, dense vegetation, and many plant and animal species. The soil is poor for agriculture, and the population density is low.

### Boreal
Boreal forests (also known as taiga) are found only in the northern hemisphere. Boreal forests have long, cold winters and short, warm summers. They have low precipitation, little agriculture, a low population density, and a good source of forest products and minerals.

### Tundra
The tundra region is located north of the taiga. The tundra has long, cold winters, **permafrost**, little if any soil, and very low population density.

### Polar
The polar region is very cold and dry, mostly unsuitable for human settlement.

### Desert
Desert regions have low and infrequent rainfall. Some deserts are cold, others hot. They have very low population density.

### Savannah
The savannah region is located north and south of tropical rainforests. Savannah has wet and dry seasons, some trees, grassland, many animal species, and low human population density. Some of these areas have been transformed into desert because of such human activities as pasturing domestic animals.

### Monsoon
The monsoon region is naturally forested and has both a wet and a dry season. It has been substantially changed by agriculture, especially rice cultivation, and has a very high human population density.

**permafrost** Perennially frozen subsoil and bedrock; underlies large areas in cold environments.

## Let's Get Physical!

Knowing some facts about global physical geography helps us understand many aspects of human geography, including population geography. Knowing about the 10 global environmental regions provides a foundation for understanding many aspects of human geography.

We are intricately linked to the world around us. Many of our life choices—such as the crops we choose to grow, the clothes we wear, and the sports and pastimes we enjoy—are related to local physical geography, such as the climate and landforms of that place. There are very few southern Californians who like to snowshoe, for instance, and few Manitobans who regularly surf.

Recall our definition of human geography—the study of peoples and places on the surface of the earth—and recognize that such a study could not be done by someone who does not know about physical geography.

But, while there is a close relationship between physical geography and human geography, much more than physical geography is needed as a basis for understanding the peoples and places of the world. We also need to know a lot about ourselves, about our needs, wants, and values, and about the cultural, social, economic, and political structures that we have gradually constructed.

### World Environmental Regions

Legend:
- Temperate forests
- Temperate grasslands
- Mediterranean
- Tropical rain forests
- Taiga
- Tundra
- Polar
- Desert
- Savannas
- Monsoon

0    5000 km
scale at the equator

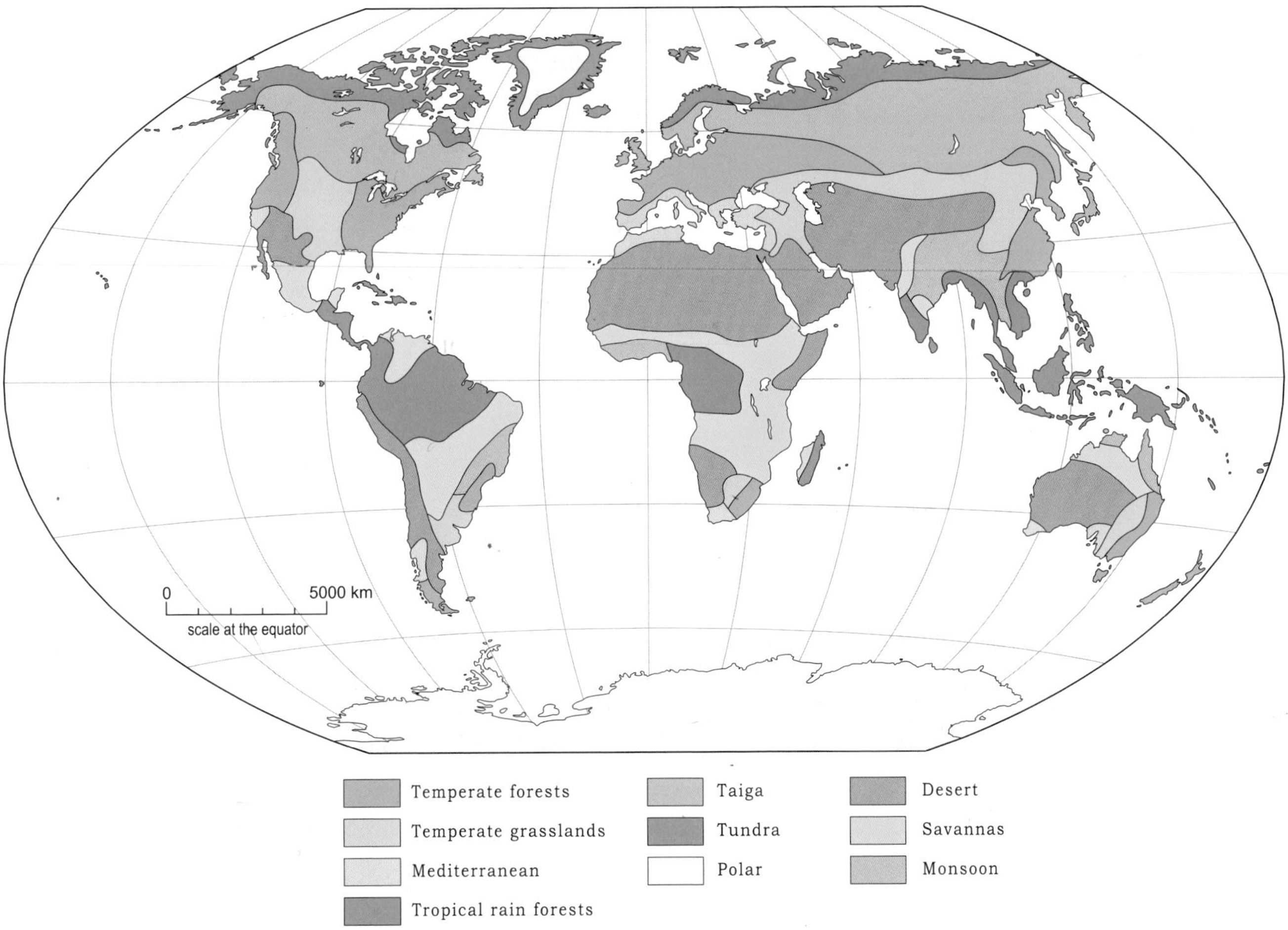

FIGURE 2.16. This is a map that you may choose to refer back to from time to time as you study this text. It shows the 10 global environmental regions described in the text. In common with many other maps drawn at the global scale, it is, of course, a generalized description.

# OUR HUMAN WORLD

**3**

## Guiding Questions

1. In human terms, why is the world an unequal place? Why are some countries more developed than other countries?

2. At what rate is world population growing today?

3. How many people are projected to be living in the world by about the middle of this century?

4. In what part of the world will most future population growth occur?

5. On the global scale, why do people live where they do?

6. Is the map of countries a fixed and unchanging fact?

## We Live in an Unequal World

Your country of birth and its world location probably influence your development as a person more than almost any other factor in your life. They determine whether you will be well-fed as an infant or you will suffer from malnutrition. They determine whether you will be educated or not. They determine challenges you will face and obstacles that will get in your way. This is because there are "have" countries, and there are "have not" countries. This is the single most important fact of human geography today.

The "have" countries are grouped together as the **more-developed world**. The "have" countries are better off, in economic terms and in quality-of-life terms, than are the "have not" countries, which are grouped together as the **less-developed world**. As table 3.1 shows, more-developed countries have a higher **standard of living** than do less-developed countries.

**less-developed world** Comprises countries characterized by low standards of living.

**more-developed world** Comprises countries characterized by high standards of living.

**standard of living** Physical level of comfort determined by the goods, services, and luxuries available to an individual, group, or nation.

"A new vision of development is emerging. Development is becoming a people-centered process, whose ultimate goal must be the improvement of the human condition" (Boutros Boutros-Ghali, b. 1922, 6th secretary-general of the United Nations).

## Locating Our Unequal World

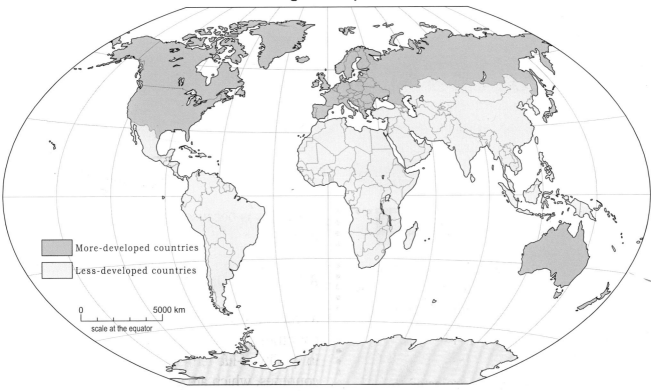

More-developed countries

Less-developed countries

0          5000 km
scale at the equator

FIGURE 3.1. The distribution of more- and less-developed countries is shown on this map. The more-developed countries include all of Europe, the United States, Canada, Australia, New Zealand, and Japan. The less-developed countries include all of Africa, all of Asia (except Japan), all of Latin America and the Caribbean, and all of Oceania (except Australia and New Zealand).

 Discuss your ideas about why there might be more-developed countries and less-developed countries. How do countries become more or less developed? (This topic will be explored later in this chapter.)

## TABLE 3.1. Some of the Differences between More-Developed and Less-Developed Countries

|  | More-Developed Countries | Less-Developed Countries |
|---|---|---|
| average income | high | low |
| energy use | high | low |
| number of births | low | high |
| number of deaths | low | low (in most countries) |
| rate of population growth | low | high |
| life expectancy | high | low |
| percent literate | high | low |
| percent urban | high | low |
| percent rural | low | high |
| leisure time available | high | low |

## World Population

### How Many People?

There have never been as many people living on the earth as there are today, and this number is increasing every year by about 75 million. Most of the people in the world live in less-developed countries, and nearly all the growth is happening in less-developed countries. Consider these numbers: In 2005, there were 6.5 billion people in the world. Only 1.2 billion of these were living in more-developed countries, while the other 5.3 billion were living in less-developed countries.

**Millions and Billions** You will see the words *million* and *billion* quite often in this chapter. What do they mean to you? Here is a question that will help you understand *millions* and *billions*. Your rich uncle has died and left you with two choices: you can have one million dollars with no questions asked, or you can have one billion dollars. But, if you choose the one-billion-dollar option, you must first count it at the rate of one dollar per second for eight hours each day. Only when you have finished counting all the money can you can begin to spend it. Which do you choose? Your teacher knows which is the better option.

### Population Growth

About 10 000 years ago, the world's population was about 5.3 million people. This number had most likely remained about the same for thousands of years. During this time, people fed themselves by hunting animals, collecting food such as berries, and fishing in lakes, rivers, and coastal seas.

As people began to farm—growing crops and raising animals—the population began to increase slowly but steadily, mostly because the **domestication** of plants and animals provided more food and a more consistent supply of food than did hunting, collecting, and fishing.

About 2 000 years ago, world population reached 300 million people and by 1800 was 1 000 million (one billion) people.

**domestication** The process that involves bringing wild animals and plants under human control in order to breed them to possess some specific desired characteristics, such as providing more milk or bearing more fruit.

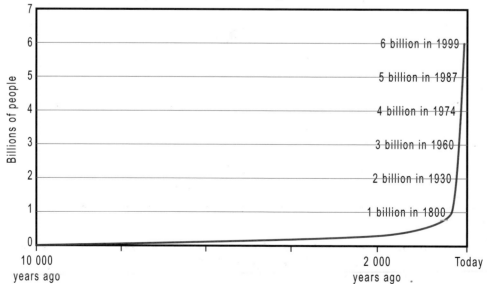

**World Population Growth during the Past 10 000 Years**

- 6 billion in 1999
- 5 billion in 1987
- 4 billion in 1974
- 3 billion in 1960
- 2 billion in 1930
- 1 billion in 1800

*y-axis: Billions of people (0–7)*

*x-axis: 10 000 years ago — 2 000 years ago — Today*

FIGURE 3.2. This graph clearly shows the very slow growth of human population until about 1800 and the very rapid growth since about 1800.

Since 1800, the growth in world population has been much more rapid than previously, mainly because of increases in agricultural production, improved nutrition, better hygiene, and improved public sanitation. These changes combined to support larger and larger numbers of people.

The rapid growth of people since 1800 is described as **exponential**. During the 20th century, some people referred to this exponential growth as a *population explosion.* For instance, while it took 14 years to add one billion people between 1960 and 1974, it took only 12 years to add another billion between 1987 and 1999.

Notice in figure 3.2 that it took thousands of years for the world population to reach one billion, in 1800. Figures 3.2 and 3.3 show the rapid increase in world population that occurred between 1800 and 2000. When you compare the two graphs, do you see that the slopes of the two lines are very different? Discuss why this would be.

**exponential** Growing at an increasing rate; more specifically, a constant rate of growth applied to an increasing base. But what does this mean? Here is a question to help you understand exponential growth. You have a choice of either receiving a monthly allowance of $20 or of receiving 1 cent for the first day of the month, 2 cents for the second day, 4 cents for the third day, 8 cents for the fourth day, and so on, through a 31-day month. Which do you choose? Again, your teacher knows which is the better option.

For the most up-to-date population figures, visit <www.theworldtoday.ca> and click on updates.

Figure 3.3 shows that the rate of future additions of one billion is beginning to slow. This is because of a number of factors, the most important of which is that women are choosing to have fewer children.

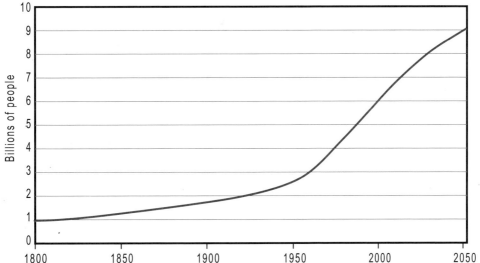

**Recent and Predicted Future Population Growth**

FIGURE 3.3. This graph shows population growth from 1800 onward in greater detail than is shown in figure 3.2. It shows the accelerating growth since about 1950 and the possible slowing down of growth by about 2050.

## Births and Deaths

Population grows when more people are born than die. To understand past and future population growth, it is necessary to consider the number of births, which add people (fertility), and the number of deaths, which remove people (mortality).

The simplest way to measure fertility is to use the **crude birth rate** (CBR). Look at table 3.2 and consider the greater population of the less-developed world. If 24 out of every 1 000 women are giving birth each year, and the population is already 5.3 billion, think how large it could be in another decade!

Another useful way of measuring fertility is to use the **total fertility rate** (TFR); this is the average number of children a woman gives birth to. The TFR introduces the interesting concept of **replacement rate**—that is, a couple that has two children "replaces" the parents when they die. Geographers measure not only fertility but also mortality. The simplest way to measure mortality is to use the **crude death rate** (CDR). The **rate of natural increase** (RNI) is the difference between the CBR and the CDR. Unlike the CBR and the CDR, which are expressed per 1 000 people, the RNI is expressed as a percentage (that is, per 100).

**crude birth rate** The number of live births in a year per 1 000 people. This rate is affected by age structure; it will be relatively high if a large percentage of the living population is of child-bearing age.

**crude death rate** The number of deaths in a year per 1 000 people. This rate is affected by age structure; it will be relatively high if there are many elderly people.

**rate of natural increase** The annual rate of population growth. It is equal to crude birth rate minus crude death rate and is expressed as a percentage.

**replacement rate** The number of children needed per woman to maintain population at the current level.

**total fertility rate** In general terms, the average number of children a woman gives birth to.

 In the less-developed world, women tend to have more children than in the more-developed world. Discuss your ideas about why this is the case.

### TABLE 3.2. World Population Data, 2005

|  | Crude Birth Rate | Total Fertility Rate | Crude Death Rate |
|---|---|---|---|
| world | 21 | 2.7 | 9 |
| more-developed world | 11 | 1.6 | 10 |
| less-developed world | 24 | 3.0 | 8 |

Source: Population Reference Bureau, *2005 World Population Data Sheet* (Washington, D.C.: Population Reference Bureau), 2005.

## Two Interesting Points in Table 3.2

1. Some of the numbers may look a little strange to you. The CDR in the more-developed world is higher than that in the less-developed world. Why? The answer is that there is a higher percentage of older people in the more-developed world than in the less-developed world, and older people are more likely to die than younger people.

2. "Crude" rates count how many people are born or die each year per 1 000 already living. They do not take into account how many people in total are born or who die. There are, of course, many more deaths in the less-developed world than in more-developed countries. If eight in each 1 000 people are dying but the population is 5.3 billion (the number of people in the less-developed world), that will add up to more people than if 10 in each 1 000 people die and the population is only 1.2 billion (the number of people in the more-developed world).

## Declining Fertility

A key fact about population today is that fertility is declining. While growth continues, people no longer see it as the "population explosion" that was feared in the 1970s. In fact, the world RNI is slowing down. So, while the world continues to experience continuing population growth, it is also experiencing declining fertility (measured either as CBR or TFR).

It is possible to have declining fertility and population growth occurring at the same time. This happens because recent population growth creates a momentum for further growth: many women are entering their childbearing years. Even though women are having fewer children, there are more of them giving birth.

### TABLE 3.3. World Fertility Decline

| Year | Total Fertility Rate |
|------|---------------------|
| 1950 | 5.0 |
| 1995 | 3.0 |
| 2005 | 2.7 |

Source: Population Reference Bureau, *2005 World Population Data Sheet* (Washington, D.C.: Population Reference Bureau), 2005.

In 2005, the TFR in the more-developed world was only 1.6. This is below the replacement rate of about 2.0, and the population of the more-developed world will decline if this trend continues. In the less-developed world, the TFR is much higher, at 3.0, which means that the population is increasing.

 Why is fertility declining? Generally, fertility is declining in the more-developed world because many women choose to enter the workforce, postpone having children until they are older, and have fewer children. As well, when people worry about the future, they tend to have fewer children. In the less-developed world, the lives of women have improved in terms of literacy and education, and women have increased access to birth control, which has resulted in reduced fertility. Discuss some other reasons showing that people are having fewer children.

## The Demographic Transition

A good way to summarize world population growth with reference to CBR, CDR, and RNI is by looking at the **demographic transition**.

**demographic transition**
A sequence of four stages of fertility and mortality change through time. Involves moving from a situation of high birth rates and high death rates to a situation of low birth rates and low death rates.

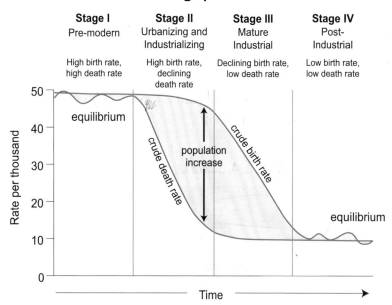

**The Demographic Transition**

FIGURE 3.4. Most countries in the world today are either in stage III (continuing growth with birth rates that are falling but that are still higher than death rates) or stage IV (stable population with birth and death rates approximately equal).

 The four stages of fertility and mortality change as indicated in figure 3.4. For each stage, write a two-to-three-sentence summary, referring to CBR, CDR, and RNI.

"Don't worry about the world coming to an end today. It's already tomorrow in Australia" (Mark Twain, 1835–1910, American author).

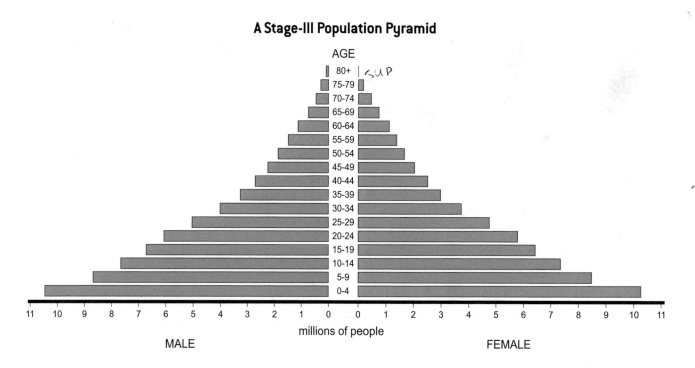

**A Stage-III Population Pyramid**

FIGURE 3.5: Population pyramid for a country in stage III of the demographic transition. This pyramid is for Nigeria in 2004.

Along with total size, important demographic characteristics of a population are the age and sex structure—that is, the proportion of people at each age, by sex. One useful way to show age and sex structure is with a **population pyramid**.

> **population pyramid** A horizontal bar graph of a population with data for males on the left and females on the right, usually grouped into five-year increments.

## A Stage-IV Population Pyramid

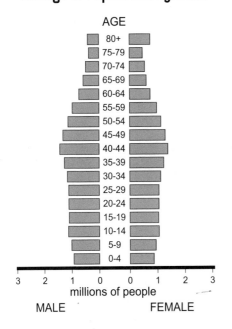

AGE

MALE · FEMALE

millions of people

**FIGURE 3.6. Population pyramid for a country in stage IV of the demographic transition. This pyramid is for Canada in 2004.**

Do you think you will have children? How many? How many children have your parents had? Do you know how many children your grandparents had? Discuss some of the positive things about having a large family and some of the negative things. If possible, interview the adults in your life to find out why they had the number of children they did.

## An Older World

People everywhere are living longer. Viewed over the long term, both the growth of world population and increases in **life expectancy** are triumphs of human ingenuity. Fewer people die now because of the progress in standards of living we have made (e.g., in quality of life, medicine, health, and nutrition).

> **life expectancy** The average number of years a newborn can expect to live under current conditions.

### TABLE 3.4. Some Life Expectancy Numbers

| Area | Life Expectancy (in years) |
|---|---|
| World | 67 |
| More-developed world | 76 |
| Less-developed world | 65 |
| Japan (highest life expectancy) | 82 |
| Botswana (lowest life expectancy) | 34 |

Source: Population Reference Bureau, *2005 World Population Data Sheet* (Washington, D.C.: Population Reference Bureau), 2005.

Life expectancy is increasing, but we continue to face many challenges. The differences between the quality of life for those in the more- and less-developed worlds are unacceptable. The lives of people living in the less-developed world must be further improved. As well, a health challenge for us in the early 21st century is the HIV/AIDS epidemic, which is especially affecting countries in sub-Saharan Africa. This will be discussed further later in this chapter and also in chapter 14.

List three reasons showing that Japan has the highest life expectancy and three reasons showing that Botswana has the lowest life expectancy.

## Are There Limits to Population Growth?

There is no single answer to the important question of whether there are limits to population growth. As people have developed new technologies, **carrying capacity** has increased. Agricultural lifestyles were able to support greater numbers of people than were hunting, collecting, and fishing lifestyles. Industrial societies were able to (and do) support an even greater number of people.

Geographers are asking more and more questions about population growth and carrying capacity. For example:

- Will the earth be able to support the approximately 9.3 billion people that may be living by the middle of this century?

- Is the earth supporting the current number of people in an adequate way?

Some geographers think that there are insufficient resources (especially food) for the number of people living in the world. They believe that world population growth should be slowed. Others feel that there is no problem in producing enough food to feed 9.3 billion people, or even more. They believe our world's problems can be solved by better distribution and by sharing our resources.

**carrying capacity**  The number of people that the earth or a part of the earth can support.

 Discuss three facts that show that there are insufficient resources (especially food) for the number of people living in the world today. Discuss three facts that show that there are sufficient resources (especially food) for the number of people living in the world today.

**FIGURE 3.7. Starving children line up for food during one of the many recent famines in Somalia. This photo was taken in August 1992, during a famine that killed an estimated 300 000 people.**

# Population Distribution and Density

Figure 3.8 shows both population distribution (where people are) and population density (how many people there are in an area). Note that population density is shown only in relative terms (high, medium, low, very low) and not in absolute terms (using a specific density statistic). The map shows that people are distributed unevenly around the world.

**TABLE 3.5. Population Density of Selected Countries (number of people per km²)**

| Country | Population Density |
|---------|--------------------|
| Bangladesh | 981.0 |
| Netherlands | 399.0 |
| Japan | 338.0 |
| India | 330.0 |
| China | 136.0 |
| Canada | 3.1 |
| Australia | 2.6 |
| Mongolia | 1.5 |

Source: Calculated from population Reference Bureau, *2005 World Population Data Sheet* (Washington, D.C.: Population Reference Bureau), 2005.

Some areas have many people (densely populated), while other areas have few people (sparsely populated). There are even some areas where nobody lives permanently. Table 3.5 shows that Bangladesh is the most densely populated country in the world and Mongolia is the least densely populated. (There are a few very small countries whose population density is higher than that of Bangladesh.)

**Population Density** Sometimes facts about population density can be misleading. For instance, according to table 3.5, Australia has a population density of 2.6 people per square kilometre. Looking at figure 3.8, you will see that the population density of most of Australia is very low; only the eastern coast has high and medium density. The average statistic does not really apply to most of the country. Similarly, Canada has a population density of 3.1 people per square kilometre. There is a medium density close to the border with the eastern United States and a very low density in the north.

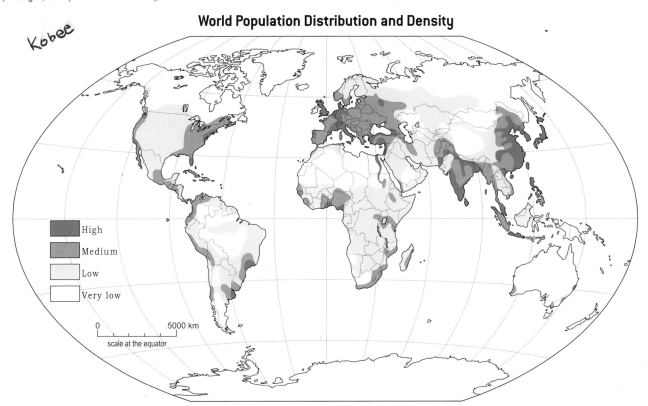

**World Population Distribution and Density**

Kobee

High
Medium
Low
Very low

0    5000 km
scale at the equator

**FIGURE 3.8. This generalized map shows both where people live (distribution) and how many people live there (density). The key is intentionally nonspecific; it describes density in relative terms only.**

## Why Do We Live Where We Do?

We choose to live in some areas but not in other areas. Glance back at figure 2.16. For each of the ten regions shown on that map, make an educated guess about whether the density will be high, medium, low, or very low. Discuss your estimates with classmates. Then check your estimates by looking at the world map of population distribution and density (figure 3.8, page 69). You will quickly see that the harsher the environment (especially as measured by precipitation and temperature), the less likely it will be that people live there.

Why are global environmental regions and population distribution and density related? It all comes down to natural resources, especially how the natural resources in an area do or do not support agriculture in that area; some environmental regions are good for agriculture, and others are not. Humans have chosen to live primarily in areas where food is plentiful and where the climate and soil support agricultural activities. One good way to assess the agricultural potential of an area is to take a look at the length of the growing season. Areas with a long growing season provide opportunities for food production; areas with a short growing season (or no growing season at all) do not provide these opportunities.

## Population Density and Distribution in 2050

Between now and 2050, there will be changes in population distribution and density by region. This page and the facing page include some predictions of what those changes might be. The details of these predictions will change, but the general trends will probably not. For example, the population of India may not be 1 628 million in 2050, but it will increase significantly. The population of Ethiopia may not be 170 million, but Ethiopia is likely to be one of the top ten most-populated countries in 2050.

By 2050, the population of the more-developed world will increase only slightly (from 1.2 to 1.3

 Discuss three reasons other than the length of the growing season that can help make an area suitable for agriculture.

### TABLE 3.6. The Ten Most-Populated Countries Today

| Country | Population (in millions) |
| --- | --- |
| China | 1 304 |
| India | 1 104 |
| United States | 297 |
| Indonesia | 222 |
| Brazil | 184 |
| Pakistan | 162 |
| Bangladesh | 144 |
| Russia | 143 |
| Nigeria | 132 |
| Japan | 128 |

Source: Population Reference Bureau, *2005 World Population Data Sheet* (Washington, D.C.: Population Reference Bureau), 2005.

### TABLE 3.7. The Ten Most-Populated Countries Predicted for 2050

| Country | Population (in millions) |
| --- | --- |
| India | 1 628 |
| China | 1 437 |
| United States | 420 |
| Indonesia | 308 |
| Pakistan | 295 |
| Brazil | 260 |
| Nigeria | 258 |
| Bangladesh | 231 |
| DR of Congo | 183 |
| Ethiopia | 170 |

Source: Population Reference Bureau, *2005 World Population Data Sheet* (Washington, D.C.: Population Reference Bureau), 2005.

billion), and the population of Europe (part of the more-developed world) will decline. However, during this same time period, the population of the less-developed world will increase from 5.3 to 8.0 billion, and much of this growth will occur in Asia and Africa.

Tables 3.6 and 3.7 show data for specific countries. Note the differences between the figures in these two tables. Discuss three reasons showing that these changes are occurring. Discuss three challenges that these changing numbers might bring to the people living in these countries.

 On the global scale, between today and 2050, the relatively high-density areas will remain relatively high, and the relatively low-density areas will remain relatively low. In specific countries, changes will occur because of changes in the numbers of births and deaths in those countries.

It is possible that the fastest growing country between now and 2050 will be Niger, where it is expected that the population will increase from 12 to 53 million. This prediction will be incorrect, however, if famine occurs. It is likely that the country losing the most population will be Bulgaria, where it is expected that the population will decline from 8 to 5 million.

## Possible Effect of Disease

The population of the world has a net increase of about 75 million people each year. However, there is one circumstance that might change this fact, and that is the growth and spread of disease, most notably of HIV/AIDS. Today, the countries most affected by this epidemic are in sub-Saharan Africa: Botswana, Zimbabwe, Swaziland, Lesotho, Namibia, Zambia, South Africa, Kenya, Malawi, and Mozambique. In these countries, mortality is rising and life expectancy is declining. Disease-related deaths in this region are not, however, sufficient to significantly reduce world annual growth.

But, if the epidemic spreads to other regions—especially to highly populated countries like China and India—then predictions of future growth in those countries, and for the world more generally, will be invalid.

**Three Types of Prediction** Predicting world population growth is very difficult. Death rates are low, about as low as possible, in many parts of the world. Birth rates are declining generally but remain high in many less-developed countries. The most difficult part of any population prediction is knowing what will happen to birth rates in less-developed countries. It seems likely that they will continue to fall, but the big unknown is how quickly this will happen and how low the rates will fall. Will they reach the replacement-rate level of two children per couple? The three types of prediction are:

1. an optimistic prediction, which sees birth rates falling rapidly to replacement-rate level
2. a current-trend prediction, which sees birth rates falling slowly but eventually reaching replacement-rate level; this is what is happening now
3. a pessimistic prediction, which sees birth rates falling but stabilizing at a level somewhere above the replacement rate

 The human cost of the HIV/AIDS epidemic is tragic. Look at current newspapers and news magazines and find stories about this epidemic. Bring these to class for discussion. Also consider what other epidemics might occur in the near future.

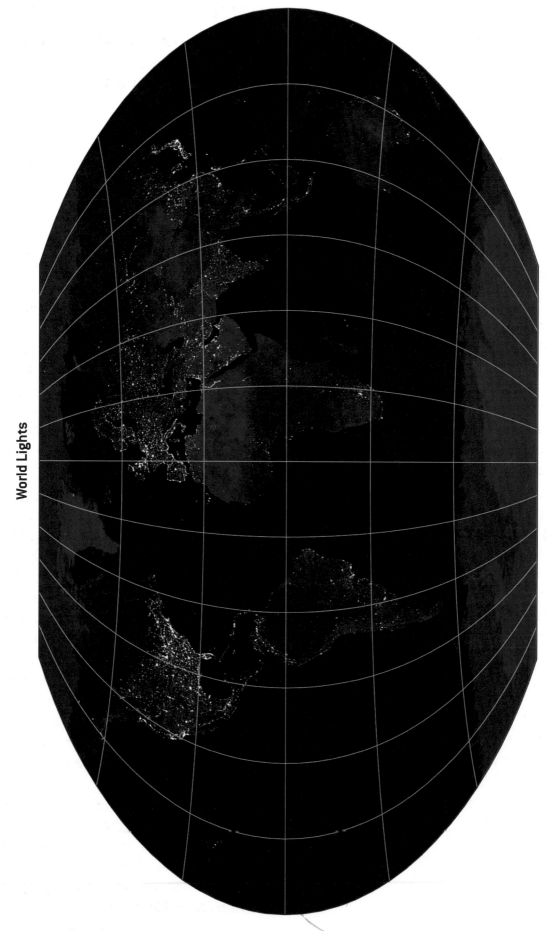

**World Lights**

FIGURE 3.9. Have you ever flown over a city at night? What you see is an amazing collection of lights. This satellite view of the earth at night tells part of the story of geographic patterns and population density.

## Migration

Changes in population distribution and density occur not only because of changes in births and deaths but also because of **migration**. Migration—both **emigration** and **immigration** —does not make a difference when we consider world population, but it does matter when we consider population distribution and density for specific countries or regions.

**emigration** The movement of people out of a country.

**immigration** The movement of people into a country.

**migration** The movement of people from place to place.

Much of Canada's population growth has come from immigration, and, in turn, much of the western provinces' population growth has come as people have migrated west from the eastern provinces.

 Discuss three reasons for someone wanting to move from one country to another. Do you know anyone who has immigrated to Canada? Why did they move? Do you know anyone who emigrated from Canada? Do you know why they left?

 Look through newspapers and news magazines during the next few weeks for articles about immigration into Canada. What countries are people emigrating from to come to Canada? List three reasons showing why people might have to emigrate from a country. List three reasons showing why people might have to immigrate to Canada.

## World Lights

Figure 3.9 is a very interesting map of the world. It shows each region of the earth as it looks at night, and, because there is no sunlight, the earth is in darkness. But not everywhere in the world is dark at night; some areas are clearly lit up. This map does not show the distribution of all the people in the world. However, it does show the distribution of some people, specifically where people live close together in large numbers (especially cities), where there are many artificial lights.

Many of the more-developed countries in the world use lighting all the time: office towers never shut their lights off completely; street lights turn on automatically as soon as the sun goes down; many people leave at least one light on at night in their homes. In the more-developed countries, the greater the population density, the brighter the night view. Some people call this *light pollution*.

*Light* and *pollution* are probably not words that you might think belong together. But, if you have ever looked up at the night sky in a large city and at another time looked at the sky in an uninhabited area, you know what an effect city lights have. There are three forms of light pollution. First, there is *skyglow*, which is the result of wasted light from poorly designed light fixtures that do not direct light effectly to where it is needed (e.g., some street lights cast light skyward rather than to the ground below). Second, there is *light trespass*, which occurs when light crosses property lines and illuminates an unintended place (e.g., when someone else's light illuminates your living room). Third, there is *glare*, which is caused by too much lighting and results in eye irritation.

In less-developed countries, some densely populated areas do not have reliable supplies of electricity, so they are in darkness. Many slum areas on the edges of large cities in less-developed countries have huge populations but virtually no electricity.

# Understanding Our Unequal World

Look at the question-and-answer box on this page and consider the incorrect answer. Not only is it incorrect, but it is also racist, and we now reject it. We know that different groups of people do not have different levels of ability. All over the world, both in the past and now, different groups of people show initiative and creativity. People everywhere—in tropical Africa, the steppes of Asia, the Australian outback—have demonstrated the ability to identify and solve problems. It is inappropriate to suggest that the people who live in what are less-developed countries are in some ways less intelligent, less able, less thoughtful. We are all members of a single species—human beings—and there are no meaningful differences between groups in intelligence and creativity. We will discuss this issue again in chapter 13.

**Question** At the beginning of this chapter, we stated that the world is an unequal place. It contains both more-developed countries and less-developed countries. But why? Why do some countries "have" while others "have not"? This is not an easy question to answer.

**Incorrect Answer** Some parts of the world are settled by groups of people who have been unable to achieve high levels of development because they lack the necessary intelligence and creativity to develop technologically.

**Finding the Correct Answer** Can you suggest what might be the correct answer to this very important question?

## The Importance of Physical Geography to Human Lifestyles

Let us consider three important facts about the relationship between physical geography and agriculture: latitude; the shapes of continents; and climate, wildlife, and plant life.

### Latitude
Latitute is one of the key determinants of climate generally. At or near the equator, for example, the length of a day is about 12 hours, and there are no seasonal changes. On the Canadian prairies, at about latitude 50°N, however, daylight hours vary significantly at different times of the year, and there are significant seasonal differences in climate.

### The Shapes of the Continents
Europe and Asia together spread east-west a great distance (latitudinally). Africa and the Americas spread north-south a great distance (longitudinally). Continents that spread east-west have large areas of similar climate, which means that technological developments related to agriculture will spread across the area at about the same latitude. Continents that spread north-south lack large areas of similar climate; therefore, technological developments related to agriculture will not spread.

### Climate, Wildlife, and Plant Life
Some parts of the world (e.g., those that are home to wild plants cultivated by humans, and animals that humans can use to provide labour, milk, meat, and clothing) have a physical geography that is well suited to agriculture. Other parts of the world (where it is too cold or too dry, or lack suitable wild plants and animals) have a physical geography that is not well suited to agriculture. Those parts of the world with a physical geography suited to the development of agriculture (both growing plants and raising animals) have

a competitive advantage over parts of the world with a physical geography unsuited to the development of agriculture.

If agriculture develops in a continent with a substantial east-west extent, then new agricultural technologies can spread latitudinally. If agriculture develops in a continent with a substantial north-south extent, then new technologies cannot spread latitudinally.

When agricultural development happens in a continent that stretches east-west, the new ideas associated with it can also spread latitudinally. Generally, this is what happened in Eurasia. But, because Africa and the Americas are geographically organized north-south, the new ideas associated with agricultural development did not spread.

### Shape and Size of Continents

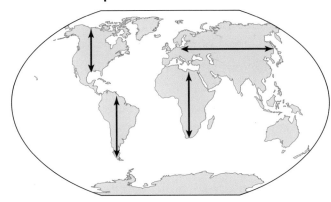

FIGURE 3.10. This map highlights the shape and size of four of the continents. It shows the considerable latitudinal extent of Eurasia compared to the considerable longitudinal extent of Africa, of North America, and of South America (*latitudinal* meaning west to east, across a specific zone of latitude; *longitudinal* meaning north to south, along a zone of longitude).

### The Effects of Colonialism

We have not quite finished answering the very important question Why is the world an unequal place? We know that, in some parts of the world:

- because of the physical geography, agriculture did not develop

- agriculture did develop but, because it occurred on a continent with limited latitudinal extent, agricultural and other technologies did not spread a great distance

- agriculture developed and, because it occurred on a continent with considerable latitudinal extent, it and other technologies spread a great distance; these extensive agricultural regions became home to politically powerful groups

But we also need to consider the effects of **colonialism**. Colonialism was the final factor that led to the unequal division of the world as it currently exists. By the 15th century, Europe and China, both of which are in Eurasia, were the most powerful regions in the world.

Of these two, it was Europe that advanced in ways that permitted some European countries to begin a series of global voyages and eventual occupation of much of the rest of the world. Overseas movement allowed Europeans to colonize other areas and to dominate those areas militarily, culturally, socially, politically, and economically. European colonialism allowed for further achievements in Europe and usually prevented achievements in the areas they colonized. For example, Britain encouraged cotton production in Egypt, which enabled Britain to develop a flourishing cotton industry but did not benefit Egypt. Most countries that are now more developed achieved this through their occupation and domination of those countries that are now less developed.

**colonialism**  The process that involves one country establishing and maintaining political, and usually economic and cultural, control over another part of the world.

## Dividing Our World into Countries

Close your eyes and picture the world. For most of us, the picture in our heads will be of a world with basic physical boundaries, especially land and sea boundaries, and a world divided into countries.

Figure 3.11. The countries of the world today.

The world map shown in figure 3.11 uses an interrupted Winkel-Tripel projection. The other world maps in this book use the more usual standard Winkel-Tripel projection, which is centred on the prime meridian (0° longitude).

The interrupted version of the projection, with the western hemisphere centred at 100° west and the eastern hemisphere centred at 80° east, is more suited to a map that spreads over two pages of a book.

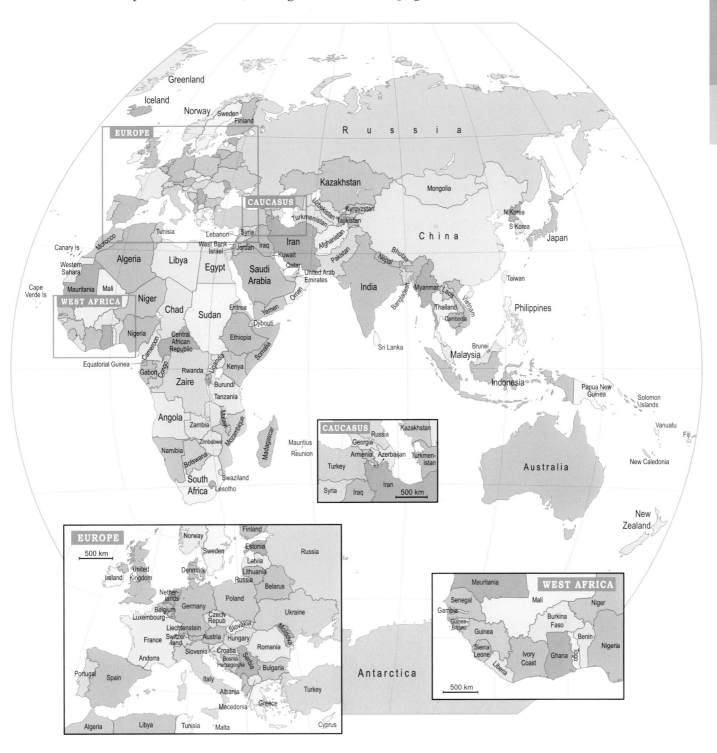

One of the most important ways in which we organize our world is by creating countries. Countries can be thought of as places that house a group of people who share some characteristics: perhaps language, perhaps religion, perhaps a more loosely defined sense of identity than language or religion. Two points are important here:

1. The division of the world into countries is not a fixed pattern. Consider that in 1900 there were about 57 countries, whereas today there are about 193. The number has increased mainly because the world of 1900 included several empires that have now collapsed, allowing many former colonial areas to become independent countries. As of 2005, the world's newest country is East Timor.

2. Many countries today experience internal tensions that threaten their stability. These internal tensions can sometimes lead to a breaking up of one large country into several smaller countries. For example, this happened to the former Soviet Union in 1990.

 Two countries that were on the world map in 1990 but are not today are the Soviet Union and Yugoslavia. Both comprised very diverse population groups and accordingly broke up into several countries. Use an atlas or the Internet to locate the area of the former Soviet Union and of the former Yugoslavia. Prepare two lists:

1. containing the countries that were previously part of the Soviet Union

2. containing the countries that were previously part of Yugoslavia

 Discuss three reasons that the Soviet Union and Yugoslavia broke up into smaller countries.

## The Changing Political Geography of Africa

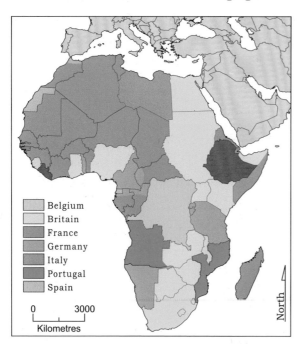

Belgium
Britain
France
Germany
Italy
Portugal
Spain

0    3000
Kilometres

North

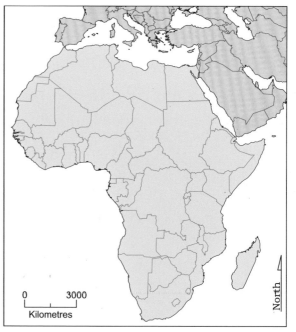

0    3000
Kilometres

North

FIGURE 3.12. Left: Africa about 100 years ago, when European countries controlled large areas (the political boundaries on this map are present-day boundaries). Right: Africa in 2005. The colonial empires have disappeared and all countries are now independent (the individual countries are not named).

The greatest increase in the number of independent countries during the 20th century occurred in Africa. About 100 years ago, European countries controlled much of Africa: Britain, Spain, Portugal, Belgium, the Netherlands, Germany, France, and Italy. As these empires collapsed, the areas they dominated became independent countries.

 Select one of the countries shown on the 2005 map in figure 3.12 (on the right) but that is not shown as an independent country on the earlier map (on the left). Use library sources and the Internet to learn more about its colonial past. Check to see if some of the place names used during the colonial era have been changed to better reflect the African identity.

 The peoples and places of the world show great differences, some of which might be thought of as good and interesting differences and others of which are clearly unacceptable. Suggest three acceptable differences and three unacceptable differences evident in the world today.

"The reasonable man adapts himself to the world; the unreasonable one persists in trying to adapt the world to himself. Therefore all progress depends on the unreasonable man" (Anthony Burgess, 1917–1993, English author).

## Six Key Facts about Our Human World

This chapter has introduced six key facts about the world:

1. The world is an unequal place: some countries are more developed, other countries are less developed. As you work your way through this book, you will find that this distinction appears frequently.

2. The world population today is increasing by about 75 million people each year, but the rate of increase is declining because birth rates are declining.

3. Current projections suggest that the world's population will reach about 9.3 billion by the middle of this century. Later in the century, it will stabilize or possibly begin to decline.

4. Most future growth in world population will occur in less-developed countries, because there are already more people in those countries and because fertility is higher in less-developed countries than it is in more-developed countries.

5. On the global scale, there are close relationships between world environmental regions and population distribution and density among those regions.

6. The current map of the world is not a fixed and unchanging fact.

Perhaps the greatest challenge facing the world today is that of undoing the historically recent creation of more-developed and less-developed parts of the world to make this a fairer world for all people.

 Discuss three ways that we could reduce or even eliminate the divisions between the more- and less-developed worlds.

# WELL-BEING AROUND THE WORLD

People experience very different levels of well-being in different parts of the world. Human geographers describe and analyze these differences and encourage all of us to contribute to making the world a more just and equitable collection of places.

In chapter 4, there is a discussion about how we measure fundamental human needs and about the discrepancies in the quality of life of citizens around the globe. You learn about some organizations and some individuals, especially those in Canada, that are working toward narrowing the gap between the less-developed and the more-developed worlds.

Chapter 5 focuses on the fundamental rights and responsibilities of citizens around the world. We introduce the history of human-rights documents and discuss violations of these rights. We introduce some of the individuals who have worked toward the creation of a just and equitable world.

Chapter 6 details the values and principles of democracy. We present the history of democratic institutions and the benefits of living in a democratic society. We discuss some of the "movers and shakers" who have shaped our democratic institutions today. We conclude the chapter with a reminder that it is our responsibility to exercise our democratic rights and responsibilities each and every day.

You will have noticed that the word *rights* is often accompanied by the word *responsibilities*. This is an important lesson in itself.

Chapter 7 outlines the distribution of wealth and power in today's world. We explain the ways we measure a nation's wealth as well as how equitably this wealth is distributed. We outline who holds the wealth and power and how this power is used and (sometimes) abused. As individual citizens, we must empower ourselves to ensure that the world is a just and equitable place that enables all its citizens to survive and thrive.

Chapter 8 outlines the necessity of working together to ensure that human rights are maintained and enhanced universally. We show how individuals and groups can and do make a difference in the political, economic, and social lives of others. More and more, the world is becoming a global village, connecting all people; we need to work together for a equitable future.

On 15 April 2005, the design for the Canadian Museum for Human Rights was unveiled (see photo on facing page). The museum is to be located in Winnipeg, and the mandate of its founders is that it become a beacon for informing and educating the world about human rights. It will display the history of human-rights movements and their leaders and promote the advancement of human rights worldwide.

It was a long-held dream of Dr. Israel Asper (1932–2003) (the founder of one of Canada's media empires) and his family to establish the centre. As stated by Mrs. Asper when the design for the centre was unveiled, "This is a moment Israel dreamed of as he appealed to all of Canada to look beyond ourselves, and our parochial interests, to reach for the stars and create an iconic structure that would symbolize Canada's commitment to human rights." The museum was designed by Antoine Predock (b. 1936), an American architect whose design reflects the principle that human rights begin "from the ground up." His design enhances both the physical and human geography of the surrounding landscape.

# QUALITY OF LIFE

## Guiding Questions

1. What is the "good life"?

2. Which are the best places to live in the world?

3. How do we decide where the best places to live are?

4. What roles do individuals and governments, particularly our Canadian government, play in ensuring the "good life" for all people around the world?

## Our Basic Needs

What are your most basic needs? Are your video games as vital to you as food and water? Is your recorded-music collection as important to you as having access to medical care? Is driving the family car as important to you as having a shelter to provide warmth and protection from wind, rain, and snow?

The answers to these questions are obvious. There are several basic human needs that enable us to continue living—to survive. These basic human needs include food, clean water, health care, and shelter. Needs are clearly different from those things that we desire: our wants—such as video games, recorded music, and driving a car.

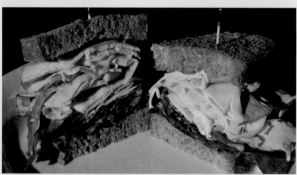

FIGURE 4.1. When the goal is life itself, which are needs and which are wants?

# Our Standard of Living

We have needs and wants. When we talk about quality of life, we are talking about the extent to which both our needs and wants are satisfied. One way to measure our quality of life is to think about the idea of *standard of living*.

> **Standard of Living** As defined in chapter 3, standard of living is the physical level of comfort determined by the number and quality of the goods and services available to us. Goods are the products of a country's economy: food, clothing, and machines, for example. Services include what people do for other people in return for income: providing health care, selling products, coordinating travel, and teaching, for example. Standard of living is expressed in statistical terms.
>
> The more-developed countries, such as Canada, the United States, Japan, Australia, New Zealand, and all European countries, have the world's highest standards of living.
>
> The less-developed countries, such as those located in Africa, Central and South America, and Asia, have the world's lowest standards of living.

How useful is the measure of standard of living as an indicator of quality of life? In Canada, the average person consumes lots of goods and services—that is, we buy a lot of food, clothing, and machinery, and we also use the services of doctors, shop assistants, travel agents, and teachers on a regular basis. This means that Canada has a high standard of living. But this simple statement ignores two important points:

1. Not all citizens of Canada have the same high standard of living. It is important to recognize that factual (statistical) statements about countries are averages. A national measure of standard of living does not tell us if all of a country's citizens' needs and wants are satisfied.

2. The measure of the standard of living of a country does not tell us if there are other factors influencing the quality of life of its citizens. For example, pollution and overcrowding are negative outcomes of too much consumption.

Clearly, standard of living is only a partial measure of quality of life. There are many factors other than production and consumption of goods and services that contribute to quality of life. For example, how do we feel about where we live, about our government, schools, and recreational facilities? Unfortunately, these factors cannot be measured. Different people value them in different ways.

>  Discuss three reasons that show how the statistical measurement of standard of living might not really capture what we mean when we talk about quality of life. Consider also whether our seemingly insatiable appetite to consume is addressing all of the needs of a society.

> "We make a living by what we get, we make a life by what we give" (Sir Winston Churchill, 1874–1965, British politician).

## Human Development

Fortunately, there is a better way to understand what we mean when we talk about quality of life—the idea of **human development**.

> **human development** More about creating places in which people are able to lead full and productive lives of their choosing than about how much we are able to produce and consume.

In the same way that you receive a report card at the end of each term, almost every country in the world receives its quality-of-life report card once a year. The people who prepare these report cards work for the United Nations, an organization that represents the interests of almost all of the countries in the world (we will discuss this topic again in chapter 8). The reports are published together in the annual *Human Development Report*. The report covers the following four areas:

1. Political and military; the number of seats held by women in government; the number of people in the armed forces; military expenditures

2. Economic: what is produced; the value of goods and services received from (imported) and provided to (exported) the rest of the world; development assistance to other countries; the national unemployment rate

3. Environmental: electricity and fuel consumption; carbon dioxide emissions; efforts to protect the environment

4. Social: health factors (such as the percentage of people under the average height and weight for age, the number of people undernourished, the probability of a newborn dying within one year, and the percentage of people infected with life-threatening diseases such as tuberculosis, HIV/AIDS, and malaria); educational factors (such as the percentage of people aged 15 and over who can read and write; the amount of money government spends on education; and the number of students enrolled in preschool, primary, secondary, middle-years, and post-secondary schools); living conditions (such as sanitation facilities; water sources; the percentage of people victimized by crime; the percentage of cell phone subscribers and Internet users)

Look at figure 4.2 and table 4.1. The ranking of countries shown in them highlights what we already know: there is a tragic difference between life in rich and life in poor countries. Notice that, except for Canada, Australia, the United States, Japan, and New Zealand, the top 20 countries are all in Europe. All of the bottom countries are in Africa. Just as some students receive a failing grade in some of their courses, many countries receive a "failing" grade in human development.

 Discuss three aspects of life other than those listed on this page that should be considered part of the measure of human development. Discuss your list with your classmates.

 "Wealth is evidently not the good we are seeking, for it is merely useful for the sake of something else" (Aristotle, 384–322 BCE, Greek philosopher). Discuss whether this statement highlights the terms we are using to measure quality of life: *standard of living* and *human development*. You may wish to think about whether the word *good* in Aristotle's quote has more than one meaning.

## The State of the World

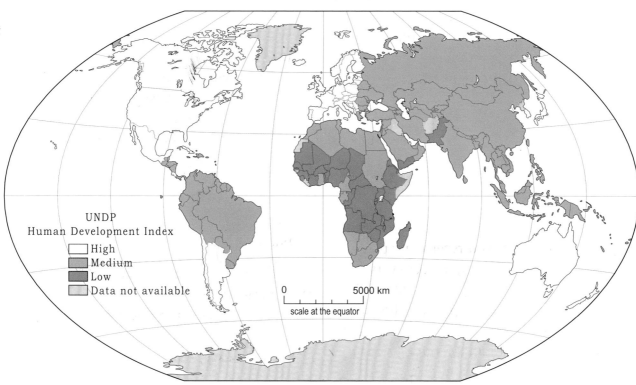

FIGURE 4.2. See table 4.1 and locate on this map the countries that are listed in the table.

## TABLE 4.1. The Best of Worlds, and the Worst of Worlds

| The Top Twenty Countries in Terms of Human Development, 2003 | | The Bottom Twenty Countries in Terms of Human Development, 2003 | |
|---|---|---|---|
| 1 | Norway | 158 | Nigeria |
| 2 | Iceland | 159 | Rwanda |
| 3 | Australia | 160 | Angola |
| 4 | Luxembourg | 161 | Eritrea |
| 5 | Canada | 162 | Benin |
| 6 | Sweden | 163 | Côte d'Ivoire |
| 7 | Switzerland | 164 | Tanzania |
| 8 | Ireland | 165 | Malawi |
| 9 | Belgium | 166 | Zambia |
| 10 | United States | 167 | D.R. of Congo |
| 11 | Japan | 168 | Mozambique |
| 12 | Netherlands | 169 | Burundi |
| 13 | Finland | 170 | Ethiopia |
| 14 | Denmark | 171 | Central African Republic |
| 15 | United Kingdom | 172 | Guinea-Bissau |
| 16 | France | 173 | Chad |
| 17 | Austria | 174 | Mali |
| 18 | Italy | 175 | Burkina Faso |
| 19 | New Zealand | 176 | Sierra Leone |
| 20 | Germany | 177 | Niger |

Source: United Nations Development Programme. *Human Development Report, 2005.* International Cooperation at a Crossroads: Aid, Trade, and Security in an Unequal World. UNDP: 2005.

You will have many assignments that involve researching an issue using library sources and the Internet. Here are a few suggestions about how to summarize information in your own words. Before you start writing a research paper, try to do the following:

- Read an entire article on your topic.

- Make a list of key terms and define them in your paper.

- Find and read at least one other article on the same topic.

- Compare the two articles in a Venn diagram to determine what information is the same and what information is different. You can also create a word web of the key information that you collected from the articles.

- Decide which information is important and organize it into sub-topics; each sub-topic will become a paragraph.

- Think of a catchy title for your paper and use it as a guide to write your introduction, topic sentences for your paragraphs, and your conclusion.

- If you find that the original author expressed an idea well, share it with your reader. Quote your author, and remember to give credit to the author.

- Keep track of your sources so that you can create a bibliography at the end of your paper. A bibliography encourages your audience to read more about your topic and to see if they come to the same conclusion as you did.

Some countries choose not to participate in the United Nations report, and other countries are unable to provide the necessary statistics; collecting information (e.g., by taking a census) is difficult and costly and may not be a priority in poor countries. In 2004, 177 countries were included in the report. Iraq, Somalia, and the Democratic People's Republic of Korea (also known as North Korea) are three countries that chose not to participate.

 Did you know that Canada ranked first in 1990, 1992, 1994, 1996, 1997, 1998, and 1999 on the human-development scale? Brainstorm the question of why many Canadians might think that Canada is one of the best places in the world to live and why it might not be.

 Select one of the countries that rank in the top 20 and one that ranks in the bottom 20. Use library sources and the Internet for research and then create a poster highlighting some of the differences between the two countries.

 Study the two maps in figure 4.3 carefully. Note that the countries in the less-developed world are located in sub-Saharan Africa. These maps are just two of many that might be drawn to show the very real differences in quality of life in various countries around the world. What are some other factors that might be measured and mapped to help reinforce this point?

"The goal of life is living in agreement with nature" [Zeno, 335 BCE–264 CE, from Diogenes Laertius, trans. R.D. Hicks, *Lives and Opinions of Eminent Philosophers* [New York: G.P. Putnam's Sons], 1925].

## People with Access to Improved Drinking Water

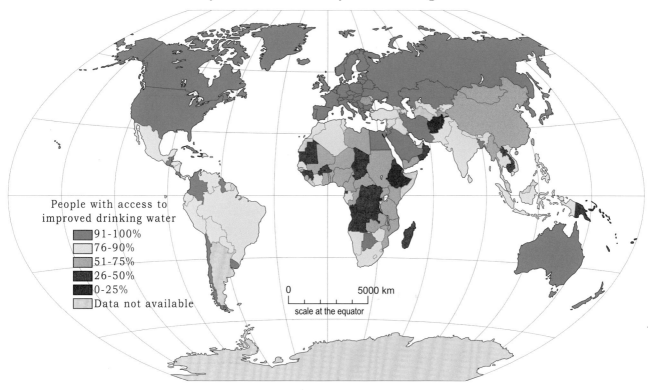

People with access to improved drinking water
- 91-100%
- 76-90%
- 51-75%
- 26-50%
- 0-25%
- Data not available

0      5000 km

scale at the equator

## Percentage of Undernourished People

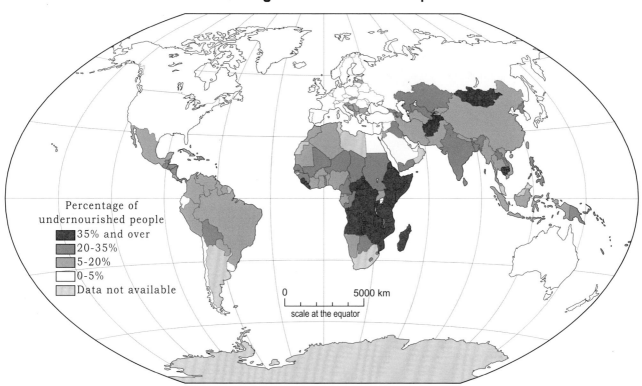

Percentage of undernourished people
- 35% and over
- 20-35%
- 5-20%
- 0-5%
- Data not available

0      5000 km

scale at the equator

FIGURE 4.3. Two maps with one message: the world is an unequal place.

## Improving the World's Average Grade

The discussion of human development in this chapter supports what you read in chapter 3: our world comprises a set of unequal places. People in more-developed countries live mostly in large cities, enjoy higher incomes and higher life expectancy, and have a greater amount of leisure time available than people do in less-developed countries. The more-developed countries are located mostly in temperate parts of the world. These countries include regions with soil that is well suited to the growing of crops and with sufficient rain and warm growing days.

**Question** Why is it important to improve human development in those countries that are less developed?

**Suggested Answer** The balance of development in the world is unfair, and it is morally right for more-developed countries to help improve development in less-developed countries. Do you agree with the suggested answer? If yes, why? If not, what answer do you suggest, and why?

One way to achieve the goal of raising the level of human development in less-developed countries is for the more-developed countries to provide aid, both short-term aid (e.g., for food shortages) and longer-term aid (build health clinics and schools, improve the water supply, and implement more efficient agricultural practices). Providing aid to a less-developed country is not an easy task. For example, the government receiving aid might be corrupt, and the aid might not reach those who are in most need; or the transport facilities to move aid to those in need might not be adequate.

So, what is being done? We look first at the work of one famous individual and, second, at the work of one Canadian organization.

### Bob Geldof

Bob Geldof's (b. 1951) contribution is an example of what one individual can do to help those in need. In 1986, the former lead singer of the Irish punk-rock band the Boomtown Rats received an honorary knighthood from Queen Elizabeth II for his efforts as a social activist and became Sir Bob Geldof. How does a performer and songwriter transform himself into a world-class humanitarian?

Geldof began to use his fame as a musician to help people in less-developed countries in 1984, when he saw a media report on famine in Ethiopia. To raise money for the victims of this famine, he collaborated with many other well-known popular singers on a song entitled "Do They Know It's Christmas?"which was released by the group Band Aid. The song, which became the biggest-selling single in the United Kingdom's chart history, raised $150 million. (A second version of the song topped the United Kingdom's charts in 2004.)

 It is is essential that more-developed countries give aid to less-developed countries, but it is also essential to provide them with the means to help themselves. One way of doing this is to help reduce the debt load of less-developed countries. Many of these countries spend a huge portion of their government budgets just paying the interest on their debt. These interest payments are often much more than the amount of money spent on education or health, for example. Check newspapers and news magazines to see if the topic of debt reduction is being discussed. If it is not, then look for reports about other means of aiding the less-developed world.

FIGURE 4.4. On 2 July 2005, a series of 10 concerts, called Live 8, was held in cities around the world. These concerts influenced public opinion and prompted world leaders to take action. One of the driving forces behind these and other concerts was Bob Geldof, who is shown here with a number of African children. The photo was taken in 2003 in Ethiopia.

In 1985, Geldof joined American pop stars Michael Jackson (b. 1958) and Stevie Wonder (b. 1950), among others, to perform a song entitled "We Are the World." Later that year, he organized a massive charity concert called Live Aid, which raised not only huge sums of money but, more important, the consciousness of many people around the world about those who were less fortunate than themselves. Furthermore, the concert prompted governments of more-developed countries to increase their famine-relief donations.

Together with another rock-band leader, U2's Bono (b. 1960), Geldof has worked to convince governments of more-developed countries to reduce the debt load of impoverished African countries. They called their program DATA (debt, AIDS, trade, Africa). For their tireless humanitarian efforts, both musicians have been nominated for the Nobel Peace Prize.

## Canada at Work Helping Others

The Canadian International Development Agency (CIDA) is one of many international agencies that are actively working to reduce poverty by promoting the economic and social well-being of less-developed countries throughout the world. Other agencies with the same goals include:

- Department for International Development (United Kingdom)

- French Development Agency

- International Fund for Agricultural Development (United Nations)

- Japan's Official Development Assistance Program

- Norwegian Agency for Development Cooperation

- Swedish International Development Cooperation Agency

- United States Agency for International Development

 Use the Internet to learn more about one of the agencies listed above and create a poster describing the agency's work. As an extra challenge, find one other agency that does similar work.

 Do an Internet search on Canadians in development work around the world. Visit <www.theworldtoday.ca> and follow "Links" to <www.citizens4change.org>. Read some of the personal stories and note the various occupations and skills represented by the workers in the field of development.

According to CIDA, development begins with meeting the most basic human needs: food, clean water, good health, and shelter. CIDA stresses as well that an **infrastructure** that provides essential services for all and underpins economic growth must be in place, along with an economy that encourages innovation and respects the environment.

Many Canadians believe in the importance of helping people in need and support these agencies. Today, television and the Internet bring images from less-developed countries directly into our homes. We can see that our own security, health, environment, and economic well-being are increasingly affected by events in less-developed countries. This is so because peoples and places of the world

**infrastructure** Refers to all those things that enable a society to function effectively: transport and communications systems, power supply, water supply, and a sewage system, for example. In many parts of the less-developed world, these things are lacking. In the more-developed world, we take these things for granted.

 For more information about the work of CIDA, as well as other aid organizations, visit <www.theworldtoday.ca> and follow "Links" to <www.acdicida.gc.ca/youthzone.htm>.

 Where should CIDA become involved in the future, and what should the agency do there? Suggest a country and defend your choice.

are becoming closely connected (see our discussion of the global village in the introduction). For example, a particular strain of influenza might spread from a poor area in Asia and overwhelm the health systems in other places around the world.

As of 2004, one branch of CIDA has been called Butterfly 208. This organization was designed by Canadian youth for teens around the world. It began with the following idea: if a butterfly flapped its wings in one part of the world, then the air disturbance caused by one flap might upset a delicate balance of nature that could trigger a storm somewhere else in the world a month later. The organization challenges students to imagine the power of ideas—one very small action could help improve the quality of life in many other countries (208 is the suggested number of places that might need help). The main idea is that our world is totally interconnected.

Butterfly 208 encourages Canadian youths to put their hearts and minds together to think about problems that people in less-developed countries must face on a daily basis.

 For more information about Butterfly 208, visit <www.theworldtoday.ca> and follow "Links" to <www.bp208.ca/main.php>.

 Debate the following question: What is more important— how much we give or how much we get? When thinking about this, consider the following:

- Does being generous always produce positive results?

- Does receiving aid have some negative effects?

## Making the Grade

The balance of wealth in the world today is unequal and unfair. There is no single explanation for this inequality. Most notable, however, are two factors (as discussed in chapter 3):

1. Most of the more-developed countries are located in temperate areas of the world; these areas do not suffer from extremes of climate and are therefore well suited to crop production.

2. Most of what is now the less-developed world underwent colonization by European countries, which limited the economic opportunities for them and enhanced opportunities for the colonizing countries.

It is essential that those of us who live comfortable and safe lives work hard to ensure that all people in the world can live in the same way. Much is being done, both by individuals and by organizations, to this end. But is the gap being narrowed? There are some reasons to be optimistic. For example, poverty is decreasing worldwide, and the current world **literacy rate** of 82 percent is higher than ever before. Also, world life-expectancy has increased since 1960 from 46 to 65 years. Improving literacy rates and increasing life expectancy are both very positive changes.

There are also reasons to be pessimistic. Far too many people have insufficient medical care, lack the opportunity to be formally educated in schools, live on insufficient money, and face starvation. Further, because of the HIV/AIDS epidemic, there are rising mortality rates and declining life-expectancy rates in some African countries. Clearly, much more needs to be done.

**literacy rate** Usually defined as the percentage of a country's people aged 15 and over who are able to read and write.

# UNIVERSAL HUMAN RIGHTS

**5**

## Guiding Questions

1. What are our fundamental rights as human beings?

2. How are our rights protected?

3. Who guards and maintains our rights?

4. When, where, why, and how have human rights been violated?

5. What responsibilities do we have to protect the rights of others within our communities?

## What Are Our Rights?

Imagine that you were in a classroom, and, after 20 minutes, the teacher has still not shown up. What would you do? Who would take control? You and your classmates have the *right* and the *responsibility* to act. You might first agree that someone—for example your class president—should take control of the class and ask everyone to take their seats. Someone would need to notify the principal. Any student who left the room would need to be called back. All students would need to wait patiently for the problem to be solved. You would not want to let chaos take control, so you would need to be a responsible citizen and take control yourself!

The United Nations *Universal Declaration of Human Rights*, adopted in 1948, makes it clear that we all have rights. The first part of the *Declaration* empowers us with the right to be able to study and work within a "foundation of freedom, justice and peace in the world." The second part of the *Declaration* articles (or lists) the *inalienable* rights—that is, rights that we all possess. These rights are described as inalienable because no one can truly give us these rights or take them away; as human beings, we are born with these rights. Our fundamental rights include political, civil, equality, economic, social, and cultural rights. The *Declaration* is a code to live by and be governed by; it is not legally binding. It is up to each of us to ensure that human rights be respected and protected. (As the saying goes, "If you are not part of the solution, you are part of the problem.")

 Our personal rights go hand in hand with our personal responsibilities. This important idea is summarized in what is sometimes called *the golden rule*: treat others as you wish to be treated. You have the right to be treated in a certain way and the responsibility to treat others in the same way. With this in mind, think about your rights and responsibilities in the classroom, and then create a classroom charter of rights and responsibilities.

Although the *United Nations Universal Declaration of Human Rights* applies to all people regardless of age, in 1959 the United Nations saw fit to develop the *Declaration of the Rights of the Child*. This document consists of 10 principles:

1. All children shall be entitled to the rights contained in this document.

2. Children shall be allowed to develop physically, mentally, morally, spiritually, and socially in a healthy and normal manner.

3. Children shall be entitled from birth to a name and a nationality.

4. Children shall be entitled to grow and develop in health and have the right to adequate nutrition, housing, and medical services.

5. A child who is physically, mentally, or socially handicapped shall be given the special treatment, education, and care that is required.

6. Children shall grow up in the care of their parents (if possible) and in an atmosphere of affection and security.

7. Children are to be educated in order to develop their abilities.

8. Children are to receive protection in times of conflict or disaster.

9. Children shall be protected against all forms of neglect, cruelty, and exploitation, and they shall not be required to work before an appropriate minimum age.

10. Children shall be protected from practices that may foster discrimination.

**John Humphrey** (1905–1995), a Canadian, was involved in drafting the United Nations *Universal Declaration of Human Rights*. In 1988, on the 40th anniversary of the *Declaration*, he was awarded the United Nations Human Rights award.

 Design a mural that depicts the *Declaration of the Rights of the Child*.

As the most vulnerable members of society, children are frequently the first to suffer during times of war. They may lose the protection of caring adults, may not be able to find nutritious food, and may be unable to escape danger. War is damaging emotionally, and, during war, children struggle to recover from the associated trauma of disease, hunger, and death. Imagine what a struggle it would be for you without the help of caring adults if you had to endure war. Here are two organizations specifically set up to help children who experience war:

1. War Child Canada, which seeks to help children living in war-affected parts of the world and has partnered with bands and entertainers like the Tragically Hip and Sum41 to call attention to the struggles of children facing war

2. The United Nations International Children's Emergency Fund (UNICEF), which works to help disadvantaged children around the world; of each 100 children, about 40 live without adequate sanitation, 30 suffer from hunger and malnutrition, 19 lack access to safe drinking water, and 17 never go to school

 For more information about what you can do to help war-affected children, visit <www.theworldtoday.ca> and follow "Links" to <www.warchild.ca>. For more information on UNICEF, follow "Links" to <www.unicef.ca>.

FIGURE 5.1. The signing of the American *Declaration of Independence* in 1776.

## Today's Rights Are Planted in the Past

The principle of a charter of rights started with the Magna Carta (Latin for "great charter"). Signed in 1215 at Runnymede, England, just west of London, the charter proclaimed that "no freeman shall be taken or imprisoned or deprived of his property or exiled or in any way destroyed . . . except by lawful judgement of his equals and the law of the land." The principle of *habeas corpus* (Latin for "you have the body"), signed in 1679, further extended the rights of English subjects by stating that no one could be imprisoned indefinitely without just cause (that is, a good reason).

Two late-18th-century revolutions—the American and the French—inspired two other important human-rights statements. First was the American *Declaration of Independence* (1776), which included these words: "We hold these truths to be self-evident: that all men are created equal; that they are endowed by their creator with certain inalienable rights; that

among these are life, liberty, and the pursuit of happiness." Second was France's *Declaration of the Rights of Man and of the Citizen* (1789), which stated: "Men are born free and equal in rights. . . . These rights are liberty, property, security and resistance to oppression." The message about human rights was as clear in the past as it is today.

 Look again at the quotes taken from the 1776 American *Declaration of Independence* and France's 1789 *Declaration of the Rights of Man and of the Citizen*. First, select one of the quotes and write a paragraph explaining what the quote means to you. Second, suggest three reasons showing that the quote is as important today as it was when first written, more than 200 years ago. Third, identify a word that is used in both quotes that would not be used this way today.

In 1982, Canada amalgamated and expanded the 1960 *Bill of Rights* that was included in our constitution, calling it the *Canadian Charter of Rights and Freedoms*. The terms of our charter are similar to the United Nations human-rights principles. There are seven categories of rights:

1. Equality rights: You have the right to be treated equally before the law.

2. Democratic rights: You have the right to vote.

3. Legal rights: You cannot be imprisoned without cause.

4. Mobility rights: You are free to travel in and out of the country (subject to your having all necessary papers in order, including a passport).

5. Language rights: You have the right to use English or French.

6. Minority language education rights: You have the right to be educated in either English or French.

7. Freedoms: Your fundamental freedoms include freedom of religion, freedom of thought, freedom of expression and freedom of the press, freedom to assemble peacefully, and freedom of association.

In other words, your Canadian government wants you to exercise your fundamental freedoms as a responsible citizen.

FIGURE 5.2. An artistic representation of France's *Declaration of the Rights of Man and of the Citizen.*

 For a guide to the *Canadian Charter of Rights and Freedoms*, visit <www.theworldtoday.ca> and follow "Links" to <www.johnhumphreycentre.org/guide.htm>.

"The destiny of human rights is in the hands of all citizens in all of our communities" (Eleanor Roosevelt, 1884–1962, first lady of the United States between 1933 and 1945).

 Many special days have been set aside to celebrate different aspects of human rights (e.g., 8 March, International Women's Day; 21 March, International Day for the Elimination of Racial Discrimination; 3 May, World Press Freedom Day; 17 October, International Day for the Eradication of Poverty; 10 December, Human Rights Day). Suggest a new day to commemorate an important human-rights action or activist. Defend your choice.

# Abuse of Human Rights

**Prejudice** and **discrimination** have always been, and continue to be, a tragic part of our human world. **Slavery**, for example, is an economic and social phenomenon that was part of many early civilizations. In some areas of the world, slavery operated openly in the 17th and 18th centuries, and people from Africa could be bought or sold at public markets.

There have been several examples of **genocide** during the past 100 years, including the Holocaust, when millions of people were killed during the Second World War. These people were denied their rights to German citizenship because of some particular aspect of their identity, including religion, sexual orientation, lifestyle, and physical disability.

## Apartheid in South Africa

South Africa's former apartheid policy is another example of human-rights abuse. From 1948 until 1990, apartheid legally established the complete separation, or "aparthood," of black people from white people. Blacks in South Africa were forced to carry a "pass book" to travel within their own country. Apartheid was evident at three levels: nationally, with the creation of separate areas for blacks; in cities, with the establishment of separate townships for blacks; locally, with separate park benches, beaches, and entrances to government buildings for blacks.

The apartheid laws placed the original inhabitants of South Africa into the category of *tenants* in their own country. In 1990, apartheid was abolished after 42 years of practice, following worldwide political pressure. Inside South Africa, Nelson Mandela was the best-known anti-apartheid activist.

**Apartheid on the National Scale**

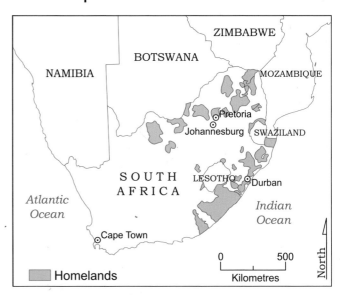

FIGURE 5.3. When apartheid was an official policy in South Africa, the government made an attempt to divide the country into two types of political unit. Most of the country was reserved for whites, and a number of scattered areas, called *homelands*, were assigned to blacks. In general, the areas assigned to blacks were outside the main cities and lacked the resources for agriculture and industry.

**discrimination** The action of treating an individual differently (usually unfairly) because the person belongs to a particular group. Discrimination is an action; it is what we do.

**genocide** Refers to the systematic killing of an entire group (or groups) of people, the group usually defined in religious or some other cultural terms. People are killed not because of who they are as individuals but because they are seen as belonging to a group.

**prejudice** Prejudging an individual on the basis of characteristics assumed to apply to all members of that individual's group. Prejudice is an attitude; it is how we feel.

**slavery** A system of forced labour, in which some people are treated as property to be bought and sold and not as persons with rights.

## Our Rights and Responsibilities

It is clear that the extreme differences found between the more- and less-developed countries are not fair or right. But it is difficult to determine just whose responsibility it is to do something about it. Should the governments around the world be held responsible for trying to balance the inequalities that exist in their own and other countries? Is it inevitable that differences will exist?

International agencies such as Amnesty International (AI) are nongovernmental human-rights watchdogs that suggest peaceful means to persuade governments to change discriminatory policies.

AI was founded by lawyer Peter Benenson in 1961. He read an article about two Portuguese students imprisoned for drinking a toast "to freedom." With the financial and moral support of fellow lawyers worldwide, he made sure that the two students were given a fair trial. Today, when human rights are violated, AI responds. With more than 1.8 million members worldwide, AI has defended more than 44 000 prisoners. Many political prisoners, including Nelson Mandela, have been freed at least partly because of the support given by AI. In 1977, AI was awarded the Nobel Peace Prize. Peter Benenson died in 2005. His legacy is a worldwide movement that has the following goals:

- Free all prisoners of conscience (people imprisoned for peacefully stating their beliefs).

- Ensure fair and prompt trials.

- Abolish all forms of harsh treatment of prisoners, including the death penalty.

- End government-supported killing of people.

- Assist people forced to leave their country because they disagree with their government.

- Cooperate with such organizations as the United Nations that also seek to put an end to human-rights abuses.

- Raise awareness about human-rights abuses around the world.

amnesty international
JUSTICE | EQUALITY | FREEDOM

FIGURE 5.4. The candle-and-barbed-wire icon for Amnesty International. The candle symbolizes peace; the barbed wire symbolizes oppression.

**Question** What happens when human rights are violated?

**Answer** It is up to each and every one of us to react, individually and through our governments, to rectify wrongs. Individuals can boycott goods produced in countries that violate human rights and can rally together to voice opinions, and governments can impose trade sanctions to call for change. In our global village, the media is an invaluable tool for shedding light on acts of inhumanity and mobilizing people to act.

 Review recent issues of newspapers and news magazines and listen to news programs on the radio and television to find out whether these media sources are highlighting issues of inequality in your community, in your province, and worldwide. List some issues that are identified and note any that you feel the media are not addressing but ought to be addressing.

 For more information and current examples of human-rights violations that are being tackled by AI, visit <www.theworldtoday.ca> and follow "Links" to <www.amnesty.org/>.

FIGURE 5.5. Dr. Martin Luther King Jr. shown during the 1963 March on Washington.

## The Many Forms of Protest

Protest assumes many forms, but the very best and most effective forms of protest are both peaceful and compassionate. One of the most universally recognized and admired human-rights activists was Dr. Martin Luther King Jr. (1929–1968). He attracted media attention in 1955 when he organized the Montgomery, Alabama, bus boycott. The boycott was in support of Rosa Parks (1913–2005), who was arrested for refusing to give up her seat on a bus to a white person. King organized and led several other marches in support of equal voting, employment, and education rights for blacks.

"You may say I'm a dreamer but I'm not the only one ..." (from *Imagine* by John Lennon, 1940–1980, musician, songwriter, and peace activist).

### Extract from "I Have a Dream"

Let us not wallow in the valley of despair, I say to you today, my friends. And so even though we face the difficulties of today and tomorrow, I still have a dream. It is a dream deeply rooted in the American dream.

I have a dream that one day this nation will rise up and live out the true meaning of its creed: "We hold these truths to be self-evident, that all men are created equal."

I have a dream that one day on the red hills of Georgia, the sons of former slaves and the sons of former slave owners will be able to sit down together at the table of brotherhood.

I have a dream that one day even the state of Mississippi, a state sweltering with the heat of injustice, sweltering with the heat of oppression, will be transformed into an oasis of freedom and justice.

I have a dream that my four little children will one day live in a nation where they will not be judged by the color of their skin but by the content of their character. I have a *dream* today!

King used nonviolent means to fight injustice, and he fought for the rights of all citizens in the United States. His peaceful approach led to the adoption of the United States Civil Rights Act of 1964. This act made racial discrimination in public places illegal, and it required employers to provide equal employment opportunities. In 1964, King became the youngest recipient of the Nobel Peace Prize. He was assassinated in 1968. His famous "I Have a Dream" speech and Martin Luther King Day, which was established to commemorate his fight for the civil rights of all American citizens, remain lasting civil-rights legacies.

Bob Marley (1945–1981) was a reggae singer and songwriter who wrote about his personal experiences living in ghettos in his homeland of Jamaica and also about the struggles of impoverished and powerless people more generally. In 1978 he was honoured by the United Nations with the Medal of the Third World. His song entitled "Redemption Song," which he wrote in 1980, summarizes his inspirational message of hope and freedom for all people. This plaintive song highlights the need for oppressed people to free themselves from self-imposed shackles; the message is that you become free if you believe yourself to be free.

 Protesting through song is an established and often-effective strategy to call attention to injustice. Do you know of singers other than Bob Marley who wrote and sang songs of political or social protest? Share the words and messages with other students.

"Freedom is like a birth. Till we are fully free, we are slaves" (Mahatma Gandhi, 1869–1948, East Indian spiritual and political leader, humanitarian).

## Making a Difference

Eleanor Roosevelt was an unusually active first lady, even challenging her husband, Franklin D. Roosevelt (1882–1945) (United States president from 1933 to 1945), when he ordered the internment of Japanese-American citizens during the Second World War. She used her knowledge and wisdom to motivate people worldwide to champion human rights. She was active in the formation of the United Nations. She also helped to draft the *United Nations' Universal Declaration of Human Rights*, which she appropriately called "the international Magna Carta of all mankind." She left a human-rights legacy for all people. It is no wonder that her husband's successor, Harry S. Truman (1884–1972), called her "the First Lady of the world."

Do you agree that the world needs more people like Eleanor Roosevelt, John Humphrey, Nelson Mandela (b.1918), Dr. Martin Luther King Jr., and Peter Benenson (1921–2005)? Who will be our next champion of human rights?

**Question** Where do human rights begin?

**Answer** "[Human rights begin in] places where every man, woman, and child seeks equal justice, equal opportunity, equal dignity without discrimination. Unless these rights have meaning there, they have little meaning anywhere. Without concerned citizen action to uphold them close to home, we shall look in vain for progress in the larger world" (Eleanor Roosevelt). Do you agree?

# DEMOCRATIC VALUES AND PRINCIPLES

6

## Guiding Questions

1. What is democracy?

2. Why is democracy important?

3. What does it mean to live in a democratic society?

4. What does it mean to live in a society that is not democratic?

5. What are some of our responsibilities as citizens living in a democratic society?

## Understanding What Democracy Is

**Democracy** is one of those words that we hear all the time. But most of us do not have a clear idea what it is. Democracy is hard to understand, because it is not just one thing; there is no neat definition. But it is important to understand democracy. One way to do so is by thinking about how it is practised in our everyday lives.

Democracy is:

- a process

- people listening to one other

- people speaking up to say what they think

- people making decisions together, either by accepting a majority vote or by consensus (that is, agreeing as a result of understanding)

- taking into consideration the opinions of those who think and feel differently from the majority

We do not have a democracy when:

- some people speak and others are silenced

- people speak but are not listened to

- one person, or a small group of people, make decisions that affect everyone else without taking the views of the others into consideration

- people vote with little knowledge and feel for the issues being considered

Democracy is one way we provide structure to our daily lives. Imagine what your life would be like if you and your family members, you and your friends, even you and your teachers, related to each other without practising democracy. How would you feel if your younger sister were allowed to make all the decisions in your family and you had no say? What would you do if your best friend always decided what the two of you would do together on a summer afternoon? What would you do if your teacher never took student opinion into account or allowed you to express your opinions?

**democracy** The way we organize how to relate to each other in order to ensure that everyone has a voice and that responsible decisions are made.

FIGURE 6.1. Informal democracy: a Japanese family enjoying beverages and conversation together.

FIGURE 6.2. Formal democracy: inside the Canadian House of Commons.

Democracy as it is practised in your family, or by a small group of friends, is informal democracy. There are no written rules, because each person understands how to relate to the others. But, as the size of the group gets larger, it is usually necessary to be a little more formal. When the group of people is very large—for example all of the people in Canada—then it becomes necessary to be much more formal.

How does democracy work when everybody in the country is part of the "family"—for example, in Canada. First, all Canadian adults have a regular opportunity (at least once every five years) to choose people to make decisions on their behalf. If we do not like the decisions that are made for us by those we have chosen (our elected representatives), then we will probably choose different people next time. We call this **representative democracy**.

Second, there is a set of rules that make it clear what our elected representatives can and cannot do and for how long. This set of rules is known as a **constitution**.

**constitution** The written agreements, contracts, or sets of rules by which the government of a country operates. Whenever groups of people need to meet, talk, and make decisions, they usually have a written constitution to help them do what they need to do in an orderly manner.

**representative democracy** Democratic countries, such as Canada, practise an indirect form of democracy because it is too difficult to gather every citizen together to discuss issues. Instead, we allow others to represent our points of view in an assembly, which may be called a *council*, a *legislature*, a *parliament*, or a *congress*. The student council at your school is a representative democracy.

# The Origins and History of Democracy

Now that we know what democracy is and what it is not, we will consider how democracy developed. To discover the original meaning of democracy, we have to go as far back as ancient Greece, about 2 600 years ago.

**Democracy** The word *democracy* originates from two Greek words—*demos*, meaning "people" and *kratos*, meaning "rule." Democracy refers both to a way of life and to a form of government. In both cases, the people living in a community or country are treated as free and equal and are either directly or indirectly involved in their government. In ancient Greece, all male citizens were expected to participate directly in making the laws for their community. Ancient Greece was not democratic in the current sense of the word *democracy*, as women and slaves were denied the right to speak up and to vote.

We also need to look at another early constitution: the British Magna Carta of 1215 (also referred to in chapter 5). The Magna Carta consisted of a number of written promises between the king and his subjects. There were 63 clauses altogether, but the most important was that, for the first time in Britain's history, the king was subjected to the law of the land, just as everybody else was.

FIGURE 6.3. Athens was one of the ancient Greek city-states. Prior to the development of democracy, a few powerful men ruled these states. Left: the Temple of Hephaiston overlooking Athens. Right: a sculpture of the eminent Greek thinker Aristotle. The Athenian constitution was written by Aristotle in 505 BCE.

For more information on the Magna Carta, visit <www.theworldtoday.ca> and follow "Links" to <www.britannia.com/history/magna2.html>.

Finally, we need to look at the 1787 American Constitution. It was modelled on these earlier ideas, including a belief in the rule of law (meaning that all members of a society must follow the law, including those who make the laws) and in a government that serves the common interest of all citizens.

## Canada's First Democracy?

The Iroquois League is considered by some to have been Canada's first democracy. It was made up of five groups of First Peoples—Mohawk, Oneida, Onondaga, Cayuga, and Seneca—that lived in the area around Lake Ontario. The League kept track of its history on beaded strings that were woven together into a wampum belt. The belts included symbols that could be "read" and make up a 200- to 300-page book written by the Iroquois that tells of their history.

The Iroquois council met at least once each year, and all women and men were invited to attend these meetings. On the first day, topics were introduced. Discussions took place the next day, giving people time to think about the topics. In order for a law to pass, the League had to speak with one voice—what we call a consensus.

For information on the Iroquois League, visit <www.theworldtoday.ca> and follow "Links" to <www.wsu.edu:8080/~dee/CULAMRCA/IRLEAGUE.HTM>.

# Democracy in Canada Today

We have talked about how democracy works in a small group such as a family, but how does it work in a large group, such as we have in Canada today?

## Six Important Components

*Freedom of Expression*
We have the right to freedom of speech, freedom of the press, and the freedom to meet or assemble.

*Free Elections*
We have the right to vote.

*Majority Rule and Minority Rights*
Decisions are made by the principle of majority rule; the majority must respect the wishes of the minority.

*Political Parties*
Voters are provided with a choice of candidates, meaning that different points of view are expressed and heard.

*Private Organizations*
Newspapers, labour unions, and businesses are examples of privately owned and operated organizations that are allowed to exist within a democratic society.

*Constitutional Government*
Constitutions provide the rules within which a government operates. Together, these documents outline the powers and duties of government and, more important, set limits to a government's powers.

 For more information on the Canadian constitution, visit <www.theworldtoday.ca> and follow "Links" to <www.canadiana.org/citm/themes/constitution1_e.html>.

FIGURE 6.4. Voting in a Canadian election.

**Question** What do our elected representatives do?

**Answer** Their main role is to write and rewrite laws by which we must all live.

**Question** What can we do if we do not like the laws that they write?

**Answer** We can elect different representatives.

 Now that you understand something about what democracy is and how it works, it is time to think about why it is important. Talk with a partner and then list three ways in which democracy improves your quality of life. Report your discussion to the class.

## One for All and All for One?

One goal of the kind of democracy we have in Canada is to balance the needs and rights of each person with the needs and rights of the society in which these people live and work. How does a democracy accomplish this balancing act? Here are four ways:

1. Democratic governments write laws that ensure the principles of equality and freedom for all.

2. Democratic goverments establish programs such as unemployment insurance, public-health insurance, civil-rights laws, and public education, which provide compassionate support for people in need and give everybody opportunities to receive income, health care, an education, and to be treated fairly. Such programs are paid for with tax dollars; it is believed that the benefits to society in general outweigh the costs to the individual who pays taxes.

3. A new government must be elected at least once every five years, which makes sure that violence and revolutions are not necessary to change who is in charge. In some nondemocratic countries, people have to resort to revolutions if they want a new government.

4. Large-scale economic and social changes, such as the establishment of medicare, are much more likely to develop in a democratic society.

For more information about Tommy Douglas, visit <www.theworldtoday.ca> and follow "Links" to <www.weyburnreview.com/tommydouglas/welcome.html>.

FIGURE 6.5. Tommy Douglas in 1965 following his re-election to the Canadian Parliament.

**Tommy Douglas, Father of Medicare** In 2004, Tommy Douglas (1904–1986) was named the Greatest Canadian in a CBC national poll. Having lived during the Depression (1929–1939), Douglas realized that the plight of citizens caused by the Depression was too great a burden to solve alone, and it was time for governments to assist the citizens they were elected to serve. He served as premier of Saskatchewan from 1944 to 1961, helped form the national New Democratic Party (NDP), and served as federal leader of the NDP from 1961 to 1971. It was through the tireless efforts of Douglas that the National Medicare Program was established in 1967. Canada's medicare program, which provides equal access to medical care for all Canadians, is admired worldwide. In 1981, Tommy Douglas was awarded the Order of Canada for his service to his fellow citizens.

 In most cases, organizations and governments that discuss things democratically arrive at decisions through voting either for or against something. The majority wins. But, in a few cases, votes are not held; rather, the people talking try to arrive at a consensus. This means that all of the people talking reach a decision that is acceptable to all group members. List three reasons showing that voting is a good way for a group to make a decision. List three reasons showing that reaching consensus is also a good way for a group to make a decision.

# Making Democracy Work

As John F. Kennedy, president of the United States from 1961 to 1963, proclaimed, it is up to each and every citizen to make democracy work. And, as the saying goes, "United we stand, divided we fall."

## Four Ways to Help

### Vote When You Can!
Eligible citizens have a duty to exercise their right to vote in municipal, provincial, and national elections. As a student, you have the opportunity not only to vote for your student council but also to be involved in school committees and to respond to school surveys. You can also volunteer to help in election campaigns. When you turn 18, exercise your right to vote, and make sure you do so municipally, provincially, and federally.

### Get Educated!
Well-educated citizens are necessary for the survival of democracy. As the saying goes, "knowledge is power," and countries that support public education have strong democratic governments.

### Do Not Discriminate!
Inclusion is key in democratic societies. Citizens must not be discriminated against based on, for example, the ethnic group they belong to, the language they speak, the religion they practise, their gender, or their sexual orientation. Allow all citizens the opportunity to participate in the economic and social well-being of the society at large.

**Voter Turnout in the 2004 Federal Election**

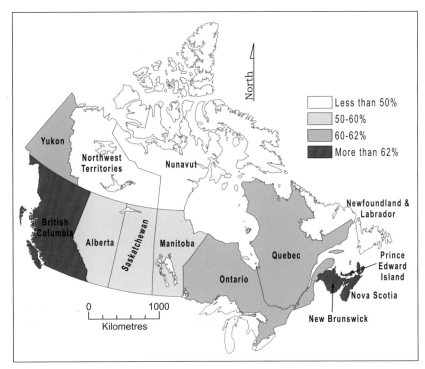

FIGURE 6.6. As this map shows, too many of us choose not to vote. Do not make this mistake. Quite often, one vote—and it may be your vote—can make all the difference. Perhaps even more important, voting is your opportunity to say, "I participated. I did my bit."

### Consider the Needs of Others!
It is essential that individuals work together for the betterment of the whole group. Installing elevators and wheelchair-access ramps in buildings may be costly, but, for the sake of those who require them, the benefits outweigh the costs.

 Look at figure 6.6. Is voter turnout higher or lower than you would have expected? On the basis of this map, is Canada a successful, thriving democracy?

 Debate whether or not democratic governments should be allowed to ban panhandling on street corners. List three reasons showing that they ought to, and three reasons showing that they ought not to.

## Alternatives to Democracy

If democracy is such a good thing, then why do not all of the countries in the world practise it? Although democracy has been practised in one form or another for a very long time, its spread worldwide is quite recent. Indeed, democracy has become popular only since the American and French revolutions of the late 18th century. Prior to these revolutions, many countries were ruled by "divine right"—the claim that a monarch had supreme control over the people in a country and could dictate laws to all its citizens. Today, there are still countries in which those who govern do not want to give up their power and be subject to the wishes of all citizens. Rather, they want to be in charge without the consent of the governed and without the restrictions of a constitution.

What is the alternative to democracy? There are many forms of nondemocratic government. In general, all such forms are **authoritarian**.

> **authoritarian** Refers generally to governments that are in power without necessarily having the support of the majority of citizens. In many countries with authoritarian governments, individual freedom is limited, citizens are subject to violence, government officials are not accountable for their actions, and freedom of expression is denied. Some notorious 20th-century examples of authoritarian governments that no longer exist were those of Nazi Germany and the Soviet Union under Joseph Stalin.

### Democracy Around the World

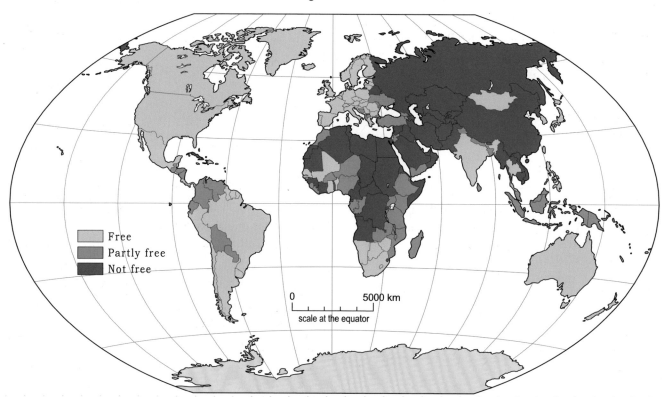

Free
Partly free
Not free

0    5000 km
scale at the equator

FIGURE 6.7. This map shows the countries of the world grouped into 3 general categories. This is one way of indicating the level of democracy practised in each country.

## Democracy Stop Signs

While people enjoy many rights in a democratic society, democracy has limits. For example, every time you enter an airport terminal, your democratic freedoms are limited for the security of society at large. At school, you have limits as to where you may eat, what you may wear, and when you may enter and leave the building. These restrictions, while they might appear to limit your freedom, are designed for our collective safety and well-being.

**Democracy Is Not Perfect** Even in a democratic society, rights may be violated. For example, following the Japanese bombing of Pearl Harbor in Hawaii on 7 December 1941, the Canadian government decided that people of Japanese descent living in Canada were a security risk and interned them. From 1942 until 1945, about 23 000 citizens of Canada, mostly from British Columbia, were forced out of their homes and placed in work camps in the interior of the province, and even as far east as Manitoba. This is an example of discrimination. In 1988, the Canadian government acknowledged that its actions were unwarranted, extended an official apology, and compensated those who had suffered property damage and loss of income.

**Components of Democracy** As you know, democracy has many components, one of the most important of which is that people are free to express themselves (usually subject to some limitations). Figure 6.7 shows countries in three general categories: free, partly free, and not free.

## Martin Luther King's "I Have a Dream"

Living in a democratic country allows us to "spread our wings." Democratic countries aim to provide all citizens with the opportunity to live and work free from discrimination and oppression. The practice of democracy has a history going back as far as ancient Greece. It is our responsibility to ensure that democracy has an equally long future. We must remember to exercise our right to vote so that our other rights of freedom and equality are preserved and maintained. Democracy ensures that the potential of all humans is allowed to survive and thrive. We may not all be as eloquent as Dr. Martin Luther King Jr., but we do each have a voice.

 Democracy is always evolving. In many countries, voting rights were initially restricted to men, and it often took considerable pressure from women to win voting rights for all adults. Using library sources and the Internet, find out when women were granted the right to vote in Canada.

 Curfews are one form of martial law. Debate the pros and cons of government-imposed curfews. Do teenagers need a curfew?

 Check newspapers and news magazines for discussions about possible human-rights violations in Canada today.

# POWER AND WEALTH IN TODAY'S WORLD

**7**

## Guiding Questions

1. What is an empire?

2. What makes a nation powerful?

3. How do we measure wealth?

4. How do nations maintain and contain wealth and power?

5. What is globalization, and what effect does it have on world wealth and power?

## What Is an Empire?

Throughout history, some countries and peoples have been so politically strong that they were able to exercise power over others and create **empires**. Empires rise and fall. Here is a simplified listing of powerful political empires over about the past 2 700 years.

- The Greeks dominated from about 776 BCE until the death of Alexander the Great in 323 BCE. Their influence extended east from Greece to present-day Afghanistan and Pakistan.

- Following a series of conquests during the previous 500 years, the Romans controlled much of western and central Europe from about 1 CE for about 500 years.

- From about 500 to 1500, Islamic cultures spread eastward from the Middle East (into what is now Iraq, Iran, Afghanistan, Pakistan, and beyond) and also westward (through North Africa and southern Europe).

- The overseas expansion that began in the mid-15th century allowed several European countries to become very powerful.

Today, there are no political empires on the scale of those of the past, but there are some very powerful countries. The United States is by far the most powerful country in the world today, although it is possible that China or a united Europe might become equally powerful.

 The creation of a political empire in the past involved the establishment of not just political control over other lands but also economic and cultural control. Suggest one example of economic control and two examples of cultural control.

**empire**  A large area that is controlled by one central authority.

## The Roman Empire

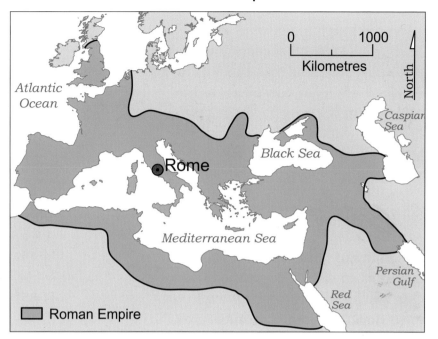

FIGURE 7.1. The Roman Empire included all of the land area bordering the Mediterranean Sea and even extended north through much of northwestern Europe and east to the Persian Gulf. The Roman Empire lasted from about 1 CE for about 500 years.

## The British Empire

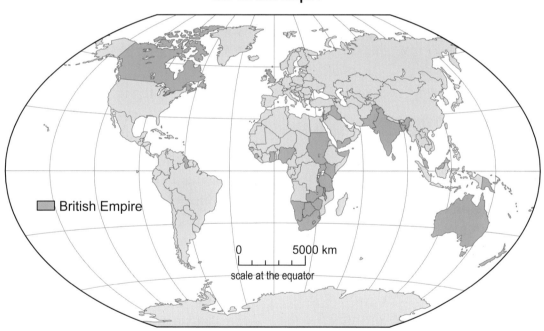

FIGURE 7.2. This map shows the British Empire at its maximum extent in the early 20th century. Some of the areas included in this huge political unit were acquired through military conquest, some were acquired by negotiating treaties with local populations, and some, which were apparently unoccupied, were simply taken over by the British. The Empire had earlier included the 13 colonies in what is now the United States, but these colonies revolted in 1776. The collapse of the British Empire began with the independence of India in 1947.

See figures 7.1 and 7.2 for examples of past territorial expansion. Note how different they are. The Roman Empire was land based. The British Empire moved overseas, outside the British Isles.

 It was often said that "the sun never sets on the British Empire." What do you think this means? Are you able to suggest two different meanings?

# Strength in Numbers

Countries today do not want to be dominated by other countries—politically, economically, or culturally. But there are many advantages to be gained from one country voluntarily linking up with another country (or other countries) as long as there is some give and take in the relationship.

An early form of union occurred in the 5th century BCE, when Athens, a powerful Greek city-state, created the Delian League. The League initially served as an offensive and defensive deterrent against Persia (now Iran). All areas under the control of Athens were obligated to belong to the League, yet each had equal voting power. To maintain this union, a "tribute," or tax, was required of all members of the League. The tribute was paid either in direct monetary aid or indirectly by providing Athens with ships, soldiers, or weapons. In return, the conquered area was offered protection from pirates and the Persians.

## Toward One Europe

In the world today, many countries are joining together. The most highly developed economic and political union is the **European Union** (EU). Forged out of a Europe ravaged by the Second World War, it is a **supranational** organization consisting of 25 European states. The EU coordinates many aspects of national policy: health, the economy, foreign policy, and defence, for example. In 1999, the EU introduced a common currency, known as the *euro*, and today boasts the largest economy in the world.

Although much of Europe was included in the Roman Empire, and although there have also existed several other important empires in Europe, for much of its history, Europe comprised a large number of independent

**The European Union**

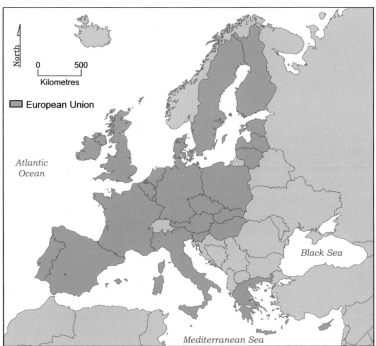

FIGURE 7.3. Unlike such political units as the Roman Empire and the British Empire, which were created at least partly through military conquest, the EU, through the process of application, has expanded. Norway and Switzerland are the only two countries "inside" the EU that are not members.

countries, and these countries were regularly at war with each other. The most devastating conflicts were the First World War (1914–1918) and the Second World War (1939–1945).

This long history of conflict makes what happened after the Second World War (that is, the beginning of European integration) all the more remarkable. In the 1950s, six European countries agreed to start working together in some aspects of their economic policy. Since then, economic ties have become closer and closer, and many new members have joined what is often called the "European club" (see table 7.1).

> **European Union** An economic union of European countries that started with six members in 1958 and by 2005 had 25 members. The economic union may become a political union.
>
> **supranational** *Supra* means "beyond," so a supranational organization is one that includes more than one country.

# Commonwealth of Nations

Today the Commonwealth of Nations is a free association of independent countries that were once colonies of the British Empire. In 1867, Canada became the first British colony to transform itself into a self-governing "dominion," a status that implied equality with Britain.

In 1884, Earl Rosebery (1847–1929), a British politician, described the Empire as a "commonwealth of nations." Other countries that became dominions included Australia (1900), New Zealand (1907), and South Africa (1910). The Commonwealth of Nations was established in 1926. The countries of the former British Empire were now equal in status.

The Statute of Westminster (1931) incorporated this equality into British law, establishing Canada and several other countries as independent nations within the Commonwealth.

Today, Commonwealth countries have economic policies that are designed to benefit not just their own, but also other, member countries. The Commonwealth is an important structure for promoting democratic principles of freedom and equality.

The Commonwealth also promotes athletic and artistic cooperation and competition among its member countries. For example, the Commonwealth Games were established in 1931, and Commonwealth countries participate in sports competitions every four years. The Booker Prize for the best novel by a citizen of the Commonwealth was established in 1969, and several Canadian authors have been nominated for and won this prestigious award.

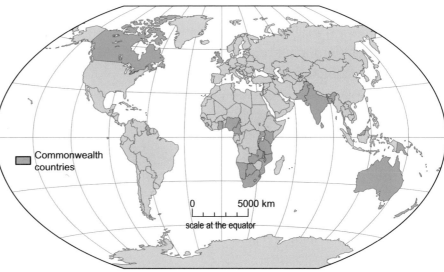

**The Commonwealth**

**FIGURE 7.4. Not all of the areas included in the former British Empire (see figure 7.2) are now members of the Commonwealth.**

## TABLE 7.1. The European Union

| Date Joined | Countries |
|---|---|
| 1952–58 | Belgium, France, Italy, Luxembourg, Netherlands, West Germany |
| 1973 | Denmark, Ireland, United Kingdom |
| 1981 | Greece |
| 1986 | Portugal, Spain |
| 1995 | Austria, Finland, Sweden |
| 2004 | Cyprus, Czech Republic, Estonia, Hungary, Latvia, Lithuania, Malta, Poland, Slovakia, Slovenia |

## National Power

There are three important sources of national political power: natural resources, people, and political organization. A country is more likely to be powerful if it has a varied natural-resource base: water; land suited to growing crops; sources of lumber; sources of hydroelectricity; coal, oil, and natural gas; and sources of the raw materials needed to support such industrial activities as making iron and steel, chemicals, and textiles. If certain natural resources are not available in the country, the country might import them.

A country is more likely to be powerful if it has a large and well-educated population. Democratic countries support the right of all citizens to free education.

A country is more likely to be powerful if the majority of its people support its political leaders. If the country is not democratic, then it is critical that the leader be supported at least by the military. Good leaders usually understand that a well-structured political organization helps a country remain stable; democracies are especially well-structured forms of political organization.

Maintaining national power once it has been established is just as important as the initial gaining of it. Some authoritarian leaders use physical force to maintain power, but such leaders rarely survive for a long time. Like school bullies, they rule tyrannically or unjustly, using violence or the threat of violence to maintain control. Leaders in democratic countries are dependent on the people to vote them into power (or out of power), so they cannot afford to act unfairly.

### Using Power Wisely

Pierre Elliott Trudeau (1919–2000) became the 15th Canadian prime minister in 1968 and proved to be a charismatic and powerful leader. He was a citizen of the world, having travelled extensively, including to China and India. As a lawyer, he championed the rights of workers. He was the founder and editor of *Cité Libre*, which advocated for social justice in his home province of Quebec. During his political career, he ensured that the principles of

FIGURE 7.5. Former Canadian Prime Minister Pierre Elliott Trudeau, wearing his signature red rose.

bilingualism and biculturalism were entrenched into the Canadian political and cultural landscape. He established the National Energy Program, which ensured that all Canadians had access to energy sources, and, during his 16 years as prime minister, he worked toward creating a "just society" for all Canadians.

 Debate the pros and cons of having elections for our Canadian government at the discretion of the governing party (but at least once every five years). Compare our system with the American system, where its citizens elect a new government once every four years.

 Trudeau once stated: "I must follow the people; am I not their leader?" What did he mean by this statement? Do you think this is a definition of democracy?

## Power in the Family and in the School

So far, we have talked about power in terms of countries, and this is called *national power*. It is also important to consider power in other situations. For example, who holds the power in your school or in your family? How did those people acquire this power, and how do they maintain it?

Power is the ability of one person or group to control the actions, and sometimes even the thoughts, of others. Teachers, parents, and employers are examples of people who exercise power. In most cases, these people maintain their power by earning your respect, but they might also do so through the threat of punishment and by penalizing those who disobey their authority. Some people, such as school bullies, wield power solely through the threat of violence and punishment, and not through respect.

Usually, those in power rarely threaten to punish. For example, the primary concern of parents or caregivers is to make decisions with the best interests of their children at heart. Most of the time, children understand that adults have to assume responsibility for making decisions about such matters as bedtime, how much television to watch, and what to eat. Similarly, your student council makes decisions about certain matters that affect you, but, again, they do so in a supportive rather than a threatening way.

Your student council has been given this power by the school board through the principal and a constitution that guides what they can and cannot do. In the classroom, your teachers have the power, and they have the responsibility, to make the classroom a safe and effective teaching and learning environment.

"Politics is not the art of the possible. It consists in choosing between the disastrous and the unpalatable" (John Kenneth Galbraith, 1908–2006, American economist).

**Power** What is needed for a country to be powerful? Natural resources, people, and political organization are needed. It is much the same if you want to become the leader of your student council. You need the ability to run a campaign with a sufficient supply of resources (such as posters and buttons), a sufficient number of supporters, and an efficient and effective campaign strategy.

"Leadership and learning are indispensable to each other" (John F. Kennedy, 1917–1963, 35th president of the United States, speech prepared for delivery in Dallas, Texas, the day of his assassination, 22 November 1963).

 Debate the famous quote "Knowledge is power" (Sir Francis Bacon [1561–1626], English philosopher). Is wealth more important than knowledge when it comes to power?

"Nearly all men can stand adversity, but if you want to test a man's character, give him power" (Abraham Lincoln, 1809–1865, 16th president of the United States).

"We thought, because we had power, we had wisdom" (Stephen Vincent Benét, 1898–1943, American author).

"The problem of power is how to achieve its responsible use rather than its irresponsible and indulgent use—of how to get men of power to live for the public rather than off the public" (Robert F. Kennedy, 1925–1968, American politician).

## Measuring and Mapping Wealth

Before we define wealth and then map the countries of the world in terms of their wealth, it is important to remember two points:

1.  There is more to wealth than meets the eye. In chapter 4 we distinguished *standard of living*, which is basically an economic measure valued in dollars and cents, and *human development*, which is much more than an economic measure, as it takes into account the way people live.

2.  Material wealth can be both a blessing and a curse. Owning a car certainly helps people get from place to place quickly, but there are high environmental costs.

There is no simple way to measure the financial wealth of a country. For example, not all work is calculated formally. On weekends many people sell unused household items at garage sales, and the income from them goes unrecorded. A parent who stays at home to look after children is not paid a wage. Volunteers assist many organizations and do not receive money for it.

When they want to measure the wealth of a country, economists often use what is called the **gross national income** (GNI). Here are four ways that our Canadian measure of GNI adds up:

1.  Every time someone buys a ticket to a movie or purchases a new outfit, that purchase adds to Canada's GNI. The more goods people buy, the more people are employed to sell us these goods and, therefore, the higher is our GNI. In Canada, personal consumption is the largest contributor to GNI (about 65 percent).

2.  Government purchases of military equipment and salaries for such essential workers as teachers and firefighters are the second largest contributor to the Canadian GNI (approximately 20 percent).

3.  Businesses add to the GNI each time they purchase a new building or buy a new machine. These private (nongovernmental) expenditures account for approximately 15 percent of the GNI.

4.  GNI also takes into account the difference between the value of all the goods exported from Canada (e.g., timber and aluminum) and all the things imported into Canada (e.g., motor vehicles and electronic goods). In Canada, only about 1 percent of the GNI is based on this difference.

**gross national income** This is not an easy term to define. GNI is the total value of a country's output of goods and services in a year. Examples of goods include food, clothing, and machines. Examples of services include the work that doctors, shop assistants, travel agents, and teachers do. Note that, regardless of the country, GNI is usually measured in US dollars.

 Create a pie graph showing the percentage contributions of each of the four ways that our Canadian measure of GNI adds up. Do you think that the GNI of a country in the less-developed world would show similar percentages? If not, why not?

# Coming Together

Have you ever heard the terms *shrinking planet* and *time-space convergence?* Both refer to the most notable change taking place in the world today: the many different peoples and places of the world are increasingly interconnected.

There have been many technological changes in recent years, which means that the time it takes to travel from one place in the world to another has become shorter and shorter, and more people are moving from place to place.

Have you ever heard someone use the following terms to describe our planet: *spaceship earth? only one earth? global village?* These three phrases highlight a very important consequence of technological change: all of us share the earth. We are coming together and beginning to share similar experiences, to live lives that are more and more similar. This coming together is what we call *globalization*: changes in global economy, global culture, and global politics. Some signs of globalization are:

- People are moving around the world in increasing numbers, crossing political borders for both work and vacation.

- Ideas, in the form of knowledge and technology, are moving rapidly from place to place because of the Internet and cell phones.

- One language—English—is increasingly being used as the language of business.

- There is an increase in trade among countries. In 1994, Canada, the United States, and Mexico took a major step toward economic globalization by passing the North American Free Trade Agreement.

- Many large companies, such as General Motors and IBM, are now multinational.

- Many of the products that we purchase have been made in more than one country.

- Popular music and Hollywood entertainment know no boundaries.

## National Incomes around the World

High income countries
Upper-middle income countries
Lower-middle income countries
Low income countries
Data not available

0 ___ 5000 km
scale at the equator

**FIGURE 7.6. This map groups countries into 4 categories based on GNI data. It demonstrates global inequalities: some countries are rich, others are poor.**

## Globalization Pros and Cons

Whether globalization is a good thing or a bad thing is a continuing debate. But one thing is clear: governments the world over need to ensure that education and vocational training are up to date to ensure that workers can keep up with the rapidly changing economic community. No country can afford to remain stagnant and isolated from the world economy. It is only through trade and aid that the global economy will be sustained and, more important, strengthened.

 Debate the pros and cons of globalization. First, consider globalization from a Canadian perspective. Then consider globalization from the perspective of a less-developed country in sub-Saharan Africa.

### Globalization Is Often Applauded

Here are some positive points:

- Globalization has seen the costs of some products drop and quality and quantity of goods increase. Fruits like kiwi, for example, were rarely seen in Canadian supermarkets until recently. Where do kiwi come from? Ask at your local supermarket.
- In a global marketplace, countries can concentrate on producing products that reflect their physical and human resources and sell to a wider market.
- In an increasingly interconnected world, countries can work together to exchange resources efficiently and effectively.
- As we discussed in chapter 4, it appears that conditions in some parts of the less-developed world are improving. For example, there is evidence that gaps in education and life expectancy are narrowing.

### Globalization Is Often Criticized

Here are some criticisms:

- Globalization may be increasing rather than decreasing inequality amongst nations. Are the rich getting richer and the poor getting poorer?
- Perhaps some multinational companies have "supersized" their power; for example, they have their own best interests in mind, not the best interests of the larger community. This is not democratic behaviour.
- Globalization may be damaging the environment. In order for multinational companies to make more and more money, natural resources are being exploited more and more and without due consideration for future generations.
- As we are all increasingly watching the same movies, eating the same burgers and fries, and listening to the same music, our world is losing some of the differences that have made it so interesting.

## Fair Trade

"Before you've finished your breakfast this morning, you'll have relied on half the world" (Dr. Martin Luther King Jr.). This is an interesting thought, but it is also a depressing one when you realize that some of the people who worked hard to produce coffee, cereal, and other breakfast items might have been exploited and oppressed. Often, multinational companies in less-developed countries pay workers low wages and buy their products at low prices, thus keeping the local people poor. The product is then sold in Canada and other more-developed countries for a much higher price.

But there is one way all of us can make a contribution to creating a fairer world. We can buy products according to the approval of the Fairtrade Labelling Organizations International (FLO). The FLO is an international movement that ensures that producers in poor countries get a fair deal. This means that the price they receive for their goods covers the cost of production and guarantees a living income. They also receive long-term contracts that provide real security and help develop their businesses and increase sales.

Fair trade benefits producers in less-developed countries by opening up new markets for their products. Fair trade allows small organizations to maintain their independence against larger corporations. Any extra money earned through the Fair trade program goes into supporting community initiatives such as building schools and hospitals.

There is a wide variety of products that are covered by the FLO—for example, cocoa, coffee, tea, honey, mangoes and other fresh fruits, juices, rice snacks, sugar, and wine. Check the labels of these items in your kitchen to see if they carry an FLO label.

 Select one of the two quotes below and discuss how it applies to the ideas in this chapter.

"Sometimes you have to use your failures as stepping-stones to success. You have to maintain a fine balance between hope and despair. In the end, it's all a question of balance" (Rohinton Mistry, b. 1952, Canadian author).

"We cannot survive as an island in a sea of change…cooperation is in our own self-interest" (Rufus Yerxa, American politician).

 Create an advertisement promoting fair trade products available at your local grocery store.

## Moving Forward

The various peoples and places in our world display significant differences in wealth and power. Some differences are related to physical geography and seem natural, inevitable, and perhaps even desirable. But the differences in wealth and power are clearly unacceptable and need to be changed.

Whether or not globalization is removing some of these differences or adding to them is debatable. Certainly, our world is a complex place, but it ought not to be beyond our collective wit and wisdom to identify what is working well, what is wrong, and to propose and implement solutions for what is wrong.

This chapter has highlighted some of the key issues evident in the world today and hopefully prompted you to think critically about how we might better plan and organize our shared world. Throughout this chapter, you have seen how the peoples and places of the world have been affected politically, economically, and culturally by changing global circumstances. The world has seen the rise and fall of many powerful nations. It seems that life is a fine balance between the rich and the poor, the powerful and the powerless.

 For more information on fair trade, visit <www.theworldtoday.ca> and follow "Links" to <www.fairtrade.org.uk/about_what_is_fairtrade.htm>.

# WORKING TOGETHER AROUND THE GLOBE

## Guiding Questions

1. What are nongovernmental organizations, and what roles do they play in our world?

2. What organizations other than government organizations are active in helping people connect globally?

3. What is the United Nations, and what role does it play in helping create a better world for all people?

4. Who are some Canadians who have helped make the world a better place, and what are their accomplishments?

5. How can you make a difference?

As discussed in chapter 4, many people, both in groups and as individuals, are working to make our world a better place for us all. In this chapter you will learn more about some of these efforts, especially about the roles played by two of the many organizations that work for the political, economic, and social well-being of all humankind: the Red Cross (which is one of many nongovernmental organizations—NGOs) and the United Nations (which is a global association of governments). You will also learn about how individual Canadians, notably Lester B. Pearson and Stephen Lewis, have made a difference, and even about how you as an individual can contribute to making a better and fairer world. Finally, you will learn about some ways that nations come together and celebrate together in friendly competitions, such as the FIFA World Cup.

NGOs help people by tackling their social and environmental problems. NGOs receive no government support; they are financially sustained by volunteers and donations. If you have ever donated used items to the Red Cross, you have supported an NGO, and you are therefore probably aware that people acting collectively can make a real difference. NGOs are truly grassroots projects, created for the people by the people!

**Question** How are groups such as the Red Cross or Amnesty International identified generally?

**Answer** They are nongovernmental organizations (NGOs), organizations that have no connection to any government. They are neither elected nor funded by the citizens of a particular country.

# The Red Cross

The Red Cross is the largest global humanitarian organization. There are 181 Red Cross societies in the world, with 97 million members. Although founded to help those who suffer during war, the Red Cross responds also to a wide range of other social and environmental problems, offering food, shelter, clothing, and medical support to those in need. Through the Red Cross, people from various countries put aside their political differences and work side by side to help those in need. In 1963, the Red Cross received the Nobel Peace Prize for its humanitarian efforts.

**Countries Affected by the 2004 Tsunami**

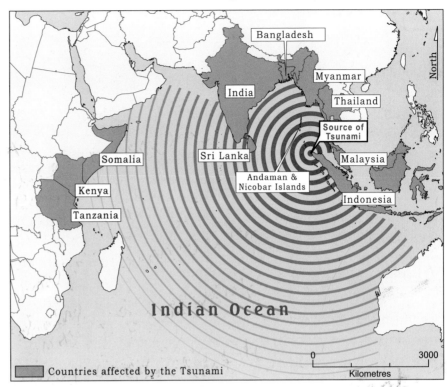

FIGURE 8.1. As shown on this map, the December 2004 tsunami affected many countries.

## Disaster Relief: The Red Cross at Work

### The Asian Tsunami

On 26 December 2004, a terrible wave of destruction swept over southeast Asia. A magnitude 9.3 earthquake, the second biggest in recorded history, ripped apart the sea floor off the coast of northwest Sumatra. The earthquake unleashed a devastating **tsunami**, which travelled thousands of kilometres across the Indian Ocean. In some coastal areas, the wave was 10 metres high when it reached land. People around the world watched in disbelief at the loss of lives, homes, and livelihoods. Although the total number of deaths caused by the tsunami will never be known, a reasonable estimate is about 300 000.

While the Red Cross and other relief agencies could do nothing to save the lives of those submerged by the wave, they responded quickly by providing shelter, medical attention, and food to the over one million people left homeless.

**tsunami** A very large ocean wave that results from an underwater earthquake or volcanic eruption.

 Select one of the countries hardest hit by the 2004 tsunami. Using library sources and the Internet, write a report on the devastation it caused. How has the country recovered from the disaster?

 For more information on the 2004 tsunami and natural disasters, visit <www.theworldtoday.ca> and follow "Links" to <www.drgeorgepc.com>.

*Hurricane Katrina*

The Caribbean islands and the southeastern area of the United States are regularly battered by hurricanes. The hurricane season extends from August until October. Hurricanes are large rotating storms, often about 800 kilometres wide, with winds greater than 120 kilometres per hour. They move at speeds of about 30 kilometres per hour. Hurricane Katrina struck the Gulf Coast region of the United States in August 2005.

After crossing southern Florida and leaving about 100 000 homes there without power, Hurricane Katrina strengthened and moved inland toward Louisiana. It reached land at Grand Isle, about 90 kilometres south of New Orleans, on 29 August 2005. The sustained wind speed was about 200 kilometres per hour. As the hurricane passed through New Orleans and the coastal areas to the east and west, many buildings were destroyed, and others were seriously damaged. Storm surges caused flooding several kilometres inland in parts of Louisiana, Mississippi, and Alabama. The cities of Biloxi and Gulfport were devastated.

But it was in the coastal city of New Orleans that the greatest tragedy unfolded. New Orleans lies below sea level in a bowl-shaped depression. It was protected by walls, called *levees* built as a defence against the sea. But

**The Path of Hurricane Katrina**

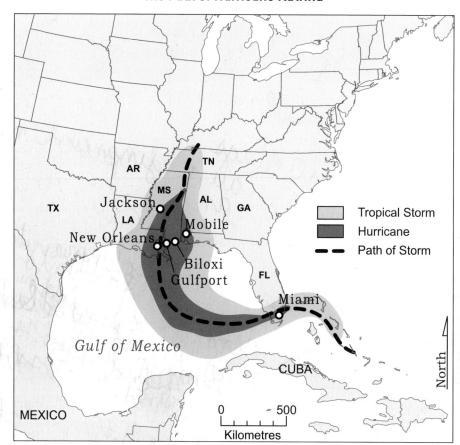

FIGURE 8.2. The movement and strength of hurricanes are usually very difficult to predict because of changing winds in the atmosphere and variable water temperatures.

the storm was so severe that the levees broke in several places, and water poured in, submerging most of the city. About a million people had left the city as the hurricane approached, but tens of thousands of people were unable to leave. These people, mostly the very poor, the elderly, and the ill, sought refuge from the flood waters on rooftops and in two large downtown buildings, the Superdome and the Convention Center. It took several days to get water, food, and medical care to many of these people, and the process of evacuation was not complete until 4 September, six days after the hurricane hit.

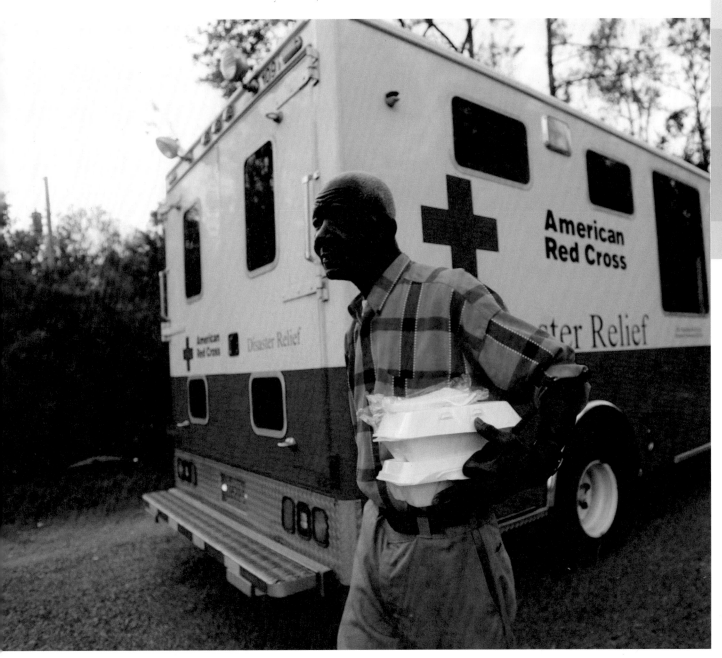

**FIGURE 8.3. The aftermath of Hurricane Katrina. This resident of Pearlington, Mississippi, lost his home. He is shown carrying meals provided by the Red Cross.**

The Red Cross was one of several agencies that responded quickly to the Katrina crisis, offering water, food, and shelter to those in need. Within five days, the Red Cross was helping about 100 000 evacuees in more than 350 shelters. Financial donations poured in, as did offers to help, and the Red Cross National Response Call Centers took more than 43 000 calls with offers of financial contributions in the five days after the hurricane struck.

 Use library sources and the Internet to research another NGO, perhaps *Médicins sans frontières*, World Vision, Care Canada, Greenpeace, the Mennonite Central Committee, or Habitat for Humanity. Describe its origin and discuss two specific examples of how it has helped people in need.

# Governing the World: The United Nations

We have local governments, provincial governments, and national governments. Why do we not have a world government? Although the world is not a poltical unit (like a city, province, or country), there is a body that is concerned with the entire world. It is called the *United Nations*. The United Nations was formed in the aftermath of the Second World War and is the rebirth of the League of Nations, which was formed in the aftermath of the First World War. By the 1930s, for various reasons—including the withdrawal of several key nations (Germany, Italy, and Japan)—the League of Nations had lost its effectiveness.

**The United Nations** In 1918, Woodrow Wilson (1856–1924), then president of the United States, identified 14 points intended to serve as the basis for world peace. Point 14 prompted the 1919 formation of the League of Nations: "A general association of nations should be formed on the basis of covenants designed to create mutual guarantees of the political independence and territorial integrity of States, large and small equally." Later, in 1942, during the Second World War, Franklin D. Roosevelt, president of the United States at that time, coined the name *United Nations* when representatives of 26 countries pledged to continue fighting together against the Axis Powers (Germany, Italy, and Japan). This became the name of the body that replaced the League of Nations in 1945.

Both the League of Nations and the United Nations were created with the goal of establishing world peace and social and economic cooperation among all countries, and both organizations were initiated by the United States. The League comprised far fewer countries than does the United Nations today and was dominated by European countries. Today, with 191 member countries, the United Nations represents almost all of the countries in the world.

Mark 24 October on your calendar. It was on this date in 1945 that the United Nations officially came into existence and, internationally, this date is celebrated as United Nations Day. It is in the United Nations that the countries of the world—large, small, rich, and poor—come together to participate in debate. The United Nations does not have the same authority that local, provincial, and national governments have—for example, the results of their debates are not binding on member countries—however, their resolutions are usually taken very seriously by most national governments.

## Everyone Can Join

The United Nations is an inclusive, not an exclusive, club of nations. A country is admitted once it convinces the Security Council that it supports the principle of peace and is willing to work to improve the conditions of people around the world. Just like in school, however, expulsions and suspensions can occur if a nation were to violate the Charter.

FIGURE 8.4. The headquarters of the United Nations in New York City. Note the row of flags of some of the member nations.

**Four Main Purposes of the United Nations**

1. Preserve world peace and security.
2. Encourage nations to act toward other nations in a just and humane manner.
3. Help nations to cooperate when problem-solving.
4. Provide a context in which nations can communicate and work together.

**Seven Guiding Principles for the United Nations**

1. All nations have equal rights.
2. All nations are responsible for carrying out their duties as Charter members.
3. Nations must agree to settle their disputes peacefully.
4. Nations may threaten or use force only in self-defense.
5. Nations must support the United Nations to carry out the purpose of the Charter.
6. Nations must work to convince nonmember states to support the principle of world peace and security.
7. Nations will not interfere with the actions of a member state within its own borders.

## How the United Nations Works

All 191 member states of the United Nations are represented in the General Assembly, a body that functions as a parliament of **sovereign nations**. However, it is the Security Council that is the United Nations' most powerful body, as it has the responsibility of maintaining international peace and security. Five powerful countries sit as permanent members on the Security Council—China, France, Russia, United Kingdom, and the United States—and there are 10 other member states that are elected for two-year terms. The Council has much authority; for example, it can engage in military operations, impose economic sanctions on countries, conduct arms inspections, monitor elections.

A third main body—the Economic and Social Council—coordinates economic and social projects, while the International Court of Justice arbitrates disputes between countries.

We know from studying geography that all the peoples and places in the world are interdependent. The United Nations provides a peaceful forum for countries to find a way to balance their national goals with the interests of the larger, international, community. Rather than meet on battlefields to settle issues, members of the United Nations can meet together in a civilized fashion to discuss a full range of issues to do with national security, justice, human dignity, the well-being of people, environment, and trade.

There are several sites around the world that house United Nations offices. New York City in the United States houses the United Nations headquarters, but the site itself is deemed international territory. The United Nations has its own flag, its own post office, and even its own stamps. The European headquarters for the United Nations are in Geneva, Switzerland, at the Palais des Nations. The International Court of Justice is located in The Hague, Netherlands. There are also regional offices in other countries.

You may wonder how all the member countries communicate. The United Nations translates all its proceedings into six languages—Arabic, Chinese, English, French, Russian, and Spanish—ensuring that all opinions are not only heard but also understood.

**sovereign nation** In simple terms, an independent country. More formally, a sovereign nation has a government that exercises authority over the country and all citizens of the country.

## The Person in Charge of the United Nations

Like the principal of a school, the secretary-general oversees the running of the United Nations. All five permanent members of the Security Council must agree upon the nomination for the position of secretary-general, and then the position must be officially approved and appointed by the General Assembly. A majority vote is necessary before the secretary-general can be selected to begin his or her five-year term. The secretary-general also oversees the office of the Secretariat, which manages the daily business of the United Nations. There are over 9 000 employees at the New York headquarters of the United Nations. Because the composition of this workforce must reflect the diversity of the world community, each member of the United Nations is allowed to fill at least six positions with citizens from its own nation.

The first secretary-general was Trygve Lie, of Norway, who served for a term and half, from 1946 until 1953. Some of the other countries that have provided a secretary-general are Sweden (Dag Hammarskjöld), Myanmar (U Thant), Austria (Kurt Waldheim), Peru (Javier Pérez de Cuéllar), Egypt (Boutros Boutros-Ghali), and Ghana (Kofi Annan).

 As of 2005, Taiwan has not been allowed into the United Nations, because China is not willing to recognize Taiwan as an independent country; China views it as one of its provinces. Use library sources and the Internet to research this topic.

FIGURE 8.5. The United Nations flag.

## The United Nations Flag

The United Nations flag was designed in 1947 and is recognized throughout the world. No matter which part of the world you reside in, the olive branch that surrounds the world means peace—for all peoples in all places.

The flag has five circles radiating out from the North Pole, and the projection extends as far as 60°S. Each part of the world is connected by a web of latitudinal and longitudinal lines. The colour blue depicts the oceans that surround our continents; white, a neutral colour, reflects the neutrality of the United Nations.

 How big is too big? Is the United Nations becoming too big? How can 191 members' voices be heard? Is there an additional language that should be represented? What about the locations of the United Nations headquarters? Should the United Nations meet in various locations as do the Olympic games? Discuss these questions.

## Responding to a World with Many and Varied Needs

Many agencies are a part of or, in some cases, closely linked to, the United Nations. For example:

- Food and Agriculture Organization (FAO)
- International Labour Organization (ILO)
- International Monetary Fund (IMF)
- International Telecommunication Union (ITU)
- United Nations Development Programme (UNDP)
- United Nations Educational, Scientific, and Cultural and Scientific Organization (UNESCO)
- United Nations High Commissioner for Refugees (UNHCR)
- United Nations International Children's Emergency Fund (UNICEF)
- World Bank Group
- World Food Programme (WFP)
- World Health Organization (WHO)
- World Trade Organization (WTO)

FIGURE 8.6. A tent camp set up in 2003 by the United Nations High Commission for Refugees on the border between Iraq and Jordan.

 Each agency has a specific mandate. The World Bank, for example, lends money to help countries strengthen their infrastructures, perhaps through building dams, railways, or power plants. Select one agency, then check library sources and the Internet to learn more about how it helps build a better world.

 So far, only one nation has ever left the United Nations. It was Indonesia, in 1965, but it asked to be reinstated two years later. Think about the following questions and suggest three answers to each:

- Why are so many countries members of the United Nations?
- What advantages does the United Nations offer to smaller countries?
- Should smaller countries be given the same vote as larger countries?
- Do you think that all countries should be part of the United Nations?
- How should the United Nations be paid for? (At present, every member of the United Nations must pay part of the operating costs.)

These are very difficult questions to answer; even the United Nations itself wrestles with finding appropriate answers to them. There really are no "correct" answers. Compare your answers with those of classmates, and work as a class to develop a set of agreed-upon answers. Is it difficult to get everybody in your class to agree? Imagine what it must be like getting 191 people to agree on a complex and controversial issue.

# Wars and Peacekeeping

Since its inception, the United Nations has been "fighting" for peace and has been instrumental in finding peaceful resolutions to many conflicts, including the Korean War and civil war in Sudan.

## The Korean War

The Korean War followed the division of the Korean Peninsula into South Korea and North Korea at the end of the Second World War. After a number of border skirmishes, North Korean troops invaded South Korea in 1950. The United States, Britain, Canada, Australia, and Turkey defended South Korea under the umbrella of the United Nations, while China supported North Korea. A cease-fire agreement was signed in 1953, but only after about four million Koreans (many of them civilians), one million Chinese, and about 55 000 members of the United Nations force had died.

**The Korean Peninsula**

FIGURE 8.7. North Korea has a long boundary with China and a very short (about 19 km) boundary with Russia.

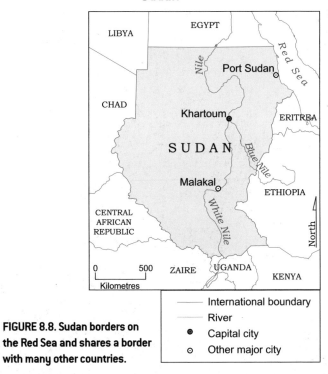

**Sudan**

FIGURE 8.8. Sudan borders on the Red Sea and shares a border with many other countries.

## Conflict in Sudan

Imagine that you have spent your whole life wondering what life would be like without war. Imagine that you have always feared raids on your home. Imagine that your mother or your sister has been sold into slavery. Imagine that your brother has joined the militia and you have not heard from him in months. Imagine that your father was killed years ago, along with many other family members. This is how life would probably be for you if you lived in Sudan in the early 21st century.

Beginning in 1983, Sudan was torn apart by fighting between a rebel group and government forces. In January 2005, an agreement was reached that put an immediate ceasefire into place, and the United Nations sent peacekeeping forces to help ensure peace. Religious differences played a part in the early years of the conflict, but the discovery of huge oil reserves in southern Sudan kept the fires of hatred burning, resulting in the death of at least 1.5 million Sudanese and the homelessness of another four million. At the same time, much of Sudan was experiencing a terrible famine.

FIGURE 8.9. Mahatma Gandhi (see arrow) and some of his followers on the Salt March in 1930. This was an act of protest of Britain's regulation of salt in India and, further, its rule. India was declared independent in 1947.

## Reasons for Wars

Why does war exist in our world? There are many reasons. Wars are fought over natural resources like water, salt, fertile land, or forests. Wars are fought for prime trading routes and new lands to be "discovered" by exploring nations. Wars are fought for reasons of religious difference, racism, power, and greed. Wars are fought because of fear that one country or state is a threat to the safety of another. Wars are fought because a group of people seeks to own and occupy a place that is in the hands of another group of people. What we do know is that less-developed countries are much more likely to experience war. Development prevents war, and war prevents development.

In 1930, Mahatma Gandhi and some of his followers undertook a march to the sea—the famous Salt March. When they got there, Gandhi scooped up a handful of salt and by doing this sent a message to Britain that India would reject British rule and have its freedom. Britain had forbidden private collection of salt—a powerful message to all Indians, who understood well the need for salt in everyday life. Before the invention of refrigeration, and later for people who could not afford it, salt was crucial for preserving foods such as meat. As well, it is a necessary part of a balanced diet. (It was so valuable that the Romans used it as a form of payment, which is where we get the word *salary*.)

 For photos taken by Sebastião Salgado (b. 1944) at the height of Sudan's famine, visit <www.theworldtoday.ca> and follow "Links" to <www.terra.com.br/sebastiaosalgado>. Click on Migrations and then Africa Adrift. Look for the story of Winnie from Sudan and other teenage refugees at <www.itvs.org/beyondthefire>.

## Crisis in the Former Yugoslavia

At the end of the Second World War in 1945, Josip Broz Tito (1892–1980), Yugoslavia's president, declared that Yugoslavia was one nation. Tito dealt with the many groups of people who wanted their own country by calling the regions *republics*. He gave each republic equal powers. Until Tito's death in 1980, his powerful personality made this jigsaw-puzzle country work, and things were relatively peaceful and stable.

By the early 1990s, regional disagreements had increased. Two of the republics declared their separate status as nations, and Yugoslavia began to fall apart. A series of conflicts saw various groups of people pitted against each other, and it was during these conflicts that "ethnic cleansing" (a polite phrase for "mass murder") began.

Over about 10 horrific years, about 2.7 million people were displaced from their homes, and perhaps 20 000 to 40 000 women were molested. When the war ended, a new set of countries appeared on the map, replacing the former Yugoslavia.

## The Suez Crisis

The Suez crisis occurred in 1956 when Egypt wanted the Suez Canal back from the

### The Countries of the Former Yugoslavia

FIGURE 8.10. This map locates and names the 6 countries that occupy the territory that was previously the one country of Yugoslavia.

European companies that had financed its construction almost 100 years before and that had run it since then. The Suez Canal is an important shipping route, because it connects the Red Sea to the Mediterranean Sea. When Egyptian President Nasser decided to claim ownership of the Canal, France, Britain, and Israel attacked Egypt. They were worried about losing a precious trading route connecting Europe to the Persian Gulf and the Far East. Canadian Prime Minister Lester B. Pearson suggested that a United Nations peacekeeping force be put in place to separate the combatants. Since that time, Canada has been involved in peacekeeping missions around the world, and many Canadians see peacekeeping as an important part of the Canadian identity.

Some people argue that besides its role in coordinating peacekeeping forces, the United Nations, to be truly effective, needs to have a permanent police force. List three reasons for and three reasons against this proposal. Discuss with your classmates the pros and cons of creating a permanent United Nations police force.

 Keep your eyes and ears open. Are the peacekeeping operations mapped in figure 8.12 being reported on a regular basis? Are some of these missions concluded? Are there peacekeeping forces in other locations?

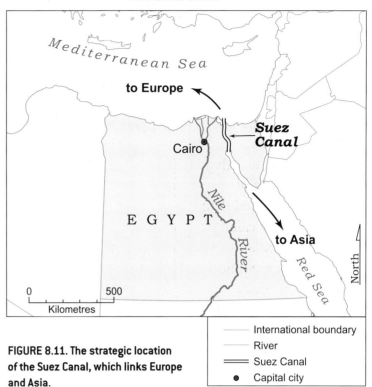

**The Suez Canal**

FIGURE 8.11. The strategic location of the Suez Canal, which links Europe and Asia.

## Location of United Nations Peacekeeping Forces in 2005

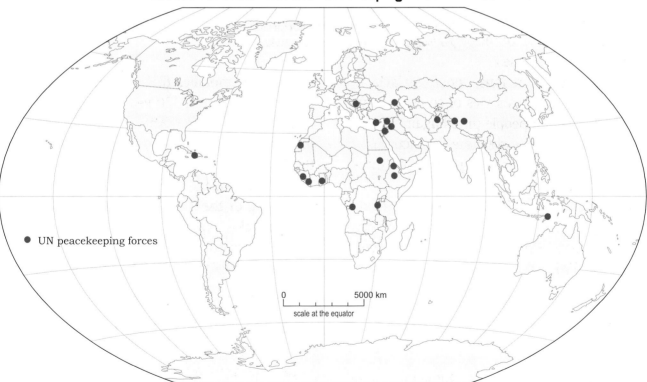

FIGURE 8.12. There are peacekeeping forces in the Middle East, Europe, Asia, the Caribbean, and Africa.

# Remembrance Day

Remembrance Day, originally called Armistice Day, was first conducted in 1919 in all the Commonwealth countries. It was intended to commemorate the end of the "war to end all wars," now known as the First World War. The Armistice, or truce, was signed on the 11th hour of the 11th day of the 11th month.

The poppy, featured in a poem written by John McCrae, became the symbol of remembrance. In Canada each year, artificial poppies are sold by the Royal Canadian Legion to raise funds for poverty-stricken veterans.

FIGURE 8.14. John McCrae (1872–1918).

FIGURE 8.13. Poppies and photographs placed in the ground at a war memorial following Remembrance Day ceremonies.

### In Flanders Fields
(Lieutenant Colonel John McCrae, MD, 1872–1918, Canadian Army)

In Flanders Fields the poppies blow
Between the crosses row on row,
That mark our place; and in the sky
The larks, still bravely singing, fly
Scarce heard amid the guns below.
We are the Dead. Short days ago
We lived, felt dawn, saw sunset glow,
Loved and were loved, and now we lie
In Flanders fields.
Take up our quarrel with the foe:
To you from failing hands we throw
The torch; be yours to hold it high.
If ye break faith with us who die
We shall not sleep, though poppies grow
In Flanders fields.

**John McCrae** was a surgeon who spent 17 days treating men who were injured in the fighting at Ypres, Belgium, during the First World War. He said, "I wish that I could embody on paper some of the varied sensations of that seventeen days. Seventeen days of Hades!" The day after he led the funeral of a dear friend and student, Lieutenant Alexis Helmer of Ottawa, he wrote "In Flanders Fields" while looking at the poppies that had sprung up in the ditches by the cemetery where his friend was buried.

John must have felt that his words did not embody the horror of what he experienced; he threw the poem away. It was retrieved from the garbage by another officer and was published in *Punch Magazine* on 8 December 1915. It became a favourite tribute and continues to be read at Remembrance Day ceremonies throughout Canada and the world.

For fascinating and interactive information about Canada's involvement in remembering the fallen from the First World War and later, visit <www.theworldtoday.ca> and follow "Links" to <www.cwgc.org> (the Commonwealth Wars Grave Commission). Also find film clips, books of remembrance and many other helpful research tools at <www.vac-acc.gc.ca> (Veterans Affairs Canada).

## Five Questions

1. "In facing the choice of peace or extinction, man must renounce predatory nationalism and look to the primacy of world concerns to bring about peace and security for all." Who is responsible for these stirring words?

2. Who helped Canada introduce the maple-leaf flag in 1964, a national pension plan in 1965, and medicare in 1966?

3. Who established the United Nations Relief and Rehabilitation Administration as well as the Food and Agriculture Organization (designed to eliminate world hunger)?

4. Who was the president of the United Nations General Assembly in 1955?

5. Who received the Order of the British Empire and the Nobel Peace Prize in 1957?

**One Answer** Lester B. Pearson (1897–1972). Lester B. Pearson served as prime minister of Canada from 1963 to 1968. He received the Nobel Peace Prize for helping create a peacekeeping force to monitor the 1956 Suez crisis between Egypt and Israel. Always an activist, Pearson once stated, "A true realist is the man who sees things both as they are and as they can be. In every situation, there is a possibility of improvement; in every life the hidden capacity for something better."

FIGURE 8.15. Lester B. Pearson at his seat in the United Nations in 1957.

FIGURE 8.16. Stephen Lewis speaking at a press conference at the United Nations in 2001 after being named Special Envoy of the Secretary-General for HIV/AIDS in Africa.

**Stephen Lewis** (b. 1937) is another Canadian who has made valuable contributions to the United Nations and to the world. In 2001, he was appointed to assist the secretary-general in a campaign to stop the spread of diseases such as HIV/AIDS and to provide treatment and care for those afflicted in Africa. Stephen Lewis served as the deputy executive director of UNICEF (1995–1999) and as Canada's ambassador to the United Nations (1984–1988). His political experience in Canada with the New Democratic Party and his diplomatic experience within the United Nations reflected and reinforced his humanitarian concerns, especially his advocacy of the rights and needs of children worldwide. Recognizing that one cannot always wait for governments to provide funding, he established the Stephen Lewis Foundation to personally assist communities in Africa plagued by the HIV/AIDS epidemic.

It is not hard to understand why *Maclean's Magazine* named Stephen Lewis as Canadian of the Year in 2003. He is both articulate and passionate: "When people are dying by the thousands every day, unnecessarily, when we've had this horrendous pandemic unfold for two decades while the world stands by and watches—you'll do anything in your power to move the process," says Lewis. "I don't care what it takes. All I know is that every time I go to Africa, I am shaken to my core" (*Maclean's Magazine*, December 2003).

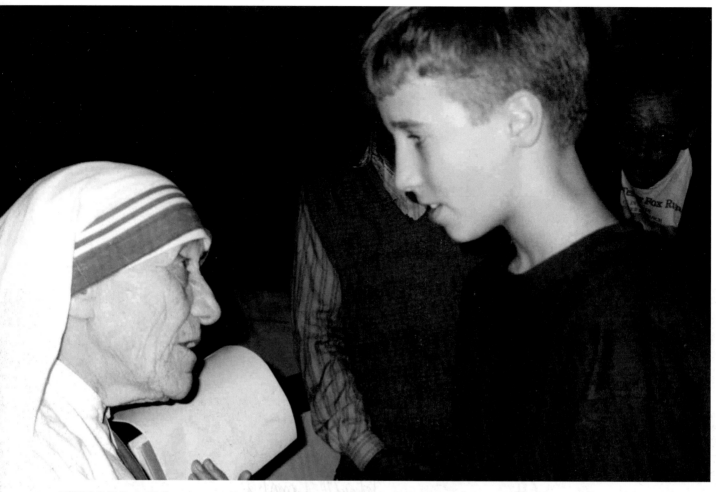

FIGURE 8.17. Craig Kielburger meets Mother Teresa. Born in Macedonia, Mother Teresa (1910–1997) devoted her life to caring for the homeless in Calcutta, India. She was awarded the Nobel Peace Prize in 1979.

## You, Too, Can Make a Difference!

Do you think that you are too young to start your own NGO? Well, here is an example of one teenager who decided to make a difference. In 1995, at the age of 12, Craig Kielburger started Free the Children. Saddened by a story he came across in a newspaper about a young boy in Pakistan who was murdered for speaking out against child-labour practices, Craig knew he had to do something. His group began to lobby governments to put an end to the exploitation of children, and it became an advocacy group for children's rights worldwide. Free the Children encourages children and young people to take action and get involved in their youth-based programs and campaigns. Through the hard work and dedication of young people, the group built more than 400 schools for children in less-developed countries around the world. Rather than simply reading the news and leaving action up to others, Craig started a youth advocacy foundation that made news on television shows such as *Oprah* and *60 Minutes.* More important, he showed how one person can make a difference.

 Hannah Taylor is Canada's youngest advocate for this country's homeless community. Research other such youth advocates and advertise their programs to students in your school. Refer to the Ladybug Foundation: visit < www.the world today.ca > and follow "Links" to <www.ladybugfoundation.ca/>.

## Working Together for a Wonderful World

Politically, economically, and socially, the Red Cross, the United Nations and its many agencies, as well as other NGOs, numerous individuals both young and old, and sporting competitions, strive to create, as Louis Armstrong wrote and sang, "a wonderful world."

 The 2002 FIFA World Cup final soccer match between Brazil and Germany was the most viewed event in sporting television history, with viewers in almost every country and with an audience of 1.1 billion—that is, more than one in every six people at the time.

Imagine—one in every six people in the world sharing the same experience at the same time. Is this what geographers mean when they talk about the global village? List three reasons showing that the world coming together to share a sporting experience might be one way in which a better world is being built.

FIGURE 8.18. Enjoying youth and making memories.

# SOCIETIES AND WAYS OF LIFE

Imagine what your life would be like if you were living in a different part of the world. What effect do you think growing up in a different place would have on you? Would you be attending school? At what age would you be preparing for initiation into adulthood? What would you think about yourself, your landscape, your religion, your weather, and your health?

Our beliefs, what we call "normal," our clothing, our food, our choice of music, even how we rebel, can be understood only in the context of those with whom we live—the larger society of which we are a part—and in the context of the way of life of that society: our culture.

In this section, we explore the societies and cultures of some of our global neighbours, from indigenous tribes in Africa to urbanites in Japan. We see how people adapt to natural environments and change natural environments. We explore expressions of culture from many different places and look at how our culture determines the way we think, feel, and say.

History and geography are closely related. The European colonial expansion that began in the 15th century has changed many societies and cultures, often beyond recognition. In some cases, traditional indigenous cultures have survived and even thrived despite great challenges and external pressures. We explore issues that arise from this far-reaching and earth-shattering expansion.

In this section, you are challenged to see the world through another's eyes. You are asked to consider how your buying and consuming habits affect your neighbours in our global village. You are invited to be a world traveller, a global thinker, and a good neighbour, all from the comfort of your own spot on the globe.

"The world is so empty if one thinks only of mountains, rivers and cities, but to know that there is someone who, though distant, thinks and feels with us, this makes the earth for us an inhabited garden" (Johann Wolfgang von Goethe, 1749–1832, German philosopher).

# SOCIETY AND CULTURE

# 9

## Guiding Questions

1. What is society, and why do human beings live in societies?

2. What is culture, and how does it relate to who we are?

3. What do all groups of people, past and present, near and far, have in common?

4. How are the human geographies of India, Somalia, and Australia similar to but different from each other?

## Society

You have heard the term *society* many times, and you probably know that you are a member of Canadian society. But have you thought about what society is or how it affects you? A look at the Latin roots of the word gives us a hint: *socius* means "companion," and *societas* means "fellowship." Society, then, is a fellowship of companions, or a group of friends. Does this mean that everyone in Canada is your friend? Of course not, but a traditional Latin understanding of the word *friend* includes the idea that a friend is someone with whom you are at peace, an ally

A society is a group of people with whom you live at peace, with whom you are connected. You share a common government, similar beliefs and values, a way to divide labour, a method for educating the young within the society, a general idea of what is right and wrong, and you share some common goals. You band together in this way because it helps you meet your material and emotional needs.

Individual members of a society usually live close to each other, so place is an important part of society. Societies live in places. There might be several different cultural groups in a single society. This is the case in Canada.

The definition is not complete, however. The society you belong to affects what you think is important in life, how you define "the good life," who you admire, how you communicate, the language you use, and even what you consider beautiful.

Finally, the term *society* applies at several different geographic scales, and it is often convenient to recognize societies within societies.

**society** A group of humans distinguished from other groups by common elements such as beliefs and values, structures of government, social organization, education, and economic activities. When we talk about social structure, we are talking about the way a society is arranged, how its parts are organized.

Society is greater than any one life, or any one life span. Our society has been influenced by people who have come and gone (lived and died) before us. Although only few of us ever know our great-great-grandparents, we are affected by the contribution they made to our family and our society.

**Nellie McClung, Society Changer** Nellie McClung (1873–1951) was one of the most important leaders of Canada's early feminist movement, and she is still remembered for her role in the famous *Persons Case*, which saw Canadian women declared persons in 1929. She also helped win the vote for women in Manitoba in 1916, making Manitoba the first Canadian province to grant women the right to vote provincially. Think about how our lives might be now if Nellie McClung hadn't been a society changer.

**FIGURE 9.1.** Above: teenage girls in Istanbul, Turkey. Upper right: friends in Iceland. Lower right: schoolboys in South Africa.

**FIGURE 9.2.**
Nellie McClung.

# Culture

We understand the term *culture* to mean the way we express ourselves. We live in a world of **cultural diversity**.

> **culture** A way of life shared by a group of people. Culture gives us our identity and then helps sustain that identity. Culture includes our language, religion, art, music, dance, dress, homes, attitudes toward work and recreation, and much more.
>
> **cultural diversity** The ways in which cultures differ from one another. When we talk about cultural diversity, we are talking about the different expressions of culture. Sometimes, as in Canada, there is cultural diversity within a single society.

Language is the basic building block of culture, because it enables people to communicate with one another. Throughout history, conquerors have used language to control and subjugate people. Time and time again, conquering groups have outlawed the language spoken by the people they conquered. When a group of people loses its language, the people lose their poetry, their stories, and their jokes. They lose the lessons they could have learned from previous generations, and they lose their distinctive cultural identity. The most effective way to combat this loss of cultural identity is to ensure that a child's first language be spoken at home and in the school setting so that he or she will grow up with it. This is especially important when the language is not a written language, when the stories, songs, and dances are transmitted orally.

> **Society and Culture** Think of *society* as the people and *culture* as the expression of who they are, and you will understand the difference between society and culture.

# Patterns of Culture

As you continue working your way through this book, you will be introduced to many different people in many different societies with many different cultural practices. There are many ways to look at the people you are researching.

## Consider their Physical Geography
What kind of natural environment do these people live in? If they go out their door and look as far as they can over the horizon, what will they see? Do they see mountains or prairies? Is water plentiful or scarce? Is the weather cold or warm? What kinds of food does the natural environment provide? Do the soil and climate support agriculture, and, if so, what types of crops are grown and what animals are kept?

## Consider their History
How did these people develop? How did they become allies? What historical circumstances contributed to making their culture what it is today? Is their past peaceful, or is it one of conflict? Is their past relatively stable, or have there been significant changes?

## Consider their Language
Language is the main way that people communicate with each other. Language is evident in the naming of the parts of the landscape; describe the landscape of Manitoba, and you will discover many languages. Language is necessary for describing the physical geography of a place; the words need to allow for clear description of the local surroundings. For example, the Spanish language includes many words that refer to landforms in dry areas, whereas the English language does not.

## Consider their Religious Beliefs

Cultures develop religious ceremonies to express their faith and ideas about gods and the unknown. Religious beliefs often bring hope and a reason for being; they offer many people a purpose to their life. They help form values and are expressed through worship, prayer, faith communities, ceremonies, and rituals. They are expressed in the stuctures, cemeteries, and shrines that are built into the society's landscape.

## Consider their Technology

How does technology affect the economy and everyday lives of these people? As technology changes, people are able to use the natural environment in new ways. For example, some cultures are predominantly agricultural, while others have technologies that allow them to practise industrial activities.

## Consider their Economy

How do these people work together to meet their physical needs and wants? What do they do to make money so that they can provide for themselves and their families? Are they working at sawmills, fisheries, farms, or computer firms? How are they using their natural resources?

## Consider the Possessions they Prize

What do these people want to own? What material possessions do they value? Usually, the more **disposable income** people have, the more they seem to want. In more-developed countries especially, people often identify themselves through their possessions.

## Consider their Politics

People need a way to be governed, make laws, keep order, and settle differences. Government

**disposable income** Personal income that remains after bills and taxes have been paid. It is the income available for consumption or saving.

provides structure to a society, keeps people safe, and allows for a basic code of conduct.

## Consider their Families

Family structure and roles within marriage help determine who is responsible for caring for those who are young, old, and weak. Some societies have a culture that believes extended family members should live together; other societies believe that only the nuclear family should make up the household. What roles do men, women, and children have within the families of these people? What living arrangements are typical?

## Consider their Artistic Expression

Art is one of the ways that people pass on traditions, express feelings, confront injustice, communicate ideas about the unknown, and celebrate important events. Artistic expression includes music, visual arts, literature, theatre, craft, dance, for example.

## Consider their Educational System

Schools help students learn so that they may contribute to their society. Are these people generally literate? Are girls educated equally with boys?

## Consider their Recreation

People in all cultures, even when they live in extremely harsh conditions, devise ways to enjoy themselves. What kinds of recreational activities do these people enjoy? How do they use their leisure time? Do men and women tend to engage in the same kinds of leisure activities?

## Consider their Standards for Beauty

Every culture has beliefs about beauty. What do these people consider beautiful? How do they adorn themselves? Why is one thing considered beautiful and another not? Do these standards change through time?

# Exploring Peoples and Places

In the next few pages, we explore three countries from which people have immigrated to Canada. You can use this information to give you ideas for your own research into peoples and places.

## Locating Canada, Somalia, India, and Australia

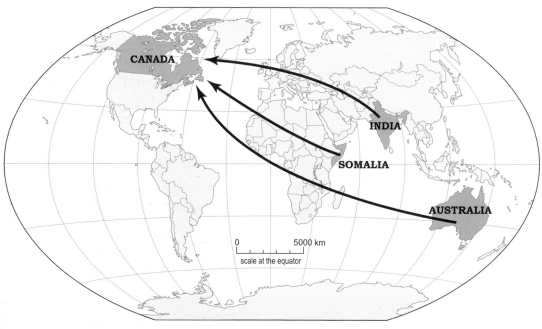

FIGURE 9.3. The world comes to Canada and adds to Canada.

FIGURE 9.4. The variety of foodstuffs is as diverse as is the variety in the regions of the world. Simply look at a banquet table. In some countries, where they are common, iguanas are known as "chickens of the trees," because (you guessed it!) they taste like chicken. A teenager born and raised in Canada would find eating an iguana unusual, perhaps, but the thought of eating venison, or deer meat, is quite "normal."

## Stereotyping

There are two very important facts to bear in mind before we begin studying the three countries we have chosen:

1. No study of a country can provide all the facts; any study necessarily includes generalizations about peoples and places. But be careful not to treat these generalizations as though they applied to each and every person in that country. To do so is to **stereotype**.

2. It is very important to avoid stereotypes because they can easily lead to prejudice and discrimination.

**stereotype** To think in rigid and inflexible categories; for example, to think that all elderly people are confused or that all Canadians are hockey fans.

**Prejudice and Discrimination** Remember the definitions of these two important words, which were included in chapter 5.
1. *Prejudice* refers to the prejudging of an individual based on characteristics assumed to apply to all members of that individual's group. Prejudice is an attitude; it is how we feel.
2. *Discrimination* is the action of treating an individual differently (usually unfairly) because they belong to a particular group. Discrimination is an action; it is what we do.

 Reports of racist, or presumed racist, activities appear frequently in the media. Look at Canadian newspapers and news magazines to see which groups of people are being targeted today.

FIGURE 9.5. Punk girl applying lipstick.

**Are You Stereotyped?** You may feel stereotyped as a teenager when you walk into a corner store and see a sign that says, No More Than 2 Students at a Time. The store owners have made a generalization that you might try to shoplift. Some common stereotypes about Canada are that it is always cold, that Canadians are always polite, and that all Canadians play hockey. While there may be some truth to some of the statements some of the time, they are not true for all individuals. Keep this in mind when you study the human geographies of India, Somalia, and Australia in the following pages. The information presented in this book is necessarily simplified. Allow yourself to wonder what might be missing and think about the kinds of information you would want to include about another country you might be studying.

## India

Many immigrants to Canada were born in Asian countries; most come from Hong Kong, China, India, and Sri Lanka. Most come to Canada because of the prospect of better-paying jobs.

### FAST FACTS
#### about India

Area: 3 287 590 km²
Population: 1 104 million (1.104 billion)
Crude birth date: 25 per 1 000
Crude death rate: 8 per 1 000
Rate of natural increase: 1.7 percent
Capital city: New Delhi
Life expectancy: 62 years
Population density: 300 people per km²
Languages: Hindi and English
   (many others are spoken)
Religions: Hinduism, Islam, Christianity, Sikhism
   (in order of prevalence)
Urbanization: 28 percent urban
Government: democracy, federal republic
Literacy rate: 60 percent
Gross national income per capita: US$3 100

### Changing Geographies

The story of India's changing geographies is best understood in the context of the Indian subcontinent, which today includes the countries of Pakistan, Nepal, Bhutan, Bangladesh, India, and Sri Lanka. One early (about 3000 BCE) agricultural and urban area was the Indus River valley (now in Pakistan) that included two major towns (Harappa and Mohenjo-Daro). Two major world religions originated in northern India: Hinduism and Buddhism. Hinduism dates back to about 2000 BCE and spread south throughout India. Buddhism became prominent in about 600 BCE, but spread from India to Southeast Asia and China. A third religion, Islam, was introduced in the 1500s by Mughals, who were Muslims (followers of Islam are called Muslims).

Life in India changed when Europeans began colonizing it in the 1600s. The Portuguese were the first Europeans to trade with India, but the British had the biggest influence, ruling for over 300 years during a period called the *Raj*. The British introduced their legal, educational, political, industrial, and transportation systems. They also introduced the English language, which is now one of India's official languages. India gained independence from Britain in 1947 after many years of peaceful resistance, led by Mahatma Gandhi. At this time, Pakistan (which is mainly Muslim) was created as one state, and India (which is mainly Hindu) was created as another. Unfortunately, millions of people now needed to relocate their homes to the "correct" side of the border, and violence broke out. Although religious differences and border disputes continue to cause unrest in India, the country is an increasingly powerful voice in Asia today.

### Basic Geographic Facts

India has a varied landscape. The Himalayan Mountain region is home to the world's highest mountains. South of the mountains lie the Northern Plains, which are fertilized by rivers, including the Indus, Ganges, and Brahmaputra. South of the plains lies the southern plateau of the Deccan. The Western and the Eastern Ghats are smaller mountain ranges that run along the coasts and frame the Deccan Plateau. The Thar Desert borders Pakistan; camels (over a million are in service at any given time) are used for transportation in this region.

The climate varies from tropical monsoon in the south to temperate in the north; the northwest is a semi-arid desert area. India has a diverse plant and animal life, from Arctic plants high in the mountains to tropical plants and flowers in the south. Most of India experiences three seasons: the cool season, the hot season, and the rainy season.

India's major exports include agricultural products, diamonds and other jewellery, clothing, machinery, and cotton. India's film industry, known as *Bollywood*, has begun to make inroads in North America and Europe.

## Representing India

Indian art is as varied as its landscape. Indian music is very different from music that developed in the west, and the primary instruments include the sitar, the vena, and the tabla.

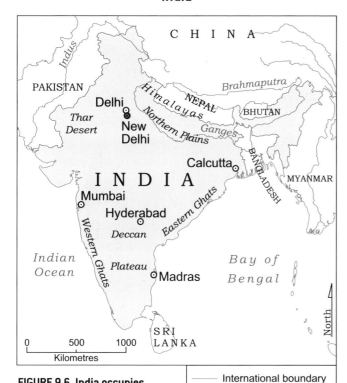

**India**

FIGURE 9.6. India occupies most of the region that geographers often label either as the Indian subcontinent or as South Asia. Other countries included in the larger region are Pakistan, Bangladesh, Nepal, Sri Lanka, Bhutan, and the small island state of The Maldives (located in the Indian Ocean southeast of Sri Lanka).

Legend:
- —— International boundary
- —— River
- ● Capital city
- ○ Other major city

## Indian Values

India's traditional roles and values are changing, especially in urban areas, but religion is important to many people, as is the outlawed **caste system**. Many Indians live in an extended family, where elders are respected and cared for. Family unity and approval are crucial throughout life, and many marriages are still arranged by parents. There are many differences in how Indians live, from the Westernized lives of the wealthy in big cities, to simple, subsistence lifestyles in rural areas.

FIGURE 9.7. Ravi Shankar popularized Indian music in other countries by blending western and eastern sounds.

**caste system** Places all Hindus into one of five social categories and sets limits on the interactions among members of the five castes. At the top of the system are Brahmans, who are mostly priests and scholars. Below them are the Kshatriyas, who are warriors and rulers. Next are the Vaishyas, who are mostly merchants and workers, and then Shudras, who are usually servants. At the bottom of the caste system are the Dalit, or untouchables, who are social outcasts. The caste system is an elaborate construction of social inequality.

 Use library sources and the Internet to research the caste system.

## Somalia

The 2001 Canadian census identified almost 34 000 Somalis living in Canada. Many came to Canada because of war and drought in their homeland. Somalia is one of the poorest countries in the world and has experienced conflict for many years.

## FAST FACTS
### about Somalia

Area: 637 657 km²

Population: 8.6 million

Crude birth rate: 46 per 1 000

Crude death rate: 18 per 1 000

Rate of natural increase: 2.8 percent

Capital city: Mogadishu

Life expectancy: 47 years

Population density: 15 people per km²

Language: Somali

Religion: Sunni Islam

Urbanization: 33 percent urban

Government: republic (but unstable and ineffective); clan-based or Islamic law prevails in some places

Literacy rate: 37 percent

Gross national income per capita: not known (very low)

## Changing Geographies

The ancient Egyptians called Somalia the "Land of God," and Somalia was famous for its frankincense and myrrh. Somalia's ownership of much of the coastline around the Horn of Africa made it an important strategic and trading location. During the 10th century, Chinese traders came to Somalia and brought back leopards, giraffes, and other exotic animals for the emperor's zoo. By the 12th century, a clan system had been established, and the conversion of the people to Islam had begun.

By the 19th century, much of coastal Africa, including Somalia, was of great interest to European powers who wanted access to new natural resources and also to extend their political and cultural influence. At different times between 1860 and 1960, coastal Africa had been under the control of Britain, Italy, and France. Colonial occupation ushered in a period of unrest; Somalis were tired of being ruled from outside, and a new nationalism took root. In 1960, Somalia declared its independence, but its problems were far from over, and clan-based violence and civil war have plagued the country in varying degrees for all of its modern history. Although Somalia is supposed to function as a republic (similar to the United States), it has no effective government, and it often seems as if it is ruled by "the one with the most guns."

## Basic Geographic Facts

Somalia is located along the coast of the Horn of Africa and is mostly hot and dry desert with frequent dust storms. The landscape is flat, with some hilly areas in the north. There are only two rivers that flow all year, the Shebele and the Juba, and these provide some water for farming. The climate is best suited for nomadic pastoralism, and the Somalis are **nomads**, herding their animals wherever they can find food and water for them. Although Somalia has two rainy seasons, drought is frequent and difficult, as people have few resources to survive extended dry periods.

**nomads** People who wander from place to place over an area in search of food, water, and grazing land for their animals. They depend on their animal products (milk, blood, meat). Pastoral nomads are found in the Middle East, North Africa, Central Asia, and parts of the Arctic. Most pastoralists engage also in some seasonal agriculture or acquire agricultural products through trade with other groups.

## Somalia

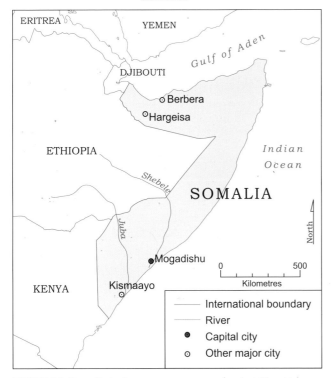

FIGURE 9.8. Somalia is the easternmost country in Africa. It occupies the tip of a region known as the Horn of Africa, which also includes Ethiopia and Djibouti. The region is called the Horn of Africa because, as evident from the map, the shape of the region is similar to that of a rhinoceros horn.

Somalia's main exports are live animals, bananas, and fish. Ironically, those who fish to make a living are held in low regard, and the nomadic people of Somalia detest fish, believing that only incompetent herders eat fish. There are some mineral resources, but these are largely unexploited.

## Representing Somalia

Nomadic cultures tend not to accumulate possessions. However, Somalis prize and decorate the woven and wooden milk jugs and other useful objects that they carry with them. Women decorate themselves with intricate patterns to celebrate important events like weddings and births, and traditional dances are important in courtship. Somalis place a high value on poetry and other spoken arts. The proverb "A man with a sense of humour is never at a loss for words or action," displays their love of puns and verbal wit.

## Somalian Values

Somalis value family and friendship. They value the ability to save face and use humour. They are generous and usually able to adjust well to new situations, such as immigrating to a new country. Because clans are so important to Somalis, and because they move around a lot, a common question is Who are your parents? Which clan are you from? Your address is far less important than your family.

**Somali Refugees** In recent years, political problems and famine circumstances have caused some Somalis to leave the country as refugees. Winnipeg is one Canadian city that has welcomed several hundred refugees from Somalia. Often, these refugees have received financial and other support from organizations such as the Canadian Lutheran World Relief, the Mennonite Central Committee, and the World University Service of Canada.

FIGURE 9.9. The Three Wise Men. In the Christian tradition, the three Magi, or wise men from the east, took gifts to the baby Jesus of gold, frankincense, and myrrh. The frankincense and myrrh probably came from Somalia, or its neighbour Ethiopia. Frankincense and myrrh are still exported from Somalia around the world.

FIGURE 9.10. A group of Somali schoolgirls.

## Australia

Australia and Canada are similar in many ways, including the value of multiculturalism, and have welcomed many immigrants from around the world. Australia's Aboriginal cultures have undergone negative experiences similar to those experienced by First Peoples in Canada, particularly loss of language and cultural identity. Most of the population of both countries live in their largest cities. They both have huge areas of virtually unpopulated land. People in Australia and Canada share a similar standard of living. Still, people do choose to move to Canada from Australia and vice versa.

### FAST FACTS
**about Australia**

Area: 7 686 848 km²
Population: 20.4 million
Crude birth rate: 13 per 1 000
Crude death rate: 7 per 1 000
Rate of natural increase: 0.6 percent
Capital city: Canberra
Life expectancy: 80 years
Population density: 2 people per km²
Language: English
Religion: Christianity
Urbanization: 91 percent urban
Government: democracy; constitutional monarchy
Literacy rate: 100 percent
Gross national income per capita: US$29 200

 Discuss how Aboriginal history in Australia is similar to that of Canada.

## Changing Geographies

Australia's first inhabitants were the Aborigines. It is not known precisely how they reached Australia. Perhaps they travelled from Africa by boat about 60 000 years ago, when sea levels were low and "island hopping" was possible, or they might have travelled through Asia and then into Australia via India or Indonesia.

Because of Australia's great distance from other large continents, it was virtually ignored by Europeans until England claimed it by establishing a penal colony there in 1788. About 161 000 convicts were sent to Australia over a period of about 80 years. Sheep farming and wheat growing became important economic activities, and a gold rush began in the 1850s. The Aboriginal population decreased to about 10 percent of its original numbers because of disease, loss of land and resources, and even massacre. Australia has expressed regret over this great loss and has begun a process called "reconciliation." While some Aborigines have welcomed this move, others demand outright sovereignty. You will learn more about reconciliation in chapter 11.

**FIGURE 9.11. A prospector pans for gold in late-19th-century Western Australia. Scenes such as this were common in other parts of the world also, including California and the Yukon Territory.**

## Satellite Image of Australia

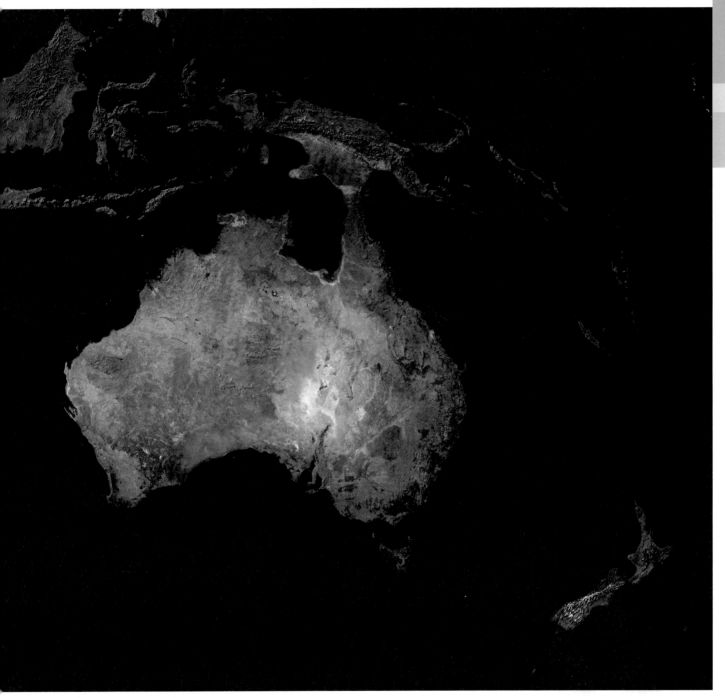

FIGURE 9.12. A satellite image of Australia showing the true colours of the continent as seen from space. Dark green areas are either agricultural crops or forest. Light green and brown areas are either agricultural crops or drier grasslands and plains. The lightest brown or yellow areas are deserts. Black or dark blue areas are oceans, except where the water is very shallow, when the colour is light blue or turquoise.

## Basic Geographic Facts

Most of Australia is desert or semi-desert—flat and dry. The Great Dividing Range runs north to south along the east coast. Other mountainous regions include the Hamersley Range, which runs along the west coast, and the Macdonnell and Musgrave ranges, which lie in central Australia. Central Australia is known as the *Outback*. There are many rivers and lakes in this region, but most of them dry up in the summer. Some of this area is suitable for grazing sheep. The area in the north and along the eastern coast is suitable for grazing cattle. The Great Barrier Reef, located along the northeast coast, is one of Australia's most famous landforms; it is the largest coral formation in the world.

Because Australia is in the southern hemisphere, winter and summer are the reverse of Canada's, winter running from June to August and summer from December to February. Summers are hot, and winters are mild. The far north (closer to the equator) experiences hot and humid conditions; the central and western areas are temperate; and the interior is hot, dry, and subject to drought. One very interesting fact about Australia is that, because it is such a great distance from other land masses, 95 percent of its native plants are found only in Australia, and many of its animals are unique to the continent as well.

Over 50 percent of the world's wool comes from Australia's merino sheep, and it is perhaps the finest in the world. Fishing and mining are also important to the economy.

**Australia**

FIGURE 9.13. Australia is the 6th largest country in the world. It comprises a continent and a number of islands in the surrounding oceans and seas. The ocean area south of Australia is part of the Indian Ocean but is sometimes called the Southern Ocean.

Before the Second World War, Australia exported most of its rich natural resources to Europe for manufacturing, but, since then, much industrial growth has occurred at home.

## Representing Australia

Australia's art scene is highly influenced by Aboriginal culture. Much of the traditional Aboriginal art was done in sand and as body painting, or created especially for specific rituals and then destroyed. In 1971, Geoffrey Bardon, a teacher in an elementary school for Aborigines near Alice Springs, began to work with his students to find ways of preserving Aboriginal heritage, identity, and artwork. The elders became involved, and they began to paint traditional designs on new media, such as canvas instead of bark (where charcoal was used). The Australian government realized the power and beauty of these new expressions and encouraged the development of Aboriginal artists. The result has been a thriving and growing artistic scene among Australia's Native peoples.

## Australian Values

Australians value freedom. They are known for liberal and freethinking views. In 1892, Australia was the first country in the world to allow women to vote. Australia is one of a handful of countries that have mandatory voting; a citizen who does not vote in an election faces fines. It is largely a country of immigrants, and so Australians today tend to be accepting of other cultures and backgrounds. But this was not always the case.

In the 1890s, Australia began restricting immigrants from some countries, especially Asian countries. These policies were put into place at least partly because there were fears that large numbers of Asian immigrants would change the British and white-skinned cultural identity of Australia. (Similar restrictive immigration policies were in place in Canada and the United States in the late-19th and early-20th centuries.) Today, many immigrants to Australia come from Europe, including Greece, and also from Asian countries. Although Australia is completely self-governing, ties to Britain are still important, and, in 2000, a referendum to cut these ties was voted down.

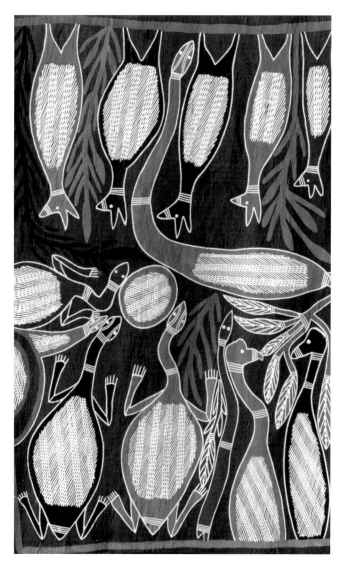

FIGURE 9.14. A bark painting made by Aborigines from Australia's Northern Territory.

FIGURE 9.15. Like Canada, Australia has received immigrants from many different parts of the world. Shown here are Muslim girls at a school in Sydney.

## When the World Comes to Canada...

Consider the photos on this page. Each of them comes from a different place in the world—the countries that we looked at in this chapter. Which photos match which countries?

a.

b.

e.

 Some people claim that you can really understand a culture only if you live within it. Do you think this is true? How has reading about India, Somalia, and Australia helped you understand these countries better? What are some of the benefits of living in a world where there are many different countries, societies, and cultures? What are some of the challenges?

g.

c.

d.

f.

i.

h.

# ADAPTING TO THE NATURAL ENVIRONMENT

## Guiding Questions

1. How are our human ways of life adaptations to the natural environment?

2. What are the principal features of the geography of Asia and of selected regions and countries in Asia?

Recall the five themes of geography that we discussed in the introduction to this book. One of these concerned relationships between humans and nature. We noted that all people change their environments all the time. We noted also that it is impossible to live in the world without changing it. Later, in chapter 3, we identified close relationships between natural environments and population distribution and density.

In short, geographers know that humans adapt to natural environments. If our ways of life are not well-adapted to natural environments, then problems arise; we will discuss some of these problems in chapters 11, 17, and 20.

In this chapter, we provide some examples of human adaptations to natural environments— as they are evident in parts of Asia. We discover the ways in which peoples and places are adapted to their natural environments— for example that people use agricultural technologies to shape the natural environment to provide the food they choose to eat and

FIGURE 10.1. Top: ancient Buddhist temple in Thailand. Bottom: Sultan Abdul Samad Buildiing in Kuala Lumpur.

that local vegetation often provides building materials for houses.

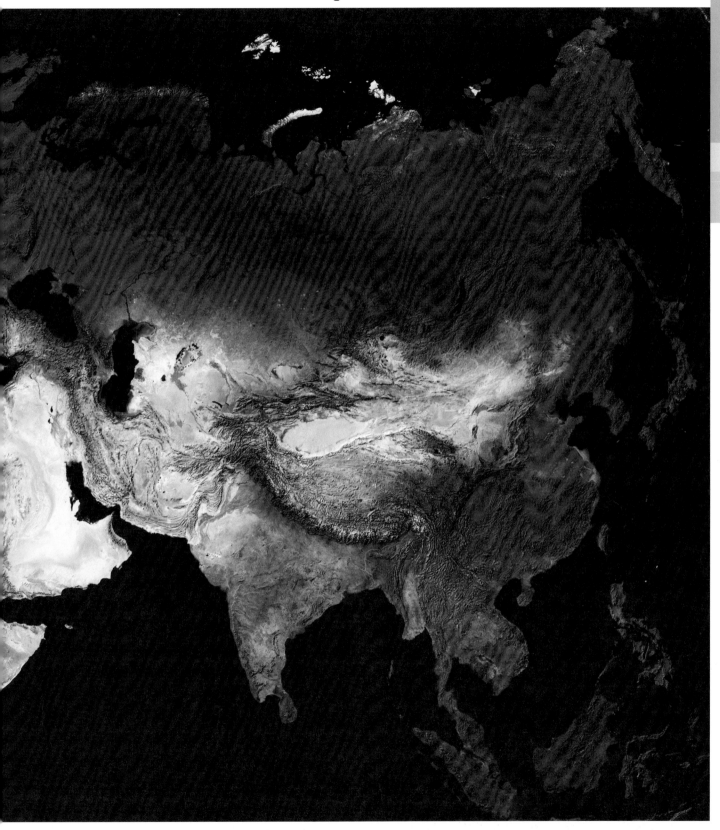

FIGURE 10.2. A satellite image of Asia showing the true colours of the continent as seen from space. White areas are glaciers in mountain regions. Dark green areas are either agricultural crops or forest. Light green and brown areas are either agricultural crops or drier grasslands and plains. Lightest browns and yellow areas are deserts. Black or dark blue areas are oceans, except where the water is very shallow, when the colour is light blue or turquoise.

# The Continent of Asia

A traveller from the Canadian prairies will find most of Asia very crowded, as almost four billion people, more than half the world's population, call Asia home. Asia contains some of the most populated countries on earth. As noted in chapter 3, China and India have by far the largest populations, each with over one billion people. Other countries in Asia with large populations include Indonesia, Pakistan, Russia, Bangladesh, and Japan (see table 3.6). Population growth continues in all of these countries except Japan and Russia, and by 2050 the population of Asia is expected to increase to about 5.4 billion people.

Asia is huge. Stretching 8 700 kilometres at its greatest north-south extent and 9 700 kilometres at its greatest east-west extent, it is the largest continent in the world. The generally accepted dividing line between Europe and Asia is along the Ural Mountains, Ural River, Caspian Sea, Caucasus Mountains, and the Black Sea. The Russian Federation is divided into eastern Russia and western Russia along this line, so 75 percent of the country is located in Asia. Large portions of Asia are desolate and difficult natural environments that cannot support agricultural lifestyles. Because of this, some regions have very dense populations, and other areas have few human inhabitants.

**Political Boundaries in Asia**

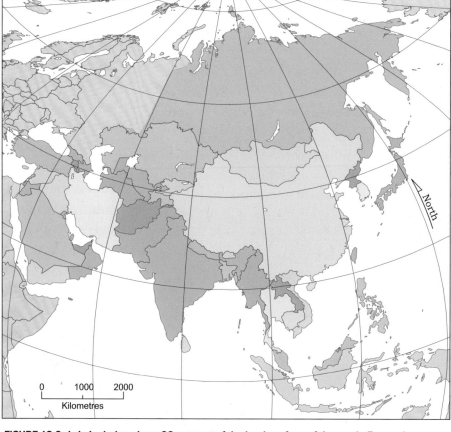

FIGURE 10.3. Asia includes about 30 percent of the land surface of the earth. Europe is effectively a western peninsula of Asia, and the two together are correctly identified as the continent of Eurasia (see figure 2.7). The many islands south and east of the Asian mainland are also considered part of Asia.

## FAST FACTS
### about the Continent of Asia

Area: 44 579,000 km$^2$

Total number of countries: 47

Largest country by area: Russia

Population: 3 921 000 000 (3.921 billion)

Most densely populated country: Singapore, 6 768 people per km$^2$

Least densely populated country: Mongolia, 1.5 per km$^2$

Urbanization: 39 percent

Literacy rate: 73 percent

Gross national income per capita: highest, Japan US$230 040; lowest, East Timor US$500

## Diverse Peoples and Places

In the east, north, and south, Asia is surrounded by water, notably the Pacific, Arctic, and Indian oceans, although the parts of the ocean areas close to land are usually identified as seas. In the west, Asia is bordered by Europe. Asia even includes three inland "seas": the Black Sea, the Caspian Sea, and the Aral Sea. Asia has a very diverse physical geography—from frozen tundra to tropical rain forests and from fertile plains to arid desert—and contains both the world's highest and lowest locations on land.

Ancient trade routes passed overland from east to west, linking different parts of Asia and linking Asia with Europe. One of the most important commodities traded along these routes was the silk produced in China and much desired in Europe. Other items included horses, fur, wool carpets, spices, pearls, and perfumes. These overland routes declined in importance in the late 15th century when a sea route was found between Asia and Europe (the route around the Cape of Good Hope). The sea route provided a much less expensive and dangerous way for goods to be conveyed.

Today, a trip through a continent as large and varied as Asia introduces you to as many cultures as there are landforms, lakes, and rivers. People who live in northern Asia are as familiar with fur and tundra as those living on the southern tip of India are with fishing and tropical storms.

 Refer to the map of Asia in figure 10.3. How many countries can you name without looking at an atlas or at other maps in this book? Don't worry if you don't know many. By the time you finish this chapter, you will know quite a few.

FIGURE 10.4. Some of the peoples of Asia. Clockwise from top left: father and daughter in Iran; Kurdish women in eastern Turkey; three Vietnamese boys; a schoolgirl in Kyrgyzstan; a Tibetan women.

## The Caucasus and Asia Minor

Three seas bound the Caucasus and Asia Minor: the Mediterranean Sea, the Black Sea, and the Caspian Sea. Much of the area is mountainous and rugged, but the valley areas are fertile, and the area is home to many plants and animals. Much land is forested, although the forests are being cut down for firewood. In addition to forest, the area is home to deserts, which require irrigation to support cultivation, and to semi-arid regions, which are used mostly for grazing sheep and goats. In more humid areas, tobacco, cotton, citrus fruits, tea, and grapes are grown. The best agricultural areas are along the coasts.

Turkey, the largest of the Caucasus countries, is located where the continents of Asia and Europe meet. Because of its strategic location, people have always met here, and the region has seen the rise and fall of many civilizations, including the ancient Hittites, Persians, Romans,

FIGURE 10.6. The rocky and desolate landscape of Mt. Ararat.

and Turks. Turkey's highest point, Mt. Ararat, is the place where, according to legend, Noah's Ark hit dry land after the Flood.

### The Caucasus and Asia Minor

FIGURE 10.5. This region of Asia is often described as a transition zone between Europe and Asia. There is a complex political geography of the area between Russia, Turkey, and Iran. The area of southern Armenia that separates the two parts of Azerbaijan is also claimed by Azerbaijan.

**FIGURE 10.7.** In this photo, the cityscape of Istanbul, Turkey, is dominated by an impressive mosque.

Turkey is a predominantly Islamic state—most people are Sunni Muslims—and most people speak Turkish. Increasingly, Turkey is looking west and expects to be the first Muslim country to join the European Union (discussed in chapter 7). Turkey is mostly an agricultural country.

**Cultural Exchange** The western end of Turkey is a narrow point of passage between two continents, and much cultural contact has occurred here. There have been exchanges of spices, of people (as slaves), of religious ideas, and of many other cultural expressions, making this a varied and interesting region.

 Using an atlas, locate the southern end of the Bosporus where it joins the Sea of Marmara. This is a particularly strategic location. The first city on this site was a Greek colony: Byzantium. Later, this city served as the capital of the eastern part of the Roman Empire and was renamed Constantinople (after Emperor Constantine). It also became the centre of the Greek Orthodox Church. The city was captured by the Turks in 1453 and served as capital of the Turkish (Ottoman) Empire. This empire survived until the First World War. Constantinople was renamed Istanbul in 1930.

# The Middle East

We do not usually think of the Middle East as part of Asia. However, it is the place where three continents meet—Asia, Africa, and Europe—making it the major natural meeting place of very different cultures. The Middle East is the birthplace of three major religions: Judaism, Christianity, and Islam. Unfortunately, much of the western part of the region has long been disputed territory, and it continues to be an area of conflict today. From about 700 to 1000 CE, Islam, based on the teachings of the prophet Muhammad (570–632 CE), began to dominate the region and also expanded east toward China and west through North Africa and southern Europe.

Because of the rugged mountains and huge deserts that cover much of the Middle East, much of the land is uninhabitable. However, there are fertile areas along coastlines and in river valleys. The area between the Tigris and Euphrates rivers, located in modern Iraq, for example, was known as the "fertile crescent" and was one of the first places where agriculture was practised.

A dramatic transformation of much of the region followed the discovery of large reserves of oil in the early 1900s. Today, the Middle East produces over one third of the world's oil. Saudi Arabia is the world's largest producer of oil, followed by Iraq. Other important producers in this region include the United Arab Emirates, Kuwait, and Iran.

Iran is the most populated nation in the Middle East. Like Turkey, Iran is an Islamic state, but most of the people belong to a sect called Shiite Muslims. Shiite Muslims also dominate in the neighbouring country of

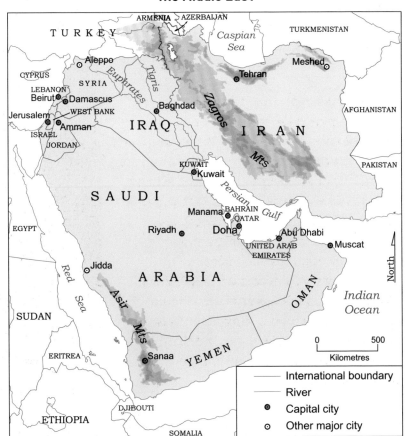

**The Middle East**

FIGURE 10.8. Also known as Southwest Asia, this region has close cultural links with Islamic North Africa.

Iraq, but most other Islamic countries are predominantly Sunni. Most Iranians speak Persian (until about the middle of the 20th century, Iran was called Persia), and other important languages are Kurdish, Baluchi, and Armenian. The majority of people live in or close to the capital city of Tehran. Most of Iran is unsuited to agriculture because of the extensive mountain ranges and desert areas. The few areas that can sustain agriculture need to be irrigated. Crops include wheat, barley, rice, beets, tobacco, and wool.

Traditionally, many of the people living in the Middle East were nomads who grazed animals and followed traditional paths from one **oasis** to the next. Because of harsh desert conditions, water was always a concern, and the practice of extending hospitality was crucial to the collective survival of the people who chose to live in the desert.

**oasis** Small area in a desert region with a natural supply of water and some vegetation.

**Various Traditions within Islam** As is the case with other major religions, there is more than one tradition within Islam. The prophet Muhammad became a messenger of Islam in the 7th century. There are two main traditions today that are quite different from each other in some of their beliefs and practices. This division occurred very early in the history of the religion and relates to different interpretations of the successors to Muhammad. About 80 percent of Muslims (a Muslim is a follower of Islam) belong to the Sunni tradition. The other 20 percent belong to the Shiite tradition. Shiites are dominant in three countries: Iran, Iraq, and Lebanon.

FIGURE 10.10. An oil refinery in Kuwait.

FIGURE 10.9. Irrigation ditch cutting through a wheat field in Iraq.

# Central Asia

The central Asian region used to be known as *Turkestan*, a region that also included much of what is now northwestern China. Turkestan was incorporated into the expanding Russian Empire in the 19th century and then became part of the former Soviet Union. The region is now home to five independent countries: Kazakhstan, Kyrgyzstan, Tajikistan, Turkmenistan, and Uzbekistan. The suffix *stan* means "place where one stays," a country. Most of the people here are Sunni Muslims.

Surrounded by Russia, China, Afghanistan, and Iran, these five countries are all **landlocked**. Today, the economy of this central Asian region is still held back by the absence of a coastline; it is a challenge to get the goods produced here to transportation hubs. In ancient times, overland trade routes were used, and several important city-states were located along those routes.

Kazakhstan, central Asia's largest country, is covered in the north and central areas by grassy treeless plains, or steppes. The south-central area is covered by desert, the east and south by mountains. Some natural resources, including various minerals, oil, and natural gas, are beginning to be developed. Some people are concerned about the environmental effect that this development will have in a country that has few safeguards in place to protect the land.

> **landlocked** A country that is entirely surrounded by other countries and has no independent access to a sea or ocean.

## Central Asia

FIGURE 10.11. This group of countries may appear isolated from much of the larger world, but the region has always occupied a strategic position between eastern and western Eurasia.

— International boundary
— River
● Capital city
○ Other major city

The other central Asian countries are similar to Kazakhstan in climate and topography; there is much potential for wealth, but, unfortunately, most people still live in poverty. Agriculture in the region, especially the cultivation of cotton, is heavily reliant on irrigation, and many of the rivers and lakes are used to supply water. One dramatic consequence of this heavy irrigation is that, since the 1960s, the Aral Sea has shrunk to half its original size. What used to be the fourth largest inland sea in the world is now mostly desert, with large areas of salt on the former seabed. Cancers, lung disease, and infant mortality are about 30 times higher than they were prior to the 1960s, because the local people drink water that is heavily polluted with salt, fertilizers, and pesticides. The Aral Sea is an environmental and health disaster.

FIGURE 10.12. Horses grazing on steppe grasslands in Kazakhstan.

FIGURE 10.13. Village children in Turkmenistan.

 The *Manas* is an epic poem that has been preserved by oral tradition for over one thousand years. It tells the story of the nomadic Kyrgyz people of central Asia. Kyrgyz scholar Roza Kïdïrbaeva says: "The epic *Manas* is not only the history of the Kyrgyz people, it is a true epic drama which widely reflects all the aspects of their life: i.e., their ethnic composition, economy, traditions and customs, morals and values, aesthetics, codes of behaviour, their relationship with their surroundings and nature, their religious worldview, their knowledge about astronomy and geography, and artistic oral poetry and language." Although many different versions exist, the longest consists of 500 000 lines of poetry! Here are a few of them:

*Longing for their Karakhan,*
*So many peoples wept.*
*The Kara Kalmyk, the Manchu people,*
*Attacked them and took their craftswomen,*
*As booty, those cursed [people],*
*Took their maidens with five braids.*
*They felled all the trees,*
*Destroyed all the houses,*
*They wiped out all people,*
*And brought the Day of Judgment,*

Think about the place where you live and the people with whom you identify. What facts and ideas might be included in an epic poem about your people and place?

## Northern Asia

Today, all of northern Asia is in one country: Russia, the largest country in the world. The Ural Mountains are the dividing line between Asia and Europe. They were formed when continental drift forced Siberia and Europe together. The Urals are estimated to be around 250 million years old and are quite worn down. They are the location of many largely untapped mineral deposits.

East of the Ural Mountains lie the West Siberian Plain, then the Central Siberian Plateau, and, finally, the East Siberian Uplands, which border on the Bering Sea. Much of the West Siberian Plain is wet and contains some of the world's largest swamps and flood plains. The Yenisey River flows from south to north through a valley between the West Siberian Plain and the Central Siberian Plateau. It

empties into the Arctic Ocean. The Central Siberian Plateau is bordered by the Sayan Mountains to the south and many other ranges to the east. In the extreme east, the Kamchatka Peninsula has many volcanic peaks, some of which are active, and because of this there are earthquakes in this area.

Much of this large region has a climate comparable to the Canadian north: the far north is tundra, similar to most of Nunavut, and south of the tundra zone is taiga, similar to northern Manitoba. Tundra and taiga (also known as boreal forest) are discussed in chapter 2. South of the tundra are **steppes**, somewhat similar to the Canadian prairies.

> **steppes** Extensive areas of open grassland with few trees or shrubs. Characterized by hot summers, cold winters, and little rainfall. The soil is often suited to cereal cultivation.

**Northern Asia**

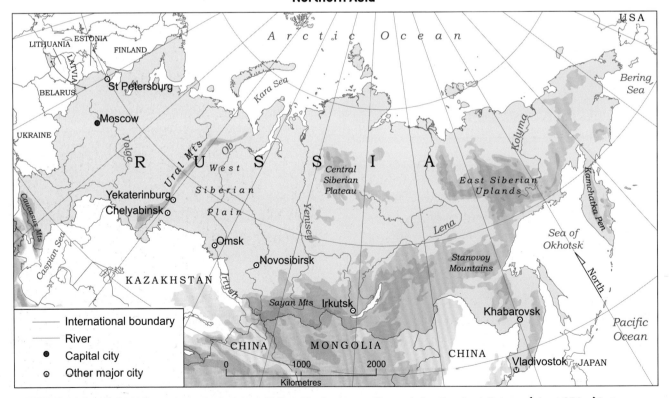

FIGURE 10.14. Russia is the largest country in the world. Note the Arctic coastline and also the short distance (about 85 km) between Russia and the United States across the Bering Sea. This map shows all of Russia, but only that part east of the Urals is generally considered part of Asia.

FIGURE 10.15. The Yenisey River, in Russia, flowing through a tundra landscape.

 Russia has over 100 000 rivers. The Ob-Irtysh river system flows north over 5 000 kilometres from western China, through Kazakhstan and Siberia, before emptying into the Arctic Ocean. There are three other major river systems: the Yenisey-Tunguska, the Lena-Aldar, and the Amur-Shilka. Research and discuss why so many river systems have hyphenated names. The region is also home to many lakes. Lake Baikal is the world's deepest freshwater lake, and the Caspian Sea is one of the largest. It is called a sea and has salt water, but it is a lake. Research and discuss the fact that large lakes are sometimes called inland seas.

 Were there early world travellers? Some of the burial sites found along the ancient overland trade routes across Asia have a decidedly European look to them; they contain Caucasian mummies with clothing that looks as if it had been made of Celtic cloth. Some people believe that these mummies are of people who crossed the Ural Mountains and entered China more than 3 000 years ago; if this were true, the East and the West would have been in contact far longer than current research shows.

 Find more information about the mysterious mummies found along the ancient overland trade routes. Visit <www.theworldtoday.ca> and follow "Links" to <www.mummytombs.com>.

FIGURE 10.16. A woman and her two children in northern Russia.

# South Asia

Northern India and its neighbouring countries were important stops on the overland trade routes through Asia. In addition to the main east-west routes, some routes led north to central and northern Asia, and others dipped down to the south. South Asia is made up of India, Pakistan, Bangladesh, Nepal, Bhutan, and Sri Lanka. The Himalayas, the world's youngest and highest mountains, are located along the northern part of southern Asia. The people who live in this region have adapted to mountains, flood plains, and plateaus.

South Asia

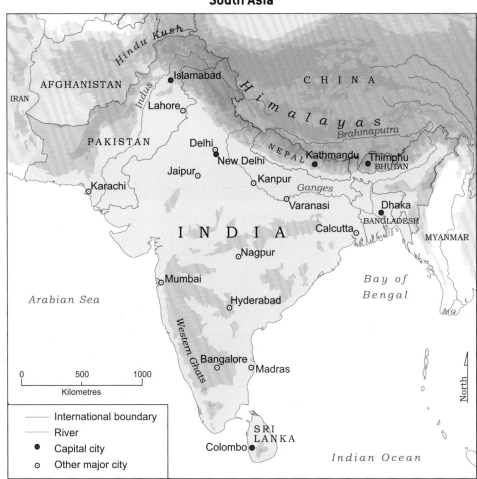

FIGURE 10.17. Although dominated by India, which is the second most populated country in the world, the region of South Asia includes several other countries with large populations, notably Bangladesh and Pakistan (see table 3.6).

Bangladesh is especially vulnerable to flooding, and almost two-thirds of the land is flooded for at least part of the year. Many rivers, known as *mouths of the Ganges*, drain into the Bay of Bengal in an area known as the *Sunderbans*. This swampy land is home to the Bengal tiger, hundreds of species of bird, and the largest mangrove forest in the world. Ask anyone to name a river in South Asia, and the Ganges will probably be named. Hindus worship it, and many cities, towns, and villages line its banks. The river provides life by providing food, water for irrigation, agriculture, and a transportation route. A common custom is to cremate the bodies of the dead and return them to the river.

This custom has resulted in much **deforestation** along the banks of the Ganges because people use the trees as fuel for the cremation pyre. People also use trees for fuel and for making bricks, which in turn are used for building homes.

> **deforestation** Cutting down and clearing away all the trees in a previously forested area.

 For more information about the Sunderbans, visit <www.theworldtoday.ca> and follow "Links" to <www.indianwildlifeportal.com>.

**Bhutan** is an extremely isolated, landlocked country located between China and India. Only a very small portion along the southern border is flat, and that area is covered with dense forest. Bhutan is a traditional Buddhist society. There is very little tourism and, until 1999, television was banned.

FIGURE 10.18. Fishing boats on a riverbank in the Sunderbans, Bangladesh.

FIGURE 10.20. Two East Indian girls.

FIGURE 10.19. Women doing laundry in the Ganges River, India. This river is worshipped by people of the Hindu faith.

# Southeast Asia

Southeast Asia is sometimes called Indochina because part of it lies between India and China. Most of the countries in southeast Asia were influenced by Chinese expansion and later became colonies of European countries. Today they are closely related to one of the three Asian giants: India, Japan, and China.

The region comprises a mainland area and over 15 000 volcanic islands. Thirteen thousand of these islands form the country of Indonesia. The region has more active volcanoes than anywhere else on earth and lies on the meeting place of three of the earth's major **tectonic plates**: the Eurasian, Indian-Australian, and Pacific.

FIGURE 10.22. Terraced agricultural landscape on the island of Bali, Indonesia.

## Southeast Asia

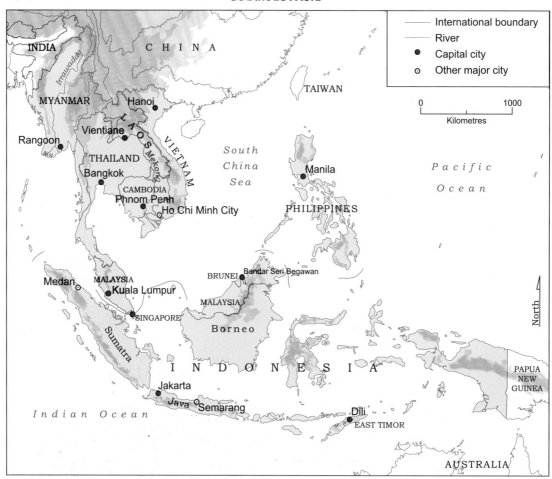

FIGURE 10.21. This region comprises several mainland Asian countries and the two large island realms of Indonesia and the Philippines.

**tectonic plates** The theory of plate tectonics dates from the 1960s and states that the earth's crust comprises a number of rigid but mobile pieces, or plates, similar to fish scales. Over the long period of geological time, these plates move, rather like ice breaking up on a river in spring, causing ocean basins to change size and shape. The Himalaya mountain chain was created by the collision of two plates.

Southeast Asia has many varied physical and human landscapes: mountains, seas, rainforests, rivers, and diverse plant and animal life. These combine to make the region very attractive for tourists from North America and Europe. However, some of the factors that create the beauty can also be dangerous. As discussed in chapter 8, in December 2004 a huge earthquake occurred in the ocean off the coast of Sumatra, setting off a tsunami that killed over 300 000 people in south and southeast Asia and left 1.5 million people homeless.

In 1883, Krakatoa, Indonesia's most famous volcano, erupted in an explosion that was heard as far away as Australia and destroyed 75 percent of the island. Earthquakes, floods, typhoons, and landslides also occur frequently in southeast Asia. The United Nations has identified this area one as of the most prone to natural disasters in the world.

FIGURE 10.24. Balinese boys preparing for a religious ceremony. They are wearing traditional dress, which includes a white head cover and yellow robe.

FIGURE 10.23. A volcano spewing smoke on the island of Java, Indonesia.

# China

China is huge. It has the third-largest land area in the world (after Russia and Canada), the second-largest economy, and more people than any other country; almost one out of every five people on earth is Chinese. For many years, China was a powerful country. It was in China that printing was invented. The Chinese held the secrets of the compass, gunpowder, and fireworks. The Chinese were the first to make kites, the abacus, paper money, and origami (a paper-folding art now mainly associated with Japan), and it was the Chinese who knew the secret of silk. During this long period of strength, China was ruled by a series of dynasties. But the country declined after the collapse of the Qing Dynasty in the 1920s. After 20 turbulent years of fighting between communists and nationalists, the communists gained control in 1948 under the leadership of Mao Zedong (1893–1976).

During the 1950s, Mao launched the Great Leap Forward, which was designed to transform agriculture and increase industrial production. However the program failed, and about 20 million people died from starvation. It is estimated that, during Mao's leadership, as many as 70 million people were killed. Mao was the most terrible tyrant of the 20th century, eclipsing even Josef Stalin (1878–1953) and Adolf Hitler (1889–1945). Mao died in 1976, and since that time, China, although still a communist state, has established increasing links with the rest of the world.

However, human-rights abuses still do occur in China today. There are more executions per capita than in any other country in the world, and many people are imprisoned for political or religious reasons. As China develops economically, concerns about the environment increase. How will the earth respond as greater and greater demands are made on the natural resources of China?

Also, as China develops economically, many countries around the world are carefully watching. About 70 percent of China's people still live on farms or in small villages; this ratio is changing rapidly, however, as people move to cities from farming areas.

China officially recognizes 56 different ethnic groups, the largest (92 percent) being Han Chinese. There are also many different regional dialects spoken in China, though the government is seeking uniformity by officially recognizing only Mandarin.

China

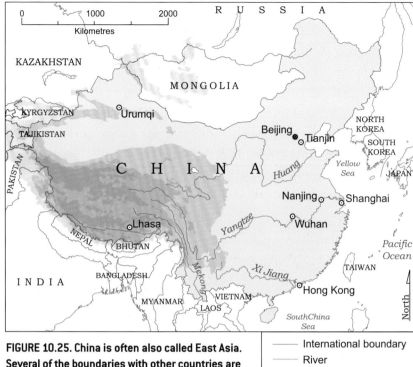

FIGURE 10.25. China is often also called East Asia. Several of the boundaries with other countries are disputed, but it is generally acknowledged that China is slightly smaller in size than Canada and slightly larger than the United States. Although China has a long coastline (about 14 500 km), it has traditionally looked inland culturally.

- —— International boundary
- —— River
- ● Capital city
- ○ Other major city

## Adapting to the Land

Because China covers such a large area, it encompasses many different climates and topographical features. About 40 percent of China is covered by mountains, 25 percent by plateaus, 20 percent by river basins, and 15 percent by plains.

Most of China's people live south of Shanghai. China's three great rivers drain this area: the Xi Jiang (also known as the His), the Yangtze, and the Huang He (or Yellow River). The south has very favourable conditions for farming. Here, rice is the dominant crop, and people, rather than machines, still do most of the work. Many hillsides have been sculpted into **terraces** to make use of as much land as possible. The warm climate allows farmers to plant two, and sometimes three, crops each year. Good farming practices throughout much of China make it possible to feed most of the population.

Northeast China has a similar topography to the Canadian prairies, but there is a much greater population. Like our prairies, northern China has severe winters that limit the growing season to less than half the year. Wheat, soybeans, and corn are grown here. Western China is home to the Gobi Desert. Very few people live in this barren and rocky land, and those who do are nomads. It is the least populated area of China.

**terraces** Flat areas cut into a hillside on which crops are grown. Terraces help prevent soil erosion on steep slopes.

**The Great Wall of China** is the only structure made by humans that is visible from space. Construction began more than 2 000 years ago, when nomadic Mongol groups invaded China. Built from local stone and earth by thousands of soldiers, prisoners, and local people, it winds from east to west about 6 700 kilometres across mountains and plateaus. There are watchtowers at key strategic locations.

### The Great Wall of China

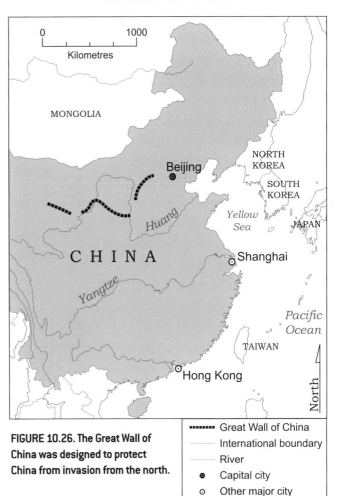

FIGURE 10.26. The Great Wall of China was designed to protect China from invasion from the north.

FIGURE 10.27. This photo of the Great Wall of China shows it stretching along a high ridge in the mountainous landscape of northern China.

# Japan

China and Japan are separate Asian countries with some shared history but very different development stories. For many years, China was a "superpower," and its ideas, technology, and commodities influenced many societies in Japan, the rest of Asia, and even Europe. But China experienced a decline by about 1900 that culminated in communist rule and is only just beginning to re-emerge as a powerful nation.

Japan is made up of a series of islands that lie east of China. Today, China is regarded as a less-developed country (although it is clearly developing rapidly), while Japan is a more-developed country; it is one of the richest countries in the world.

Japan's earliest inhabitants were an indigenous tribe called the Ainu (see chapter 11). Chinese people began arriving in Japan about 400 CE and brought their culture. Until the 1800s, Japan was ruled by military commanders known as *shoguns* ("generals") who operated with a strict code of conduct and exercised absolute authority.

Japan practised **isolationism**, even banning foreign books and refusing all foreign interest (except for a small Dutch settlement) until 1854, when an American fleet sailed into Tokyo and forced Japan to open its doors to foreign influence. It adopted Britain's industrial revolution as a model and transformed itself from a farming nation to one dominated by manufacturing and trade. Because of their histories, relations between China and Japan are at times acrimonious (the opposite of harmonious).

**Japan**

FIGURE 10.28. Japan includes several thousand islands, only the largest of which are shown on this map.

Japan entered the Second World War in 1941, when it bombed Pearl Harbor in Hawaii, the United States's primary military base in the Pacific. The atomic bombs dropped on Hiroshima and Nagasaki in 1945 by the United States damaged Japan's economy, but Japan recovered quickly to become a leader in the production of many goods, including electronics, automobiles, and appliances. Today, Japan competes with its Asian neighbours, including China and South Korea, to produce goods cheaply for export.

**isolationism** A national policy chosen by countries that wish to avoid political, economic, and cultural contacts with other countries.

## Adapting to the Land

Japan is an archipelago (group of islands) located off the Asian mainland and stretching over 3 000 kilometres. Many of the islands are volcanic. Most of the people live on one of the four largest islands: Hokkaido, Honshu, Shikoku, and Kyushu. Although Japan is a small country, there is much regional variety of physical and human geography. The climate is subtropical in the south and temperate in the north. There is generally adequate rainfall. Because it is a series of islands, Japan does not have the temperature extremes that characterize continental interiors.

Less than 20 percent of Japan's land is level enough to grow crops upon, and there are very few natural resources. Hokkaido is very hilly but supports rice farming and dairy production. Northern Honshu has a central mountain range that makes east-west movement difficult. The Tokyo region in central Honshu is the heart of Japan; it has a dense population and much industrial activity. The southern part of the island is also densely populated and supports both farming and industry. Shikoku is a small mountainous island with some irrigated farming and industry. Kyushu supports both farming and industry. Tunnels and bridges link the four main islands.

Japan is one of the most homogenous societies in the world; less than 1 percent of the population is non-Japanese. Virtually everybody speaks Japanese as her or his first language. Birth rates are very low, at about 9 per 1 000, and life expectancy is high, at about 82 years. The literacy rate is close to 100 percent, and freedom of religion has been guaranteed in Japan since 1947. Because of the occupation of Japan by the United States after the Second World War, the country has adopted many Western cultural characteristics, especially in the cities, where 79 percent of the population live. However, in rural areas, life remains much the same as it was hundreds of years ago.

## Asia: Many Natural Environments, Many Adaptations

By using examples from the varied natural environments of Asia, this chapter has shown some of the ways that humans adapt to natural environments. Asia is home to many different natural environments. Some peoples and places (particularly in rural settings) remain relatively unchanged, while other peoples and places (those in urban settings) are transforming all the time. Sometimes, as they often are in Japan, the stable and the changing environments are in close proximity to each other.

The discussions of Japan and China show how two separate cultures can affect one another over hundreds of years in both positive and negative ways. Contacts between countries throughout the world are increasing as the people find it easier to travel from place to place. Journeys that used to take many months can be accomplished in a matter of days or even hours, and virtual journeys are effectively instantaneous. In the past, a trader travelling between Europe and Asia might have been gone for years. Today, people and goods can arrive in western Europe the same day that they leave eastern Asia.

This interconnectedness can be a good thing if we value and learn from different cultures. However, if it leads to every place in the world becoming alike (which is the global-village ideal), we will be sure to lose much of what makes the world such an interesting and delightful collection of peoples and places.

# INDIGENOUS PEOPLES OF THE WORLD

## Guiding Questions

1. Who are the indigenous peoples of the world, and where do they live?

2. Why and how are indigenous peoples' distinctiveness threatened by modern society?

3. Can indigenous peoples find a place in a modern technological society without losing their identity and culture?

English natural historian and geologist Charles Darwin wrote about the Chilean Yaghan in 1832, describing a woman nursing "a recently born child . . . whilst the sleet fell . . . on the skin of her naked baby!" Soon clothes began to arrive from Europeans, who felt sorry for the Yahgan (they were cold and had no clothes). But, because of the Yaghan's close relationship to the sea, the clothes often became wet and were uncomfortable. They were warmer being almost naked. Diseases brought by European visitors decimated the population. By 1933, a tribe that had numbered close to 3 000 just 100 years earlier was reduced to around 40 people. All that remains of the Yaghans now are some photographs, a few artifacts, and the memories and writings of people who studied them. The few people of Yaghan ancestry are assimilated into Chilean culture, but the wisdom and history of their tribe are lost.

This story has been repeated many times over in various parts of the world. **Indigenous peoples** are struggling to survive, and in many cases they have already lost their language and their culture. In this chapter, we explore some indigenous peoples and where they live.

Imagine being the last of your people to have survived in the world today. There is no other person who understands the stories and legends, the values and virtues, of your culture. You are surrounded by people with whom you are familiar; you might speak their language and understand their culture, but they will never really understand your childhood language. And now, because you are the last, there is very little chance that anyone ever will.

**indigenous peoples** People who originally lived in an area, usually having developed a culture and society closely adapted to the natural environment and with their own distinctive language, history, and identity. Note: People often disagree about what constitutes an indigenous group. For the purposes of this text, *indigenous* refers to tribal and other groups who have traditional ties to the land and who identify themselves apart from the dominant culture of the country in which they live or that has surrounded them.

This is happening to people every day, all around the world. You have probably heard a lot about endangered plants and animals, but have you ever heard about **endangered languages**?

A conservative estimate is that approximately 5 000 indigenous groups make up about 5 percent of the world's population; that is about 300 million people. Other estimates range as high as 7 percent, because it is difficult (and sometimes not in a government's political interest) to identify and acknowledge indigenous groups. As well, when indigenous peoples are nomadic, they may cross political boundaries that mean nothing to them. It can be difficult to count them, difficult to know to which country they belong. Although indigenous groups make up a small percentage of the total people on earth, they account for 60 percent of the languages spoken by people worldwide and for much of our cultural diversity. Indigenous peoples live all around the world.

> **endangered languages** A language becomes endangered when it is spoken by a minority of people, when there are no people who speak only that language, and when the language is not being passed on to children, because it is preceived to be less valuable than the dominant language within an area.

 For information about *Indigenous Peoples Earth Charter* visit <www.theworldtoday.ca> and follow "Links" to <www.dialoguebetweennations.com/IR/english/KariOcaKimberley/KOCharter.html>.

**TABLE 11.1. Indigenous Groups around the World**

| Region | Approximate Number of Indigenous Groups |
| --- | --- |
| Africa | 2 000 |
| Asia | 1 350 |
| South and Central America | 800 |
| Oceania | 750 |
| North America | 250 |
| Eastern Europe and Russia | 135 |

**So Many Languages** Linguists estimate that approximately 10 000 languages have existed in the world during the course of human history. Of those, about 6 000 still exist, of which only about 3 000 are taught to children. This means that, within one generation, the other 3 000 languages will likely be lost. Only 300 languages are spoken by more than one million people, and most linguists believe that only 600 languages are stable and secure. Canada used to be home to more than 60 indigenous languages, but only four—Cree, Dakota, Inuktitut, and Ojibway—are not considered endangered.

 Some people see the trend toward fewer languages and cultures as somewhat convenient: if we all spoke the same language, we could talk to anyone, anywhere, and if we shared a similar culture, we'd understand each other better. This is a very interesting idea. List three things we would lose if we were to develop into one worldwide culture that spoke only one language. List three things we would gain. Choose the most reasonable language to which the world should adhere. Explain why you made your choice.

## How People Live in Indigenous Societies

Although the cultural practices of indigenous peoples vary greatly around the world, there are some basic similarities.

### Shelter

Indigenous peoples create their shelters based on the materials available in their environment. Those who live near large trees use trees for building houses. Where wood is scarce, people make homes out of mud bricks, cow dung, hides, or grasses. Nomadic indigenous peoples need to be able to carry their homes; plains Indians created the tipi, and Mongols use a similar shelter, called a *yurt*. Indigenous people also build their homes to best deal with local conditions, such as proximity to water and the danger of floods, high winds, heat, and cold.

### Religion

Indigenous peoples' ideas about gods and worship are based on their experiences in the natural world. Known as *animistic*, these religions see the natural world as possessing special powers; for example, indigenous cultures may ascribe special status to fish, monkeys, beaver, or other animals. Trees and other life-giving plants are also revered

FIGURE 11.2. Young men of the Hamer group in Ethiopia who wish to marry are required first to participate in a bull-jumping ceremony.

by some cultures. Other indigenous peoples worship their ancestors.

Indigenous peoples sometimes worship or revere the sun, moon, wind, and water. Much of what they come to worship is based on a tribe's dependence on the elements of nature that are important for its livelihood. While drought or too much rain may be just an inconvenience for us, a drought or flood could be deadly (or sometimes life-giving) for traditional indigenous people, and many groups developed beliefs within which they appeased the gods who controlled their environment.

Shamans, or priests, are usually the conduits (the go-betweens) to the gods within these societies, and they also function as healers. Medicine and religion are closely related, and illness is seen as a spiritual problem as much as it is a physical problem.

### Art

The art produced by indigenous peoples often has religious connotations. When the balance of nature is upset, rituals and prayers serve to restore order. These rituals are accompanied by artistic expressions such as the wearing of masks, body-painting, music-making, and dancing. Some groups use totems (tall carved logs) to honour their ancestors. Others use rock formations, carvings, or paintings to help them remember key historical events and provide places of worship.

FIGURE 11.1. In the far north of Russia, two Nentsey people construct their dwelling. Known as a *chum*, this dwelling is built like a tepee.

Indigenous peoples do not have a consumer mentality, as many of us do. They have what they need, and, especially among nomads, they acquire goods only if the goods are useful. For instance, an indigenous family do not hang paintings in frames on their walls, but they might decorate the walls of their home with paint. Other useful items—for example, cooking utensils, sleds, clothing, and weapons—are elaborately decorated with intricate designs. Art for display purposes only is rare.

## Working Together to Survive

Indigenous peoples practise a communal economy. People in indigenous communities all have to contribute to the survival of their tribes. They do not take more than they need; however, no one is allowed to shirk his or her duty to the rest of the community.

Indigenous peoples know that, when they work together, they are able to secure more reliable and plentiful food sources than if they worked as individuals. One person cannot bring down large game, but several people working together can. Still others are best suited to butcher it and make use of all its parts. Special prayers and rituals are associated with hunting, governing when and how to hunt, as well as how to divide up the kill. These rigid social expectations ensure that everyone will be taken care of. People feast and starve together.

## Ceremonies and Rituals

Many indigenous peoples perform ceremonies and rituals that celebrate birth, coming of age, marriage, and other important life occasions. Again, these rituals result from a group's close relationship with its natural environment and work to ensure the survival of its people.

Coming-of-age ceremonies in indigenous cultures usually have three stages. The first stage is one of separation, when a child is taken from his or her home and put into isolation for a time. Next is the transition stage, when the child must go through an ordeal and learn something new. Finally comes the reincorporation ceremony, when the individual is welcomed into the group as a fully adult member.

The transition stage is often painful. The youth is ceremonially scarred, tattooed, or otherwise marked to show that he or she is marriageable. Reincorporation is the payoff for all the pain; the family throws a party, with lots of food and drink.

Virtually every indigenous tribe has a ceremony for marriage that includes elaborate dress, makeup, and feasting. Usually marriages are arranged for the benefit of the two families being united, and the wealth of the bride's family increases her marriage opportunities.

Indigenous groups usually have complex beliefs and rituals surrounding deaths and funerals. Many focus on easing the passage of the person from this life to the next (almost all indigenous groups believe in an afterlife). Some erect totems. Others build a small hut in which to bury the body. Some smoke the body to preserve it then put it in a place of honour in the home. Others believe that, once a person dies, he or she should never be spoken of again.

The ceremonies performed by indigenous groups always depend on the environment and lifestyle of the group.

 The Guarani of South America believe that any hunter who eats his own kill will have bad luck in future hunting expeditions. What are the benefits of this belief?

**Dowry and Bride Price** In some cultures, the bride's family sends her off with a dowry, which is basically a payment to the groom's family. In other cultures, a bride price is paid by the groom's family to the bride's family to make up for the loss of the bride's labour in her family home.

## Food and Drink

Food and drink are key parts of many of the special ceremonies and rituals of indigenous peoples. As with all their other activities, traditional choices of food and drink have much to do with what the land provides. The Inuit people in Canada's north traditionally ate mainly Arctic animals.

In Nepal, honey is scarce and difficult to obtain, so it is highly valued. Specially trained men climb long rope ladders up to beehives high on cliff sides, under which other people have lit fires, as smoke calms the bees. After the honey is harvested, each person takes some home, the amount determined by his or her involvement during the collection.

FIGURE 11.3. Left: Men collect cattle blood; cattle blood is an important source of protein for members of the Surma tribe in Ethiopia. Right: Kangaroos are cooked after being killed and then taken back to the community for all to eat; kangaroo stew and cooked tails are favourite meals in parts of Australia.

## Oral Traditions

Storytelling and singing are important to indigenous people. Because many of them do not have written languages, stories and songs are ways of passing on the memory of important events in the lives of their people. Most indigenous people tell stories to explain how the world was created, how their people developed into a strong community, and how they perceive and interact with their gods.

Oral traditions also serve to instruct people; for example, some teach the best time to plant, to hunt, to harvest, and how to understand the tides, the phases of the moon, and the seasons.

It is through stories passed down from generation to generation that they learn the social norms of their society: what is acceptable behaviour and what is not. They hear tales that explain why one person should be honoured and another shut out. Oral traditions keep indigenous groups strong and united.

 As you have been reading about various cultural practices, you may have noticed that different indigenous peoples have many practices in common. You may also have noticed that they experience these practices in a direct and intimate way to the land that they occupy. In other words, they adapt to their natural environments. Consider how different your life would be if you were as closely related to your natural environment as indigenous peoples are to theirs. Discuss five ways that your everyday life would be different.

**The United Nations Educational, Scientific, and Cultural Organization** UNESCO (one of the many branches of the United Nations as noted in chapter 8) calls oral traditions part of an "intangible heritage" and recognizes them as "a vital factor in cultural identity." UNESCO also warns us that, "in an era of globalization, many forms of this cultural heritage are in danger of disappearing, threatened by cultural standardization, armed conflict, the harmful consequences of mass tourism, industrialization, rural exodus, migration and environmental deterioration."

 Using a library and/or the Internet, note some of the practices of indigenous tribes around the world. Reflect on why a certain practice or ritual is important to an indigenous person, how that person would feel if it were taken away or made illegal, and how an indigenous society might go about reviving some ancient cultural tradition that has been lost.

# Preserving Indigenous Cultures in Canada

After many years of trying to destroy indigenous cultures through **cultural assimilation** policies, countries like Canada are recognizing the value of preserving and encouraging these distinctive cultures. There are many government initiatives today that support First Peoples' cultures. For instance, government agencies worked together with groups like the Neeginan Foundation to build a permanent home in Winnipeg to celebrate First Peoples' spirituality and culture. In 1996, after consultation with various groups, Canada declared 21 June National Aboriginal Day, a special day to celebrate Canada's First Peoples, Métis, and Inuit cultures.

**cultural assimilation** The process by which a minority group gradually adopts more and more of the customs and culture of the larger society so that they lose their unique identity.

GREAT BOOK ALERT! For an overview about indigenous peoples, read *First Peoples* by Julian Burger. This book has short chapters about issues facing indigenous peoples today.

 "There is a fire burning over the Earth, taking with it plants and animals, cultures, languages, ancient skills and visionary wisdom. Quelling this flame and reinventing the poetry of diversity is the most important challenge of our times" (Wade Davis, Canadian anthropologist who has lived with many indigenous peoples). Discuss this quote.

FIGURE 11.4. The Circle of Life Thunderbird House, in Winnipeg, designed by First Peoples' architect Douglas Cardinal.

 On 1 April 1999, the map of Canada changed for the first time since 1949. A new Inuit territory, Nunavut, was officially recognized. Nunavut is about two million square kilometres, has a population of approximately 25 000, an elected legislature of 19 seats, and no political parties. Decisions are reached by consensus. Use library sources or the Internet to learn more about Nunavut.

For lots of information about Canada's indigenous peoples, as well as initiatives that further their culture, visit <www.theworldtoday.ca> and follow "Links" to < www.civilization.ca/aborig/aborige.asp > or < www.aboriginalcanada.gc.ca >. CBC also has news stories concerning First Peoples at < www.cbc.ca/news/background/aboriginals/index.html>.

## Some Indigenous Groups

### The Maasai

The Maasai inhabit about 160 000 square kilometres of the Rift Valley in the countries of Kenya and Tanzania (you will learn more about this valley in chapter 13). Political boundaries mean little to the Maasai, and attempts to keep them from crossing borders have been unsuccessful.

### Maasai Land and Life

The annual migration of wildebeest, zebra, and gazelles is one of the last large-scale animal migrations left on earth. As these animals migrate, they are followed by predators such as lions, tigers, cheetahs, and hyenas. Vultures take up the rear, cleaning up carcasses along the way. The lakes and rivers are home to crocodiles and hippopotami and provide water for other large animals such as giraffes, elephants, and buffalo. The Maasai consider eating wild meat disgusting, and they kill lions only when their cattle are threatened or, traditionally, to become recognized as warriors. Although lion-hunting is officially outlawed, some Maasai still believe it is their right to hunt and kill lions.

Traditionally, the Maasai are nomadic pastoralists, grazing their cattle all over Maasailand. Although they rarely kill their cattle for meat, they obtain almost everything they need from their cattle: milk and cheese for food, blood (used for emergency protein and special rituals), and dung as fuel for their cooking fires and as plaster for their walls. Cattle urine is used for cleansing gourds (bowls) used to carry milk (fresh urine is sterile and acts as a mild antiseptic), and hides are used for bedding and clothing. The wealth of the Maasai is measured by the number of cattle they own. The Maasai value their cattle and know each by name, voice, and appearance.

### The Location of Maasailand

FIGURE 11.5. The Maasai people of eastern Africa are some of the many indigenous peoples in Africa.

FIGURE 11.6. A Maasai couple work using their cattle to plough land.

**The Maasai Vision** "The development and survival of the Maasai people is a matter of grave concern to all of us in the Maasai region. We are working collectively as a community to find solutions to the problems that are undermining our community's development. We are crafting ideas, methods, projects, and programs that are culturally sensitive to our way of life. It is this vision held within the community that will enable us to eradicate poverty and to realize a sustainable future for our generations to come. Change is inevitable. We would like to be agents of our change rather than victims of change."

The Maasai resisted European influence and cultural assimilation for many years after colonization, although the British and Germans tried to recruit Maasai for military service to fight other African tribes. They also encouraged the Maasai to put their children into schools. While the Maasai are slowly adopting some Western ways, they remain determined to preserve their culture.

The Maasai still rely on their cattle for sustenance, but most also use them as beasts of burden for farming, a practice that some Maasai still resist. A decrease in grazing lands and a long-term drought have made it harder for the Maasai to live nomadically. To increase the stability of their food supply, some grow items for which they would otherwise have to trade.

## Maasai Art

Maasai women create beautiful jewellery and glass beadwork. Before European traders arrived, they used clay or bone beads, but now beads from India are favoured. They are rarely symmetrical and are made with bright colours and intricate patterns. Colour patterns have special meanings: they can identify a clan or are used for marriage rituals or other ceremonies. The Maasai have over 40 words to describe beads and patterns, and if a young woman wishes to state her interest in a particular warrior, she may give him a beaded armband or bracelet that she has made.

Stories are valued by the Maasai, and many have been passed along orally for centuries. The Maasai also use songs and hand-crafted instruments to praise a warrior's skill or a woman's beauty. Dancing will often accompany these songs.

## Maasai Family and Society

Up to 13 families live together in a *boma*, a small settlement, surrounded by a fence. The houses are built around the outside of the fence, and the cattle are corralled in the centre. Men may have more than one wife. The children are usually responsible for herding the cattle during the day. More and more children are attending school, and more Maasai are recognizing the importance of education if they want to have a say in the future of their group.

Maasai are grouped by age sets. Age sets are people who are born into the same five-to-ten-year group. Everyone in an age set undergoes initiation rites together. After these rites are accomplished, male teenagers are considered adults, and women at puberty are marriageable. Men continue through age-set rituals throughout their lives, moving in status from junior to senior warrior. There are other, smaller, categories as well, having to do with cattle ownership, marriage, and fatherhood, for example. Elders are respected and make important decisions for the entire community, such as when to move and where to graze their cattle. The entry into each life stage is accompanied by feasting and elaborate ceremonies, and it is at these events that the Maasai are most likely to eat the meat of their cattle.

Some Maasai are beginning to recognize the tourist trade as a lucrative industry, and they dance or demonstrate other aspects of their culture to attract tourists. They are seeking to maintain many aspects of their traditional lifestyle yet recognize that, in the changing world, they must adapt.

**Maasai Warriors** Traditionally, the Maasai believed that their god, Enkai, had given all the cattle on earth to them and them alone. This justified the cattle raids they made on other tribes who relied on cattle; the Maasai grew to value their warriors among them.

 For a wonderful website about the Maasai that includes some samples of Maasai music visit <www.theworldtoday.ca> and follow "Links" to <www.laleyio.com>.

## India's Bishnoi People

The Bishnoi of Rajasthan, India, have rejected the caste system and require only that members live by the 29 rules laid out by their prophet. Some of the rules are: you must never cut down a live tree; you must not partake of drugs or alcohol; you must practise kindness and refrain from swearing; and you must provide shelters for animals to keep them from being killed (the Bishnoi are vegetarian). The Bishnoi may be the world's first environmental activists. In 1847, they shielded trees in their forest with their own bodies to protect them from the army. A large number (363) of Bishnoi were killed before the king heard of their courage and declared the Khejarli region a preserve, which was off limits for hunting and logging.

The Bishnoi farm and tend animals, and they consume the milk, butter, and yogurt from water buffalo or cattle. They use dung for fuel. Their prophet believed that similarity would lead to equality, and so all the women tend to wear brightly coloured saris, while the men dress in white and wear turbans. They believe in reincarnation.

After many years of drought, some of the wells that the Bishnoi rely on dry up. People then bathe in amounts of water as small as will fit into a pie plate, and women walk for many kilometres for fresh water for their families. Droughts challenge the Bishnoi's ability to provide for themselves and have put them in closer contact with neighbouring tribes and people who do not share their commitment to preserving the environment.

 For more information about the Bishnoi, visit <www.theworldtoday.ca> and follow "Links" to <www.bishnoi.org>.

### The Location of Rajasthan

Rajasthan

FIGURE 11.7. The Bishnoi live in a semi-arid landscape with sparse vegetation and little water. They are one of several indigenous groups in the region.

FIGURE 11.8. Bishnoi people (note cattle dung drying on rooftops).

## Japan's Ainu People

The Ainu arrived in Japan over 7 000 years ago. Initially, they inhabited all of present-day Japan but now live only in the far north. They are believed to have come from Siberia over the Ural Mountains. The Ainu have been linked to Canada's Inuit and may have maintained trading relations with them. While Japan's official count of the Ainu is 24 000, the Ainu themselves believe that their number is closer to 100 000. As animists, they believe that the spirit of God inhabits the natural world, and in this regard they have a special kinship to the bear.

Several times since the 9th century, the Ainu were offered good land, only to have it taken away when it was recognized as valuable. Several times over their history, the Ainu were forced by the dominant Japanese society to find new places to live. In 1899, after hundreds of years of persecuting the Ainu, Japan passed the Hokkaido Former Aboriginal Protection Act, which was intended to assimilate the Ainu into the Japanese society. This resulted in further suffering for the Ainu. They were granted barren land and told to learn to become farmers, but they were traditionally hunter-gatherers and could not adapt to farming. The children were placed in native schools and taught Japanese culture.

Women no longer tattooed their faces, hands, and feet, a practice that signified that they were ready for marriage. As they experienced oppression, they began to lose their language and other traditional cultural knowledge. However, in the 1970s, the Ainu were inspired by stories of other indigenous cultures that were successful in reviving their identities and began to make attempts to reawaken some of their traditional beliefs and values.

For more information about the Ainu visit <www.the worldtoday.ca> and follow "Links" to <www.ainumuseum.or.jp/english/english.html>.

## The Location of Northern Japan

Ainu in Northern Japan

FIGURE 11.9. The Ainu are Japan's indigenous group.

FIGURE 11.10. Ainu people outside their home.

# COMPARING CULTURAL EXPRESSIONS

## 12

### Guiding Questions

1. In what ways do different cultures express their distinctive beliefs, values, and world views?

2. How important is it that diverse expressions of culture continue to be evident in the contemporary world?

Something to consider as you begin this chapter is whether or not cultural diversity matters. If it does matter, then why? You were asked to think about this in the previous chapter during the discussion of endangered languages. As you studied indigenous groups, your views might have been reinforced, or they might have changed. Consider again: Is it important that the world include speakers of many different languages? Is it important that groups of people retain traditional values and practices? Most of the indigenous cultures discussed in the previous chapter remained relatively unchanged for many centuries. European contact resulted in much change but also much resistance to change.

As we have seen in earlier chapters, ideas about who we are and how we should behave are not fixed and static. Rather, expressions of culture vary greatly both from place to place and through time in any one place; there are both spatial and temporal differences (the terms *spatial* and *temporal* are defined in the introduction).

For an example of spatial differences, think about how different the cultures are in Somalia and India. One reason for the variation of culture around the world is that it is related to natural environment.

For an example of temporal differences, think about your grandparents when they were young and how different their forms of cultural expression from what yours are today. Culture changes through time because it evolves in response to changing needs and values and because it is related to technology, which typically becomes more complex and sophisticated through time.

In this chapter, we look at some spatial and temporal differences in the ways culture is expressed. First, we consider language, gender, and clothing. Then we consider the way we express our culture in our everyday lives—for example, birth and death rituals, naming ceremonies, and how children are educated and socialized.

## Language

Language is the principal expression of culture. People who speak the same language are able to communicate with and understand each other; language brings them together. People who speak different languages are likely to have much less in common; differences in language pushes them apart. In short, humans organize themselves around language.

Perhaps culture is like an iceberg: some aspects are visible, and others (sometimes important foundational aspects) are beneath the surface. If culture is like an iceberg, then language is much of the part that lies underwater. People who speak the same language are also likely to share a set of customs, traditions, values, attitudes, and beliefs. It is language that allows a group of people to develop and then pass on cultural expressions relating to its way of life generally. Of course, language is not always like the part of the iceberg that is underwater; naming places within the geographic landscape does not happen outside language.

Recall from reading the previous chapter that, of the about 6 000 languages that exist today, only about 3 000 are taught to children, and only 600 of these are stable and secure. It seems likely that, as the number of speakers of a language declines, the forms of cultural expression that are related to that language will also be lost.

Language is closely related to power. In the world today, it is a real advantage to speak at least one of the major languages (preferably more); it is a real disadvantage to speak only one language, especially if it is an endangered language. The nearest thing to a global language today is English, and people who speak English have access to a dizzying array of cultural experiences and economic opportunities. The global success of the English language is one aspect of globalization. When the focus of its adoption is on culture rather than on economics or politics, it is sometimes called **Westernization.**

> **Westernization** The adoption by other societies of Western (meaning American and European) cultural ideas and practices.

FIGURE 12.1. A sign in both Hindi and English outside a post office in the Rajasthan region of northern India.

FIGURE 12.2. A place name in southern Manitoba.

---

Consult a map of Manitoba or a part of Manitoba and search for place names that reflect different languages. Make a list of names and the appropriate language. What do place names tell you about early settlement?

# Gender

The identification of **gender** is an important expression of culture, especially as it relates to inequality. As we discussed in chapter 3, the world is an unequal place, divided into more-developed and less-developed countries. But gender, too, is a very important basis for inequality that is evident in all countries.

All cultures make gender distinctions; women and men are viewed and treated differently and, more significantly, usually unequally. In most cultures throughout the world, it has been usual for women to be subordinate to men in social, economic, and political terms. Everywhere, women have fewer freedoms and rights than men.

Why is it that women have usually been assigned a lower status than men? The reasons are debated, but one possibility is that women have typically been associated with nature; it is women who give birth, which is a natural event. Humans see nature as something less than human, and, in much the same way, men in some cultures see women as something less than men. The term describing the domination of women by men is *patriarchy*.

Distinguishing between the two genders is one of the key ways in which cultures, including ours in Canada, organize their thinking about members of their group. Usually, one of the first things we notice about a person is gender. Once we notice this, we immediately make certain assumptions about what sort of person he or

FIGURE 12.3. Much of what distinguishes boys from girls is socially created. Once we know what sex a child is, we know what clothes and toys to buy and what kind of name the child will have. Here we see twin babies—one girl and one boy. With one dressed in pink and one dressed in blue, it is clear which is which. Are they being assigned gender characteristics?

she is, based on gender. While the assumptions we make may often be close to the truth, it is very clear that this is a form of stereotyping, which is not appropriate.

 Think about your perceptions of girls and boys. For example, you may think that boys are stronger than girls and that girls are more sensitive than boys. Now, write down a short list of differences that you think are generally correct. Next, reflect on the list you have made. If you see boys as different from girls, do you value one gender more highly than the other? Do the differences on your list apply equally to all the girls and all the boys that you know?

Think about these questions and discuss them with your classmates. You are likely to arrive at the following very important conclusion: although humans are biologically divided into two genders, it is of no value to attempt to assign common characteristics to each gender.

**gender** Refers to the cultural meanings that are typically assigned to the biological differences between the sexes. Sex is a matter of biology. Gender is a cultural interpretation of what that biology means.

**patriarchy** The near-universal domination of women by men.

## Clothing

Clothing customs vary greatly from place to place. While much of this variation is related to climate, the way people choose to dress is based on cultural values and on what people believe promotes good health, proper growth, and beauty.

Any Canadian department store offers a baby section full of neck-to-toe sleepers in soft cottons and terry cloth. Babies can be dressed like miniature adults in jeans and tee-shirts or in simple nighties. If you look at how a baby is dressed today, it is difficult to know whether he or she lives on the west coast or the prairies. A gradual homogenization of the way we dress has been occurring, so that people across Canada and throughout most of the more-developed world express themselves similarly by what they wear. This was not always the case.

Choice of clothing is often based on what a culture believes about health and well-being. Some cultures believe that a baby needs to be tightly swaddled for his or her first few months of life. Others believe that a child should wear as little as possible. The way a child is dressed may also reflect attitudes toward adornment and status; for example, a child in a wealthy family may wear small gold earrings, while one in a less wealthy family may not wear any jewellery. As children enter puberty, their clothing and hairstyles begin to reflect various stages of readiness for marriage. In almost every culture, it is usual for boys and girls, and men and women, to dress differently from each other.

 For a look at footwear from a variety of cultures and centuries, visit the Bata Industries website. Start with <www.theworldtoday.ca> and follow "Links" to <www.batashoemuseum.ca>.

FIGURE 12.4. An Ndebele shaman in South Africa wearing a headdress with porcupine quills. Many indigenous peoples decorate their clothing with embroidery, shells, quills, and, since European contact, with beads. The designs often indicate something about the person wearing them—e.g., what clan the person belongs to or the status of that person within the society.

 Visit <www.theworldtoday.ca> and follow "Links" to <www.muklukscanada.com> to see a page of celebrity mukluk sightings.

 What does your clothing say about you? Consider the styles that are popular among Canadian teenagers today and discuss what the choice of style says about an individual.

**Mukluks in California?** In the winter of 2004, a Manitoba company needed to hire extra workers to keep up with the demand when mukluks made it big in Hollywood, California. If you've ever worn mukluks, you know that they're warm and cozy enough for the coldest prairie winter. The earliest inhabitants of southern California would never have dreamed of wearing something so warm and impractical.

## Understanding Culture by Looking at the Life Cycle

### Ready for Learning

Recall your first day of school. You probably entered kindergarten at the age of five, probably spent only half days there, and began to learn colours and letters and maybe how to tie your shoes. Kindergarten is often seen as the year to introduce children to the idea of school and learning.

Many indigenous cultures have been affected by colonialism and enroll their children in school for at least part of their lives; this is another example of Westernization. Other cultures have resisted and keep their children away from state-run schools styled after European educational systems. When school costs money and a family is unable to send all their children to school, parents generally send their sons and keep their daughters at home to help with the domestic work. In many indigenous cultures, education for women is not seen to be as important as education for men.

Fortunately, there are many ways of learning other than in school—for example, listening, watching, and doing.

### *Listening*

Children learn about their culture through storytelling by the adults in the society. Many folk tales pass on the morals, etiquette, taboos, and customs that adults deem important for children. Stories about their origins and about their ancestors teach children about the world and serve as lessons for life.

### *Watching*

Children learn by watching their parents and other adults. Girls may pick up skills from their mothers such as weaving, cooking, building fires, beading, and sewing. Boys may learn to hunt, fish, or farm by watching their fathers. When they are ready to attempt these tasks themselves, children have watched their parents so many times that the movements are natural. Although children will not be perfectly competent at their first attempt at an adult task, they are encouraged to try when they are still young.

### *Doing*

Children learn by following adults and imitating their movements and activities. Children who are attracted to certain tasks—for example pottery-making, basket-weaving, or making nets—spend time with the adults who are engaged in such activities and copy their movements. Inuit children are given scraps of bone and antler with which to carve simple figures that they can use as playthings. Fulani boys in West Africa do not read a book to learn cattle-care; each boy is given the task of caring for his own calf at an early age. An indigenous tribe in Guatemala does not teach boys rituals and prayers; the children learn them by hearing and repeating them year after year.

**FIGURE 12.5. Children in Kenya learning how to hunt by listening, watching, and doing.**

## Ready for Adulthood

Many families within indigenous cultures around the world have different expectations for teenagers than do many Canadian families. While you may complain about having to do homework and tasks around the house, some indigenous cultures expect that a person is ready to take on adult responsibilities shortly after puberty.

In many cultures, such as in India, children may be betrothed (engaged) at a very young age, though a couple will not live together as a formally married couple until they have experienced a coming-of-age ceremony. At this point, they are ready to live together and have children.

 For more information about the Maori of New Zealand and their traditional rituals, visit <www.theworldtoday.ca> and follow "Links" to <www.maori.org.nz>.

 At what age are most Canadians considered adult? Are there any special rituals or celebrations that mark the coming of adulthood? How do people in Canada know that someone is adult? At what age are Canadians ready for marriage? Discuss these questions.

FIGURE 12.6. Many indigenous cultures use coming-of-age ceremonies to signify that a young woman or man is considered adult and is now marriageable. These rituals may be accompanied by a physical alteration to the body—tattooing or body painting, for example—that will signify to the community that the child has passed into adulthood. Here we see an elder in an Indonesian village piercing a boy's arm with wooden needles during an initiation ceremony.

## Ready for Child-Raising and Socialization

How did you learn how to behave? What does good behaviour mean to you? With whom did you spend most of your days before you began school? The way a child is raised and socialized is key to passing on the values and rules of conduct within a culture. In Canada, you are just as likely to spend much of your daytime hours during your formative years with someone other than your parents as you are with your mother or father. The concept of daycare is unique to more-developed and industrialized countries in which adults go to work and children are not welcome in the workplace.

In many indigenous cultures, however, babies are with a parent (usually the mother) at all times. They accompany their mothers to the field, market, and back home again. When the children are a little older, other members of the family become caregivers.

In indigenous cultures, young children are often given small tasks to do. For instance, the Beng of West Africa believe that asking toddlers to take small items to a home down the road will teach children about their place in the village, their relatives, and it will also give them a sense of belonging. Fulani women teach their three- and-four-year-old daughters about child care, cooking, and fetching food and water.

**FIGURE 12.7.** In indigenous cultures where a mother is working and unable to care for her child, a young relative will be enlisted to watch over the child while she is away. In this photograph from Peru, South America, we see a young girl carrying an infant.

## Ready for Work (But Whose Work Is It?)

For reasons mentioned earlier in this chapter, division of labour in most cultures—who does what—tends to be gender-specific. There are tasks that are performed mostly by men and tasks that are performed mostly by women. In most cultures today, this division of labour is less rigid, but it does continue in indigenous cultures. In Bhutan, some people believe that, if a woman did the ploughing, the oxen would cry and not be able to work properly. In Albania, it might embarrass a man to be caught doing laundry; laundry is "women's work."

In other indigenous groups, such as the Penan of Malaysia, there is no distinction between work and leisure; life is lived in the moment. Wealth—the acquisition of possessions and money—has no meaning in their traditional society. "The good life" is measured by the strength of the community. The Penan are nomadic forest-dwellers who are now being forced by commercial logging activities to settle in longhouses, working at menial jobs within the lumber industry that is destroying their homeland. Their way of life is changing, and the ideas of work and leisure as we understand them will most likely change the Penan beyond recognition.

FIGURE 12.8. Above: a woman hangs out laundry on bushes to dry in Uganda in eastern Africa. Below: men walk with their sheep and goats in search of pasture in the Kashmir region of India.

Traditional education and the work that needs to be done are closely aligned in indigenous cultures. Abstract math problems, for instance, mean nothing to a nomadic cattle herder. However, the number of cows, the amount of land needed to graze them, the resulting food and clothing gained from each cow, and the materials that can be obtained from trading a cow are all meaningful and worthy of learning. As noted earlier in this chapter, children learn to work in much the same way they learn everything else: by listening, watching, and doing what their parents do.

## Wisdom of the Elders

The cosmetic-surgery industry in Canada and the United States doubles in size every three to four years now that injections like botox to decrease wrinkles are affordable for middle-income wage earners. The trade shows that focus on cosmetic surgery are often called "anti-aging" shows. Increasingly in more-developed countries, looking old is seen as somewhat embarrassing, and people are seeking to look younger than their years. This is especially the case for women; 85 percent of cosmetic surgery in Canada is performed on women.

However, in many indigenous cultures, aging is not seen as negative. Rather, the advice of elders is sought out and respected. Elders pass on the wisdom of the society, recall and tell stories, and teach the next generation. White hair commands respect, and wrinkles are a map for future generations to follow. Grandparents take a vital role in the raising of children and in making decisions for the society. Grandparents almost always live within their extended family. The idea of a special home for elders, like a retirement or personal-care home, is unheard of. Grandparents and elders remain vital workers within the community until they experience ill health or die. Retirement as we know it does not exist.

**Westernization** The world is changing, and Westernization is affecting the world of work everywhere. Pressure to change traditional ways of working often results when American and European companies want to access natural resources, such as timber and minerals, or build new markets for their goods. When people now work for a company, they are required to work to a time clock, to buy goods rather than to barter for them, and to work for the company rather than for themselves. Together these changes cause other changes, as life becomes more consumer oriented. Very few cultures are managing to resist these changes completely, and all the signs today point to increasing Westernization in most of the world.

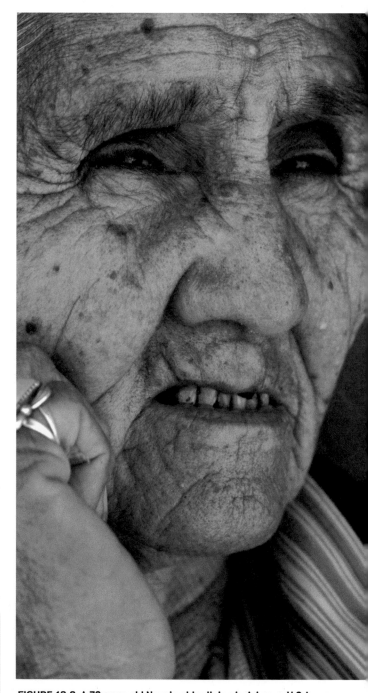

FIGURE 12.9. A 73-year-old Navajo elder living in Arizona, U.S.A., who practises tribal medicine.

 Look for news stories about elderly people in our culture and in other cultures. Consider what each article tells you about elderly people. Are they portrayed in a positive light or a negative light? Are there any elderly people to whom you go for advice? Why or why not?

## Ready for the Afterlife

Most groups of people have well-developed theories about the afterlife. Some groups believe in a spirit world and an afterlife. The rituals surrounding death reflect what the culture believes about the afterlife.

Customs, too, help prepare people who are close to death for their trip into the next world. For example, according to traditional Chinese custom, it is necessary that a dying person be helped into a sitting position; these people believe that the soul can leave the body more easily if the person is sitting up.

Body preparation and burial vary among cultures. Many cultures bury their dead along with tools and equipment to help them live in the afterlife. Other cultures adorn and dress the body, remove organs, and close the mouth and eyes.

How people mourn, how they speak about the deceased, and how they behave during a burial are all culturally mandated and therefore vary widely from culture to culture. People in some cultures weep and wail, others paint their bodies with ashes or clay. Some traditional Hawaiians tattoo their tongue to honour a father or mother who has passed on. People in some groups shave their heads, and others will not cut their hair for a specific period of time after the death of a loved one. Some societies believe that a person's name must not be mentioned after death, or that person will come back to haunt you. (When this happens, someone with the same name as that of the deceased may be forced to change his or her name.) Dances, special foods, and other offerings accompany mourning rituals.

## Understanding across Cultures

Cultures differ widely from each other, but there are also many underlying similarities. All cultures have language, religion, an understanding of gender differences, a sense of identity, and a complex set of rituals and traditions. Specific expressions of culture, however, vary greatly from place to place and from people to people. Gestures, art, literature, food, and clothing are all parts of culture.

People in all cultures cherish babies. Each person is given a name, people need food and shelter, and people seek to beautify themselves and their surroundings. These are common to all cultures.

It is clear that many of the cultural differences in the world are becoming less distinct. Westernization is a powerful force in globalization, especially in the spread of the English language and of aspects of American popular culture. Wherever we live in the world, it is getting harder and harder not to have heard of McDonald's or to have watched CNN on television. Some indigenous societies work hard to resist these outside influences, but resistance is becoming less and less effective, and certain aspects of some cultures, particularly their languages, are seen as endangered.

# 13

# CHANGING PEOPLES AND PLACES

## Guiding Questions

1. How do the events of the past influence a society's present way of life?

2. What are some effects of the period of European colonization of Africa?

3. Why do most countries find it important to be independent and self-ruling?

## "What's Past Is Prologue"

To understand the peoples and places of the world today, we need to know some history. The facts of human geography are always changing; a temporal viewpoint is used alongside our favoured spatial viewpoint, as stated in the introduction. This chapter emphasizes aspects of past geographies and how they help us understand the present.

The focus here is on Africa. We discuss African geographies prior to the arrival of Europeans, then we look at the slave trade and the colonial period when Europeans ruled most of Africa, including some of the geographical changes associated with the decolonization of Africa.

Understanding our African origins is important because it highlights the fact that we all belong to the same species. Discuss why this fact is relevant to the discussion of human rights in chapter 5.

**African Origins** Most scientists believe that the human species—known as *Homo sapiens sapiens*—originated in eastern Africa about 160 000 years ago and then slowly migrated around the world. During the past 160 000 years, the principal changes have been cultural, such as learning to use fire and developing language for communication. Different groups of people developed different ways of life in relation to different physical environments. Some minor biological changes have occured, too, during the past 160 000 years, as groups have adapted to their physical environments. The most obvious adaptation is that of skin colour; dark skin is an adaptation in warm environments, and light skin is an adaptation in cool environments. However, differences in skin colour, along with other differences, such as body size and shape, hair colour and texture, and facial features, do not alter the fact that all humans belong to the same species: *Homo sapiens sapiens*.

FIGURE 13.1. These children look different from each other, but they are biologically the same.

# Satellite Image of Africa

FIGURE 13.2. This satellite image of Africa shows the true colours of the continent as seen from space. Dark green areas are either agricultural crops or forest. Light green and brown areas are either agricultural crops or drier grasslands and plains. Lightest browns or yellow areas are deserts. Black or dark blue areas are oceans.

# African Geographies

## North Africa

The countries of North Africa are Western Sahara, Morocco, Algeria, Tunisia, Libya, Egypt, and Sudan. Most of the people are Sunni Muslim, and there are close cultural links with mostly Muslim southwestern Asia. Because several of the countries in North Africa have a Mediterranean coastline, there are also close cultural links with Europe. The arid Sahara Desert dominates the physical environment, and most people live on the desert margins. The Nile Valley in Egypt was one of the world's earliest **cultural hearth** areas.

## West Africa

The countries of West Africa are Mauritania, Mali, Niger, Senegal, Gambia, Guinea-Bissau, Guinea, Sierra Leone, Liberia, Ivory Coast, Burkina Faso, Ghana, Togo, Benin, and Nigeria. The region is bounded by the Atlantic Ocean to the west and south, the Sahara Desert to the north, and merges into Central Africa to the east. This was the first African region to be penetrated by European slave traders and by those searching for gold and ivory. During the 19th century, the British and French established **plantation agriculture** here.

**Major Geographic Regions in Africa**

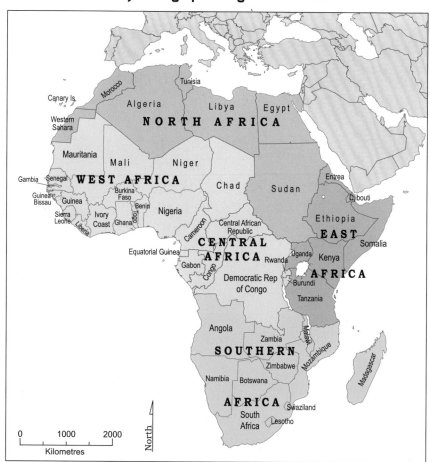

FIGURE 13.3. In addition to these general regions, geographers often identify sub-Saharan Africa. Sub-Saharan Africa includes all of Southern Africa, all of East Africa, Central Africa (except for Chad), and West Africa (except for Mauritania, Mali, and Niger).

**plantation agriculture** An agricultural system for the commercial production of tropical and subtropical crops that began during the colonial era. Plantations usually grew only one crop. Typical plantation crops in West Africa were palm oil, cocoa, and bananas. In other parts of Africa, plantations produced sugar cane, coffee, tea, cotton, and pineapple. Plantation agriculture used European organization and capital combined with cheap local labour. In some areas of plantation agriculture, where local labour was considered unsuitable (often because of the effects of diseases introduced by Europeans), as in much of the Americas, slaves were imported from elsewhere, most often from West Africa.

**cultural hearth** The place of origin of a culture. Today the origin area is also often the location where the culture is most fully developed.

## Central Africa

The countries of Central Africa are Cameroon, Central African Republic, Chad, Equatorial Guinea, Gabon, Congo, Democratic Republic of Congo, Rwanda, and Burundi. This region stretches from just south of the Sahara Desert in the north to the Algolan Plateau in the south. There is one major river basin: the Congo. There is a vast tropical rainforest and a large savannah region south of the Sahara, and one north of the Kalahari. Perceived as almost uninhabitable by Europeans, this region was colonized in the late 19th century, later than most other areas in Africa.

## East Africa

The countries of East Africa are Eritrea, Djibouti, Ethiopia, Somalia, Uganda, Kenya, and Tanzania. This region includes high plateaus that are dissected by rift valleys. Much of the region lacks adequate supplies of water. There are few minerals, and most of the people rely on agriculture for survival. Kenya is the only country within East Africa that has good transportation links between coastal and interior regions.

## Southern Africa

The countries of Southern Africa are Angola, Zambia, Malawi, Namibia, Botswana, Zimbabwe, Mozambique, Madagascar, South Africa, Lesotho, and Swaziland. Much of Southern Africa is well-suited to agriculture, and there are areas of mineral wealth and of industrial activity. European settlers were attracted to Southern Africa especially, because of the favourable climate. Today, the region includes the richest country in Africa (South Africa) and two of the very poorest (Malawi and Mozambique).

### The Great Rift Valley

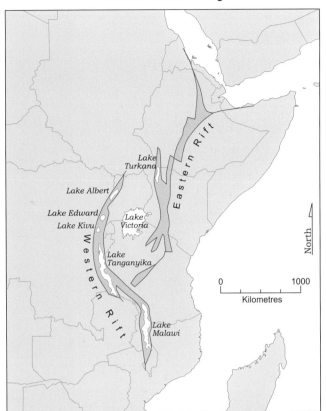

FIGURE 13.4. The Great Rift Valley resulted when the earth's crust pulled apart, and it is possible that the eastern part of Africa will eventually pull away from the rest of the continent in much the same way as it did when the Red Sea was created. The physical landscape, as shown in the photo, is varied: there are rivers, lakes, valleys, and volcanic mountains that provide stunning views.

## Africa before Europeans

Africa has a long and interesting history. The human geography of Africa developed as a mosaic of over 3 000 societies speaking over 1 000 languages. For many years, trade among the peoples in Africa and the peoples in other continents was minimal. Most African groups developed either in isolation or in contact with only a few neighbouring groups.

One of the earliest known societies in Africa was the Nok. Artifacts recovered from ancient town sites in present-day Nigeria show that the people there were sustained by agriculture and lived in homes of mud and branches. They mined gold, used iron axes, and seem to have had a great interest in art. Present-day Nigerian statues share some of the characteristics of the early sculptures and murals. Around 100 BCE, other hunting and herding societies began to move into their region, and the Nok were assimilated into these societies over the next 100 years.

One of the societies believed to have absorbed the Nok was the Yoruba. The Yoruba have lived in the southwestern area of Nigeria, as well as in Benin and Togo, for thousands of years. Although no pre-colonial written records exist for them, archaeological evidence suggests a well-developed society with walled cities containing palaces and courtyards and surrounded by agricultural land. These cities shared many characteristics and were ruled locally, not centrally, by an *oba*, who usually had a team of advisors to help him govern.

FIGURE 13.5. Nok terra-cotta head.

Another African group was the Shona, who developed a great civilization between the 11th and 15th centuries in what is now Zimbabwe. The ruins that can be seen today are those of a city that was known as Great Zimbabwe. This was an important trading centre for gold and ivory and the centre of a large agricultural region. Today the site is a UNESCO world-heritage site.

 For much more detail on the Zimbabwe ruins, visit <www.theworldtoday.ca> and follow "Links" to <www.worldheritagesite.org/sites/greatzimbabweruins.html>.

## The Slave Trade

Some African societies were frequently at war with their neighbours. Some conducted raids to take slaves, a practice that increased during the 1500s when European trade began. The Europeans who had colonized the Americas considered the indigenous peoples there to be unsuitable workers, especially since many were weakened by disease, so they began a slave trade between Africa and the Americas. For example, Yoruba people were brought as slaves to Brazil in the 16th century and to the Caribbean in the 17th century. By the 18th century, the slave trade between Africa and North America was in full swing, and many Africans were sold to plantation owners in the North American south.

In 1807, a campaign led by English humanitarian William Wilberforce (1759–1833) successfully banned slavery in Britain and its colonies. The importation of slaves was made illegal in the United States at this time as well. Slavery was a lucrative trade and supplied cheap labour. For Britain to remain competitive in the world market, it needed to make sure that its trade partners did not continue trading for slaves. Fortunately for Britain, its navy controlled the seas at the time and patrolled the coasts of Africa, effectively blockading all slave ships.

For information about slavery in our world today, visit <www.theworldtoday.ca> and follow "Links" to <www.anti-slavery.org>. For a more historic understanding of the transatlantic slave trade, follow "Links" to <http://school.discovery.com/schooladventures/slavery/equiano.html> or to <www.nationmaster.com> and search for "slave trade."

**Focus on Slavery** The phrase *slave trade* immediately brings to most people's minds the slavery of Africans in the colonial United States. But slavery is almost as old as humankind and has been practised in all parts of the world. Ancient Hebrew and Arabic texts refer to slaves and slavery, including guidelines on how to treat them. Egypt, one of the most advanced cultures in the ancient world, had a large slave population, and some slaves even had the "privilege" of accompanying a pharaoh or other ruler into the next life; they were killed when the ruler died and placed in the tomb of their master. African people themselves sometimes conducted raids in the African interior and took potential slaves to sell at seaports where European ships were waiting. Slavery was a well-established practice all over the world when Europeans began the exploration and expansion of their empires. The word *slave* is derived from the Slavic peoples of eastern and southeastern Europe who became slaves in the Holy Roman Empire in the 9th century (the Holy Roman Empire covered much of central Europe from about 800 CE until about 1800). In the African countries of Sudan and Mauritania, slaves are controlled by the slaveowners.

FIGURE 13.6. The impressive stone ruins of Great Zimbabwe.

## Colonizing Africa

The end of the slave trade in about 1820 did not end European interest in Africa. The Industrial Revolution in Europe increased demand for raw materials, and Europeans saw that much of what they needed was available in Africa. They shifted their trading focus from people to natural resources, such as gold, diamonds, ivory, gum, cloves, coffee, peanuts, cotton, rubber, and palm oil. At first, some Africans benefited from receiving European goods, but Europeans wanted to be more directly involved so as to make more profit for themselves, so they began to establish colonies.

By about 1800, several European powers had established small colonies along the coast of Africa. Most of Africa, though, was controlled by Africans themselves. The major European powers, including Britain, Germany, Portugal, Belgium, Spain, France, and the Netherlands, met in 1884 at the Berlin Conference, agreed to colonize Africa and established political boundaries that suited their own needs. No African groups were involved in this agreement. Central Africa was the region most affected by this phase of colonialism, and the major occupying countries were France, Italy, Germany, Britain, Belgium, Portugal, Spain, and the Netherlands. They signed treaties with African rulers, and offered them protection, but imposed colonial rule.

Look back at figure 3.12, which shows the European political presence in Africa at the height of the colonial period. The boundaries were determined by Europeans and do not reflect the realities of African physical or human geographies. A political map of Africa prior to European occupation is a patchwork of many small units that bears little resemblance to this map (there were about 3 000 societies).

## Why Did Europeans Begin the Process of Overseas Expansion?

Throughout history, people have waged war against and enslaved each other. Dominant groups note differences in others and assume that their own culture and society are superior.

There are a number of specific reasons that led to European overseas expansion and to colonization of the Americas, Africa, and parts of Asia. Some of the motives were admirable and good, others were not so.

### New Ideas and Attitudes

The Age of Exploration began during the European Renaissance, a time of scientific experimentation, philosophical thought, religious renewal, and, most important for our purpose, geographical exploration. New ideas in science and new inventions encouraged new ways of thinking.

The size and shape of the world was being questioned, and maps were being redrawn as information brought back from explorers collided with long-held ideas about what was where in the world.

The hopes and aspirations of Europeans were changing as its agricultural economy grew and diversified, industrial capacity increased, more detailed maps were drawn, new and improved ocean-going vessels became available, and navigational techniques improved, including more accurate measurement of latitude.

FIGURE 13.7. An inset from an 18th-century map of North America showing cod drying in Newfoundland.

### Accessing Natural Resources

As we discussed in chapter 10, trade with Asia for spices and other products had long been of interest to the people of Europe. Before refrigeration was available, food was preserved with spices, and spices made bland (and sometimes inedible) food taste better. An easier route to Asia was, therefore, a top priority for Europeans, and they began to look westward.

### Interest and Curiosity

Along with the invention of the printing press in the 14th century came an increase in the number of books available. As more and more people were able to read, new knowledge and ideas became widespread. Travel diaries became popular, too, and Europeans wanted to hear two types of exploration stories. One type was about strange and bizarre people living in faraway places—for example people with one leg, people with their faces on their bellies, people who were gigantic, and people who were very small.

The other type of story was about the idealized indigenous peoples who lived in a setting like the garden of Eden, where no disease, shame, or hunger existed. European intellectuals asked a fundamental question: were these people—who seemed so different from Europeans and who were able to walk around naked without shame—human or animal? The answer was important, because it helped them decide how these "strange" indigenous peoples would be treated.

### Empire-Building and Mercantilism

As European countries recognized the natural resources in many of the places that they were discovering, they realized that control of these areas would make them rich. Political power and wealth are what make countries strong, and those countries that were able took what they could. The Industrial Revolution began in the 18th century and progressed rapidly. An

FIGURE 13.8. A painting of an Apache family that reflects the story of idealized indigenous people in the Americas.

increasingly wealthy public, ready to buy more and more products, and services, demanded more and more inventions. Increased consumer demands, in turn, increased the need for more natural resources.

According to one theory of mercantilism, a country's wealth and strength are measured by its reserves of gold and silver. This theory was held in high regard for a long time. When precious metals were no longer available, the colonial powers controlled the trade of their colonies, ensuring that they remained stronger than their colonies. They used whatever resources the colony produced for their own industrial activities. The British colony that eventually became the United States of America grew tired of this control and fought the War of Independence in 1776.

### Christianity

Christianity motivated many European leaders to occupy other parts of the world, and Christian missionaries were often at the forefront of the exploratory process. Christianity is a "universalizing" religion— that is, it claims to know the truth about God. Many Europeans felt that it was their responsibility to introduce Christianity to other people, and to convert them, so that they might lead a more enriched life.

## Decolonization of Africa, Asia, South and Central America

The scramble for Africa that followed the 1884 Berlin Conference was the last period of European colonization. Although the period of time that most of the countries in Africa were colonized was only brief (usually under 100 years), the consequences of colonialism in many places, including political boundaries, have been far-reaching.

After the Second World War, the peoples of the colonized areas of Africa (and Asia and Central and South America) began seeking more national sovereignty; they wanted to be in charge of their own destinies. The process of decolonization thus began.

The process of decolonization proved to be far from straightforward, however. Recall from chapter 5 that it was in 1948, shortly after the end of the Second World War, that the United Nations *Universal Declaration of Human Rights* was adopted. Its charter influenced decolonization: some European countries gave up their colonies relatively willingly, while others were more reluctant. Some leaders in colonial areas, like Gandhi in India, were able to push for sovereignty without bloodshed; others inflicted violence and bloodshed on their country and the other people in it to gain independence.

The process of decolonization began in 1948 when Pakistan and India became independent from British colonial rule. The first African country to become independent from colonial authority (Britain) was Ghana, in 1957. After that, decolonization proceeded rapidly and was essentially complete by the 1980s.

### Toward Democratic Governments

The years since decolonization have been challenging and turbulent times for many newly independent countries, both in Africa and elsewhere. These countries needed to organize themselves politically, to find ways to govern, and to determine who was "in charge."

In some countries, like Canada and Australia, the movement away from colony status was peaceful and marked by negotiation that resulted in the establishment of democratic institutions (as discussed in chapter 6). In other countries, including many in Africa, independence came with a form of authoritarian political rule. Some African countries are still struggling with very difficult transitions from authoritarian rule to democracy. They are still emerging, taking new shape from the 19th-century boundaries imposed on them. Some African countries are struggling to accommodate several distinct African societies within one political unit; some traditional societies find themselves spread across two or more countries—for instance, the Yoruba, whose people are located in three different countries. How, then, does a person of the Yoruba tribe make a decision about voting? To which country do the Yoruba see themselves as belonging?

 Look back to the map of free, partly free, and not-free countries (figure 6.7). Are most of the countries that are partly free or not-free former colonies? Are most of these countries in Africa?

**Slow Move toward Democracy** Since achieving independence in 1960, the Democratic Republic of Congo, a large country with a wealth of natural resources, has been involved in a series of civil wars and conflicts with neighbouring states. A peace agreement in 2003 may or may not bring stability to this country and its people. This is just one African country that faces the challenge of moving toward democracy.

## Saying Sorry

Another difficulty that some former colonial countries face is in the ways in which indigenous peoples were treated during, and sometimes even after, the colonial period. However, the concerns of indigenous populations are now being taken into account, and efforts are being made to correct past injustices. The colonial powers have been replaced by national systems of government.

However, in Canada, Australia, New Zealand, and the United States, the responsibility lies with those who committed the injustices, as these are the groups (people of European descent) that hold political power today. In Australia, National Sorry Day (or the Journey of Healing) focuses on the "stolen generations" of children of indigenous families who were removed by force from their homes. National Sorry Day was first held in 1998 after the Human Rights and Equal Opportunity Commission recommended a special day be set aside to acknowledge the negative effect of Australia's forced removal of indigenous peoples. It is a day to express sorrow but also to celebrate a new relationship between Australia's indigenous and non-indigenous peoples.

FIGURE 13.9. In Australia, the first National Sorry Day was held on 26 May 1998. The intent of Sorry Day is to highlight past injustices committed against Aboriginal peoples and to foster reconciliation.

## The Past Is Indeed Prologue

The human geography of the peoples and places of the world depends on what happened in the past. Therefore, it is important that we understand the story of the colonization by Europeans. Here in Canada, for example, because both the French and the British were colonizers, we have two official languages. Many other countries around the world have an official language that originated in Europe.

Schools and social systems were changed as colonial systems moved in on age-old customs. Not every age-old custom would necessarily have been a good and helpful one. Some of the changes may have been beneficial. Rather, it was often the speed with which these changes were made by the colonizers that caused a social backlash from which some countries are still recovering.

Knowing who we are and what group we belong to is very important to each of us. Consider, for example, how the loss of traditional ideas about tribal identities and their replacement by national identities would have affected the people of Africa. As Europeans imposed new country boundaries, many Africans lost their age-old sense of local group identity.

The colonizing countries, too, were changed. Many European countries became richer and more powerful than they had been before they began colonizing other countries. They adopted foods and clothing from their colonies, and, in some cases, there was much migration from the colonial power to the colony.

 Discuss with classmates whether or not Canada should have Sorry Day, as Australia does. If yes, why? If not, why not?

# HEALTH AND WELL-BEING ACROSS THE WORLD

**14**

## Guiding Questions

1. How does poverty affect health and well-being?

2. How do most people in the world earn a living?

3. Can technology help solve some of the problems associated with health and well-being?

4. What are some of the major challenges to quality of life in the populations of Asia and Africa?

The fact that the world is divided into more-developed countries and less-developed countries was discussed in chapter 3. Some of the human geographic implications of this division are discussed in other chapters of this book, especially chapters 4 and 7. This chapter focuses on health and well-being, and how they are related to these divisions in the world. The various peoples and places of the world experience very different levels of health and well-being. Some people have sufficient and good-quality food, and others do not. Some people have ample supplies of clean drinking water, and others do not. Some people have basic medical care, and others do not. Some people are employed in safe workplaces that respect human rights, and others are not. In this chapter, we review some of these inequalities and discuss how things might be changed.

## Feast and Famine

Close to 85 percent of the world's people live with moderate to severe hunger. Maybe you think there simply is not enough food to go around. But that is not the case. There is enough wheat, rice, and other grains to provide every single person with 3 500 calories every day.

Maybe you think that there are too many people in some countries. But that does not answer the hunger question. While some countries, like Bangladesh, are densely populated and the people are hungry, many other densely populated countries—such as the Netherlands—have more food than they need for their populations. Hunger usually results from certain inequities that deprive people of the means to buy food and prevent farmers from producing food. Women in particular are often excluded from land ownership, education, security, and jobs.

 For an interactive map about hunger in the world, visit the site of the United Nations World Food Program (WFP). Go to <www.theworldtoday.ca> and follow "Links" to <www.wfp.org/country_brief/hunger_map/map/hungermap_popup/map_popup.html>.

FIGURE 14.1. Scattering seeds in a field in Kenya. This photo highlights the limited farming technologies used in much of the less-developed world.

Maybe you think nature is to blame. This is perhaps true in some cases, but we know that food is always available to people who can afford to buy it. Starvation hits the poorest millions who are already living on the edge of survival. People's attitudes and actions are the real cause of starvation, especially those of governments that believe hunger and starvation cannot be avoided and that the lives of some are more important than the lives of others.

Maybe you think that there is nothing that can be done. Hunger can seem like another one of those problems that is just too big for one person to solve. But world hunger can be beaten. For many of the world's poor, what it would take to end the cycle of poverty, hunger, and despair is justice, education, fair trade, irrigation, and land ownership.

 For more information about how Canadians are working to transform the lives of people in less-developed countries, visit <www.theworldtoday.ca> and follow "Links" to <www.foodgrainsbank.ca>.

## Water

Interrelated with the struggle for food is the struggle for water. People in areas affected by drought, who are without a ready supply of clean water for irrigation and drinking, are often also in the midst of famine. To fully understand food-security issues, we must also understand issues surrounding water availability.

**Such a Big Difference** Eddy was a development worker for the Mennonite Central Committee for three years. He lived in a remote village far from any cities and was visited by other North Americans only occasionally. He often felt discouraged, but one thing he felt very positive about was his work on building wells for several neighbouring villages. The villagers banded together to purchase equipment, and they worked together to dig wells in each village. The improvement in people's health was immediately obvious, and fewer children were dying. The cost to bring a well to each village was less than $400. This is small change for such a big difference.

 Imagine that every time you needed water, you had to walk 20 minutes to get it. What if you had to get your water from a building down the street? A little more convenient, but still a nuisance.

Now, imagine walking 10 kilometres, fill up a 20-litre jug, and then carry it 10 kilometres back home. This would be the water for all your family's needs for one day. Even though your water is likely clean, pretend that it is dirty, muddy, and harbours bacteria. You need to boil it to ensure that it is safe to drink.

Such inconveniences are a reality for about one in every six people in the world—that is, about one billion of your global neighbours. Bathing in and drinking unclean water results in diarrhea, dysentery, and even death for approximately two million people in the world per year. That's 3 000 people per day, and many of them are the most vulnerable people: children.

FIGURE 14.2. If you are a boy, you are probably off the hook for fetching water. In many less-developed countries, carrying water is seen as women's work, and when girls and women have to spend up to 8 hours a day carrying water, they are not able to attend school or obtain paid employment. Seen here are women with children pumping water from a well in southeastern India.

**Lake Victoria in Danger** We were visiting Kenya and stopped to see Lake Victoria, the largest inland lake in Africa and the source of the Nile. The lake is huge, but as an ecosystem it is sick. Non-indigenous species of fish introduced to enhance commercial fishing have had just the opposite effect—they have virtually wiped out the **endemic** species. For example, creeping water hyacinth, a plant introduced from South America, had at one point taken over the coastline in many regions, causing problems for boating, fishing, and using water generally. Local people got rid of creeping water hyacinth by introducing another non-indigenous species, a weevil that eats the water hyacinth (and, thankfully, it doesn't seem to have done any harm).

The lake still provides a livelihood for many  people who live along its shores, but when we came, it looked so muddy and dirty that the more cautious people in our group didn't even wade in. I did, thinking, How can I not put my toe into the source of the Nile? Plus, it was so hot that the water felt cool and refreshing, even though it was dirty. Close by, a woman was doing her laundry in it.

School was ending for the day, and a bunch of kids stopped by the lake as well. We watched as they walked right in and filled up their water jugs to bring home. Some of them drank the water right out of the lake.

I suppose, when water is as precious as it is in this hot, dry country, you take it as you get it. I thought of the relatively clear, pure little lakes we camp at in the summer at home and wondered what those kids would think if they were exposed to a summer in a Canadian provincial park. I would never consider drinking water from Lake Victoria, but after seeing people drinking straight out of the lake, it doesn't seem so bad.
—*Heather*

**endemic** Means more than indigenous. Not only is an endemic species indigenous to a certain place, but it is also found there exclusively. Therefore, when non-indigenous species of fish were introduced into Lake Victoria, other species that were found nowhere else in the world became extinct. This was another colonization disaster.

FIGURE 14.3. A canoe on Lake Victoria, Kenya. In the foreground are empty passenger boats.

## Sanitation and Health

The stories about water in this chapter raise another issue: sanitation. For many people in the less-developed world, the water used for drinking is contaminated because of poor sanitation and improper waste-control management.

Good sanitation simply requires proper disposal of human and industrial waste. In 2004, about three billion people around the world had no proper sanitation facilities. With increasing urbanization, the problem of where to put waste continues. For example, it is estimated that about two million tonnes of human excrement seeps into urban water supplies every day around the world, as well as a large amount of untreated industrial waste.

Poor sanitation leads to ill health and disease, but much of the world's population cannot afford, nor do they have access to, the drug therapies that could help them.

You have probably read and heard quite a bit about Canada's health-care system. On the one hand, we are proud of our health-care system and feel that universal health care is important. On the other hand, we expect it to work better than it does; it seems as if there is just not enough money to keep it working smoothly. A little research on this matter offers an interesting picture.

In 2003, Canada spent $2,931 per person on health care. South Africa spent $689, India spent $96, Benin spent $44, and Liberia spent $11 (which is about the price of a big bottle of ibuprofen in Canada).

 Look for sanitation- and health-related articles in local and national newspaper and news magazines. Are there articles about health care in other countries? What do they say about the health-care system in Canada?

As of 2004, per 100 000 people:

- Canada had approximately 1 000 nurses and midwives and 209 doctors.
- The United States had 773 nurses and 548 doctors.
- South Africa had 388 nurses and 78 doctors.
- India had 61 nurses and 51 doctors.
- Benin had 28 nurses and five doctors.
- Liberia had 10 nurses and midwives and only two doctors.

There are lots of numbers here, and they send us an important message. Because of the shortage of money and health-care providers, up to 80 percent of people in Africa use traditional medicines as a first approach to illness. Women giving birth have traditional birth attendants. Traditional approaches to illness can certainly be helpful, but improved education is needed so that people can make choices concerning their health—that is, to decide when modern medical intervention might be appropriate. The evidence is clear: as education improves, so does health. A population's knowledge about how to prevent disease is the best method of ensuring its good health.

### HIV/AIDS

The problem of HIV/AIDS goes well beyond the scope of any illness faced by our world in recent history. The growing numbers of HIV/AIDS-infected people are putting an even greater strain on the already stretched health-care resources in the less-developed world, especially in Africa. The number of people with HIV/AIDS is not declining, and countries outside Africa, notably China and India, are seeing increasing numbers of infected people.

## AIDS in Africa

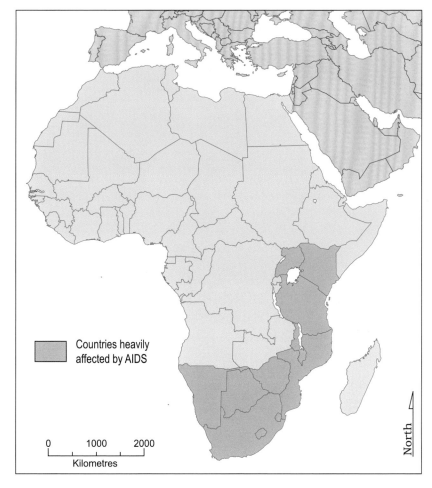

FIGURE 14.4. This map shows the countries in Africa that are most affected by the HIV/AIDS crisis.

### What Is HIV/AIDS?

AIDS is the acronym for (a quick way to say) *acquired immune deficiency syndrome.* You acquire AIDS when you are infected with the human immunodeficiency virus (HIV). HIV is a retrovirus that attaches itself to cells in your immune system and makes them unable to do their work. Your immune system is what your body needs to fight off illness (e.g., colds, cancer) and infections; when the system is weakened, you are vulnerable to many illnesses and you have little capacity to fight them off.

### Who Is Dying of AIDS?

By 2004, the number of people in the world who had died from AIDS was about 20 million, and the number of people living with AIDS was about 40 million. Sub-Saharan Africa is the hardest-hit region; about two-thirds of its people are affected. (Recall from chapter 13 that West, Central, East, and Southern Africa are often labelled together as sub-Saharan Africa.) Botswana is the worst-affected country, where about 40 percent of the population is infected.

Think about your friends and family. How many people do you know who are orphans? Now imagine that each person in your class was an orphan. In 2004, 13 million of your global neighbours became orphans because their parents died of AIDS.

Not only are those infected with HIV at risk, but their children are also at risk. They may not be able to go to school, because many of their teachers are dead or dying. In 2001, over one million African children lost teachers because of AIDS, and these numbers are generally climbing, not diminishing.

Many of the hardest-hit countries are on the very edge of survival because so many adults are dying. In Zambia, the life expectancy for a child born today is only 35 years. Table 14.1 provides data on life expectancy for some of the other hard-hit countries.

## Women and AIDS

Especially troubling is the increasing number of women who are infected. During the 1980s, most of those infected were men, but, by 2004, 60 percent were women. Of teenagers and young adults who are infected, 76 percent are female. Why?

Also very troubling is the fact that many children are infected. In 2004, as many as 640 000 children worldwide contracted AIDS from their mothers during birth or from breast-feeding. Ninety percent of these children live in sub-Saharan Africa.

FIGURE 14.5. Young AIDS orphans in Zambia. One boy comforts his younger brother while their sister sits quietly. Their grandmother cares for these 3 children.

## AIDS and the Workforce

AIDS is affecting the workforce in many African countries. How does a country produce food if those people who normally work in the fields are ill or dying? Loss of labour means loss of food production, and this is especially crucial in areas that already have an insufficient food supply. Here are some specific examples of how AIDS is affecting the workforce:

- Between 1993 and 1997, a Kenyan sugar plantation reported a 50-percent drop in output, while demands for funeral services increased five-fold and health-care demands increased ten-fold.

- Malawi had 10 times more vacancies in their national ministries of Agriculture, Water Management, Education, and Health from 1990 to 2000. Some services have only half of their positions open.

- In Thailand, rural farming families report a 50-percent drop in agricultural output in areas where AIDS exists.

### TABLE 14.1. Life Expectancy in Selected HIV/AIDS-Affected Countries

| Country | Life Expectancy, 2004 |
|---|---|
| Botswana | 36 |
| Mozambique | 40 |
| Zimbabwe | 41 |
| Malawi | 44 |
| Uganda | 45 |
| Tanzania | 45 |
| Namibia | 47 |
| Kenya | 51 |
| South Africa | 53 |

Source: Population Reference Bureau, *2005 World Population Data Sheet* (Washington, D.C.: Population Reference Bureau), 2005.

 A child born in Botswana today has a life expectancy of 36 years; a child born in Canada today has a life expectancy of 79 years. Think about this situation and talk about what it means to live in such an unequal world; talk about what might be done to change this tragic state of affairs.

## Education

Education is the key tool in the fight for social and economic development, especially for women, who are usually less educated.

Research shows that the more education a woman receives, the better able she is to care for her family. Educated women usually marry later, have children later, have fewer children, and have healthier children. Better education for girls and women is clearly linked to lower birth rates, higher incomes, and better health.

Because education promotes understanding and tolerance among people, countries with high educational standards experience less conflict and are more likely to promote democratic decision-making processes than countries with poor education standards. It is estimated that life expectancy increases two years for every 1-percent rise in literacy rates. Further, sustainable development and efficient agricultural practices are more likely to be found in countries with high standards of education. Education is clearly key to a better quality of life.

FIGURE 14.6. An outdoor classroom in Sudan. The teacher is using a portable slate.

 Visit <www.theworldtoday.ca> and follow "Links" to <http://cyberschoolbus.un.org/mdgs/index.html> for more information on education and why it can make such a difference in health and well-being in the world.

 Get to know some of your global neighbours. For example, research RESPECT, an international organization based in Winnipeg, which brings attention to the challenges faced by refugees. Their mission states that its members are committed to raising awareness among international youth about refugees and their issues. They help empower refugee children and their communities through exchanges of letters and through the donation of education-related materials.

 For more information about RESPECT, visit <www.theworldtoday.ca> and follow "Links" to <http://respectrefugees.org>.

## The Unequal World of Work

### Shop 'til You Drop?

Do you know what is in that chocolate bar you are eating? You might be surprised to find out that there is a lot more than nougat, nuts, and cocoa butter. It might have more than its fair share of blood, sweat, and tears.

Much of the world's chocolate comes from countries in Asia and Africa, from countries like Côte d'Ivoire, where children are frequently purchased from their families in neighbouring countries and put to work in the cocoa fields. Many of these children and their families are led to believe that they will be given good jobs at fair wages. Sadly, they find themselves working long hours with little pay, food, or comfort. Running away is an option, though a difficult one, because the children may be beaten if they are caught. After many years in the fields, some are allowed to go home, others are not.

Injustice and poor working conditions are part of much more than your chocolate bar. Coffee, tea, bananas, rugs, and even the shirt on your back may have come from plantations or factories where labour practices are unfair and even dangerous, where children younger than you are forced to work long hours for little pay, where wealthy Western companies capitalize on this cheap labour, and where few government regulations are in place to control the exploitation. While we "shop 'til we drop," people in other parts of the world are paid less for a day's work manufacturing the goods we buy than we probably spend on a cup of hot chocolate in the middle of a day of shopping.

If you are thinking about global citizenship, and if you want to be a good neighbour to the people in your global village, you are likely to wonder what you can do. Can you find out where your clothes are made, who made them, and how those people were treated? Maybe not, but by asking those questions you may

be forcing companies to realize that justice is important to many of us.

In chapter 7 we discussed fair-trade products—products that are made by people who are paid a stable, living wage for their work in manufacturing those products. You may pay a little more for fair-trade items, but you can take comfort knowing that you are not benefiting from your global neighbours' poverty.

FIGURE 14.7. This 13-year old girl is working in a fireworks factory in Sivakasi, in southern India. Most of the workers in this factory are girls aged between 8 and 16, and many suffer from tuberculosis.

 Now that you have read about the unequal world of work, try this: Select one of your favourite brands of clothing, or a favourite chocolate bar, and then use reliable media and Internet sources to collect information on working conditions in the less-developed countries where the product is made, or (in the case of the chocolate bar) where the cocoa comes from. Then, if you can, write and ask the company if they ensure that the people in the factories or farms are treated fairly. You may find that the information from the media and Internet sources on the one hand, and from the company on the other hand, are different. How do you decide which source is closer to the truth?

## Working in Agriculture

Farming and farm labour still account for approximately 70 percent of rural household income in Asia, and about 60 percent in Africa. In particular, there are very few people in East Asia and sub-Saharan Africa that work in non-agricultural jobs. Worldwide, agriculture employs 50 percent of the workforce.

However, earning a living from agriculture in many less-developed countries is not really earning a living. In the United States and Canada, one farmer can expect to produce enough to feed more than 100 people. But a farmer working in Russia can produce enough to feed only about five people. A farmer in a less-developed country might feed only one person or, at the most, two people.

FIGURE 14.8. Two very different agricultural landscapes. Top: dairy cows feeding on a farm in the Fraser Valley of British Columbia. Bottom: a woman milking a cow, and other cows drinking from a water trough, in northeastern India.

**Comparative Milk Production** It takes about 15 East Indian cows to produce the same amount of milk as is produced by one American or Canadian cow, and it takes about seven hectares of rice in the Philippines to produce the same amount as is produced on one hectare in the rice-growing areas of the United States. (Canada has no rice-growing areas.)

## Working in Tourism

Tourism as an economic activity is growing around the world. Approximately 200 million people, or about 8 percent of the world's workforce, had jobs in the tourism industry in 2004, and these numbers are rising. Careful and respectful tourism, especially ecotourism, can be a boon to indigenous communities. As noted in chapter 11, the Maasai in Africa are a prime example of an indigenous people who have been able to make tourism work for them.

FIGURE 14.9. Tourists and their guide riding on an elephant to view the ruins of Angkor Thom in Cambodia. This royal city was built in the 12th century.

However, the tourist trade can also harm peoples and places. In some cases, it works as a form of economic colonialism.

Tourism often "sells" certain images and experiences that are stereotypical and, therefore, harmful to the cultures they are representing. It is important that the less-developed countries and the people who live in them make sure that the "picture" presented of their own history, culture, and environment be accurate and be preserved and protected.

Companies headquartered in the more-developed world are in control of the tourist industry. For example, of the 10 largest hotel chains in the world, eight are American, one is British, and one is French.

 For more information about the status of work around the world go to <www.theworldtoday.ca> and follow "Links" to <www.ilo.org> (the International Labor Organization).

## Moving to Cities

Many people picture the rural lifestyle as idyllic, peaceful, and quiet. However, more and more of our global neighbours are moving to cities to find jobs and shelter. Today, half of our neighbours live in cities. By 2025, two-thirds of the world's population is expected to live in cities.

Rapid and unplanned urban growth stretches the resources of national and local governments. This is especially the case in the less-developed world, where city governments find it impossible to keep pace with such requirements as health, sanitation, water, transportation, and shelter. Unfortunately, it is too often the case that people who move from a rural setting to a city find themselves living in shanty towns with few opportunities. See chapter 18 for a fuller discussion of this topic.

The urban poor face many health hazards because of the pollution, lack of health care, and density of population that are characteristic of urban living, all of which facilitate the spread of disease. Mortality rates are therefore higher in urban areas than in rural areas.

Urbanization in the more-developed world has taken place slowly, over the course of several hundred years. This slow movement has allowed people to adjust without undue turmoil.

In the less-developed world, colonization introduced urbanization and new industrial technologies, which in turn caused indigenous peoples much turmoil because they were forced to absorb so many changes in such a short time. What took perhaps 500 years to accomplish in Europe took only about 50 years in parts of Africa. Most people do not adjust easily to such rapid changes.

Many indigenous peoples who were removed from their historic lands found themselves in areas unsuited to their traditional way of life, and many found themselves on the margins of the colonizing society, unable to stop urban encroachment and such new technologies as logging of forests and damming of rivers. However, urbanization and industrialization do not have to destroy indigenous cultures. What is needed is great care to ensure that any new technologies introduced are helpful and culturally appropriate.

FIGURE 14.10. Two images of cities in the less-developed world. Left: a part of the clustered residential landscape of Abidjan in the West African country of Ivory Coast. Right: the thick haze of toxic pollution, caused by smoke from nearby forest fires mixing with traffic emissions that sometimes envelops many of the large cities of Indonesia and Malaysia. Shown here is Kuala Lumpur in Malaysia. This air pollution is a major health hazard, and many residents wear masks when they venture outside. The fires are lit outside the cities to clear land for agricultural purposes.

1. Imagine going to the centre of a city and finding a comfortable place to sit, looking around and making mental notes: Where and how is energy being used? What forms of energy are being consumed, and what work is that energy doing? Notice the details of buildings, cars, buses, streetlights, and so on. Also notice the activities of the people around you. What kinds of occupations do these people have, and how do they use energy in their work?

2. After you have spent at least 20 minutes appreciating the role of energy in the life of this city, imagine what the scene you are viewing would look like if there were 10 percent less energy available. What substitutions would be necessary? What choices would people make? What work would not get done? Now imagine the scene with 25 percent less energy available; with 50 percent less; and with 75 percent less (see Richard Heinberg's book *The Party's Over*).

3. Now imagine this part of the city as it would have been before settlement. Access old maps and archival photos, if possible, and your imagination. Do you know what was growing before the concrete was poured? How has life changed for the inhabitants of this geographical area over the past 100, 200, and 400 years?

## Improving Health and Well-Being

There is no better way to end this chapter, and this section, than by highlighting what needs to be done to improve health and well-being of people around the world. As noted in earlier chapters, especially in chapter 4, much is being done by individuals and by organizations. Perhaps the most ambitious statement of need and intent is contained in the Millennium Development Goals, developed by the United Nations with the hope that they can be achieved by 2015. To summarize:

1. Reduce by half the proportion of people living on less than a dollar a day. Reduce by half the proportion of people who suffer from hunger.

2. Ensure that all boys and girls complete a full course of primary schooling.

3. Eliminate gender disparity in primary and secondary education by 2015.

4. Reduce by two-thirds the mortality rate among children under five.

5. Reduce by three-quarters the maternal mortality ratio.

6. Halt and begin to reverse the spread of HIV/AIDS. Halt and begin to reverse the incidence of malaria and other major diseases.

7. Integrate the principles of sustainable development into the policies and programs at national levels. Reverse loss of environmental resources. Reduce by half the proportion of people without sustained access to safe drinking water. Achieve significant improvement in the lives of at least 100 million slum dwellers by 2020.

8. Develop a global partnership for development.

# ECOLOGICAL EFFECTS OF MODERN SOCIETIES

Canada's recent history and modern developments are closely tied to those of Europe. In some areas of Canada, a large portion of the population is of European descent, and the fact that our money still holds the image of British royalty speaks to our ongoing ties to a country many of us have never even visited.

Those of us who live in the more-developed world are by the nature of our birthplace offered opportunities and a starting point that seems like wealth beyond compare to those in the less-developed world. Imagine your life if digging a well and getting a hand pump on your street were considered a life-changing moment! Imagine your life if being able to go to school were a privilege reserved for only one child in your family. Imagine your life if you were forced to flee from your home because of war, drought, or government corruption.

Canada and other more-developed countries are not perfect: life is not always easy, our governments do not always act with integrity, and people do not always enjoy long and healthy lives. But we expect these things, and we wonder what is wrong when they do not happen. In many cases, we have designed and built machines that have taken over our mundane, repetitive, and back-breaking chores; from washing dishes to collecting garbage, we have ways of making physical demands less taxing.

However, in terms of the environment, sometimes we are victims of our own success. We have learned how to drain wetlands and create some prime agricultural or urban landscapes, but this has done damage to the water in nearby rivers and lakes. We have learned to harness the energy of coal, oil, and natural gas to power many of our activities, but this has damaged our atmosphere.

Canadians use natural resources and non-renewable energy sources with abandon. Few countries can "out-consume" us; we use more than twice the energy of the average Dutch person, four times that of the average Brazilian, and approximately 18 times that of the average Bangladeshi. Only the United States and the United Arab Emirates consume more than we do. Should we really be so wasteful?

In this section, we will explore some of the cities and the geography of Europe and the Americas, their history, the urbanization of these continents, the resulting effects on environments, and what we can do to reduce the effect we have on the physical world around us. Throughout this section, we will look at why some of these countries have developed into the most powerful in the world, and we will investigate how we can be more aware of our global neighbours by cutting our own consumption and sharing the planet.

"Every day you may make progress. Every step may be fruitful. Yet there will stretch out before you an ever-lengthening, ever-ascending, ever-improving path. You know you will never get to the end of the journey. But this, so far from discouraging, only adds to the joy and glory of the climb" (Sir Winston Churchill, 1874–1965, English politician).

"We shall never understand the natural environment until we see it as a living organism. Land can be healthy or sick, fertile or barren, rich or poor, lovingly nurtured or bled white. Our present attitudes and laws governing the ownership and use of land represent an abuse of the concept of private property. . . . Today you can murder land for private profit. You can leave the corpse for all to see and nobody calls the cops" (Paul Brooks, *The Pursuit of Wilderness* [Boston: Houghton Mifflin], 1971).

# PEOPLES AND PLACES OF EUROPE

**15**

## Guiding Questions

1. What are some of the distinguishing characteristics of the geography of Europe?

2. Why are the countries of Europe among the most developed and most powerful in the world?

In this chapter, we will take you on a whirlwind trip around Europe. Watch for excerpts from a travel journal and postcards home to get a young person's perspective about some of the peoples and places of Europe.

> It seems that just about every plane that goes to Europe from western Canada stops in Toronto. Here I am, stuck in the airport, plane delayed for three hours! Why do all airports have the same uninteresting stores? And how can they get away with charging so much for a chocolate bar?

**continental** Climate that occurs in high- and mid-latitude areas that are remote from oceans and, therefore, lack the moderating influence of the oceans on air temperature. Characterized by a large annual temperature range and also a large daily temperature range. This is sometimes called the *continental effect*, or *continentality*.

## Introducing Europe

All of Europe is part of the more-developed world. The history of much of Canada and of many other places is connected to Europe because of the European expansion and colonization that began in the 15th century.

Geographically, Europe is a western extension of Asia. It is a collection of islands, peninsulas, mountains, fertile plains, rivers, lakes, and seas. The mountainous Scandinavian peninsula is in the north. Several mountain chains, including the Pyrenees, the Alps, the Carpathians, the Balkans, and the Caucasus are located farther south. The central European lowlands—comprising plains, steppes, forests, lakes, and tundra—make up much of the land area, from France to the Urals. Much of the lowland is fertile and well-suited to agriculture. Some of the major river systems in Europe include the Loire, Rhine, Danube, Don, and Volga.

Europe's climate varies from Mediterranean (much like southern California) to polar (much like Nunavut). The Mediterranean region (in the south) is warm and dry. The west and northwest are mild and quite humid because of the moderating influence of prevailing westerly winds, a lot like coastal British Columbia. In central and eastern Europe, the climate is more **continental**, with hotter summers and colder winters, like the Canadian prairies. The northeast is tundra and subarctic, similar to the Canadian north.

FIGURE 15.1. This satellite image of Europe shows the true colours of the continent as seen from space. White areas are either glaciers in mountain regions or are ice sheets. Dark green areas are either agricultural crops or forest. Light green and brown areas are either agricultural crops or drier grasslands and plains. Lightest browns and yellow areas are deserts. Black or dark blue areas are oceans.

## Europe's Regions

In Europe, geography and history combine to form many different countries. Although their histories are intertwined through wars, occupations, and population movements, most countries in Europe retain long-standing cultural traditions, including languages. This is possibly because of the early Roman influence (from the 1st to the 5th centuries CE): when the Romans conquered a region, they did not evict the inhabitants or force them to stop using their own language or change their way of life, they just absorbed them into the greater Roman Empire. This may have this led to a general attitude of tolerance toward other cultures and language use in Europe.

Most of Europe is **multicultural**—that is, it is home to immigrants from other parts of the world, including the Caribbean, Africa, and parts of Asia.

> We'll be landing in London in 20 minutes. I can't believe I'm in Europe! Finally boarded this plane yesterday at 6:45 p.m. (or, to use the 24-hour clock like they do at airports, 18:45). I talked to the woman sitting beside me. She's visiting her son, who lives in Bath, England. She told me Bath is named for its "baths" that are fed by 3 natural hot springs. When the Romans invaded Britain almost 2 000 years ago, they built temples and bathing complexes there. Maybe Aunt Margaret will take me.

There are many different ways to divide Europe into distinct regions. The way we do it for this chapter considers both political and geographical boundaries. We can travel to these regions by bike, train, car, bus, boat, plane, or foot.

**Statistics** It's interesting to note that all of Europe is about 12 million km² and Canada is 10 million km².

## Dividing Europe

*The British Isles*
Two countries: United Kingdom (includes England, Wales, Scotland, Northern Ireland), and Ireland.

*Scandinavia*
Five countries: Iceland, Norway, Sweden, Finland, and Denmark.

*Central Europe*
Eight countries: Germany, Switzerland, Liechtenstein, Austria, Poland, the Czech Republic, Slovakia, and Hungary.

*Eastern Europe*
Seven countries: Estonia, Latvia, Lithuania, Belarus, Ukraine, Moldova, and the European portion of Russia.

*Southeast Europe*
Eleven countries: Slovenia, Croatia, Bosnia-Herzegovina, Serbia and Montenegro (Yugoslavia), Albania, Macedonia, Romania, Bulgaria, Greece, Cyprus, and the European part of Turkey.

*Southern Europe*
Seven countries: Portugal, Spain, Andorra, Italy, Malta, San Marino, and Vatican City.

*Western Europe*
Five countries: France, Belgium, the Netherlands, Luxembourg, and Monaco.

**multicultural** A term with three meanings. First, it refers to countries that contain more than one cultural group. Second, it refers to the idea that all cultures are equal. Third, in some countries, including Canada, it describes policies and practices that encourage minority groups to retain traditional cultural values.

# The Countries and Regions of Europe

**FIGURE 15.2. This map shows one popular way of dividing Europe into geographic regions.**

**FIGURE 15.3. Clockwise from top left: St. Basil's Cathedral, which was built in Moscow in the 16th century; the picturesque Amalfi coast of southern Italy; Hvar Island off the Adriatic coast, Croatia; Swiss Alpine landscape; lavender fields and a Cistercian abbey in Provence, southern France; sheep grazing on moorland in southwestern England; fjord landscape on the Norwegian coast.**

## The British Isles: Visiting the United Kingdom

England is primarily lowland, with low rolling hills in the south and east. There is more mountainous terrain in the northwest, though there are no peaks over 1 000 metres above sea level. There are many rivers, including the Thames, which is the major river. Wales is mostly mountainous, and Scotland has highlands in the north and west, lowlands in the south and east, and many deep lakes and bays (lochs and firths). Northern Ireland is mostly hilly and has the United Kingdom's largest freshwater lake, Lough Neagh (usually pronounced "Lock Nay" by English-speakers).

The United Kingdom has been occupied by humans for thousands of years, and sites like Stonehenge, built about 3000 BCE, are evidence of this early settlement. In 1707, England, Scotland, and Wales combined to form the Kingdom of Great Britain. By 1801,

### The United Kingdom

FIGURE 15.4. Separated from mainland Europe by the North Sea and the English Channel, the United Kingdom was often seen as different from the rest of Europe. Today, however, past differences are fewer. Outside of the cities, much of the land is used for agricultural purposes.

Ireland joined, thereby forming the United Kingdom of Great Britain and Ireland. This was an unpopular decision in Ireland, and in 1921 part of Ireland broke away to form a separate country, which was called the Irish Free State (now known as the Republic of Ireland). Northern Ireland remained within the United Kingdom. In the 19th century, the British Empire controlled about a quarter of the world, but, by the second half of the 20th century, most of the colonies had achieved independence, and the empire no longer existed.

## FAST FACTS
### about the United Kingdom

Area: 244 755 km²
(about 40 percent of the size of Manitoba)
Population: 60.1 million
Crude birth rate: 12 per 1 000
Crude death rate: 10 per 1 000
Rate of natural increase: 0.2 percent
Capital city: London
Life expectancy: 78 years
Population density: 244 people per km²
Language: English (also Welsh and Gaelic)
Religion: Christianity (Protestant, Catholic), Islam, Hinduism
Urbanization: 89 percent urban
Government: constitutional monarchy
Literacy rate: 99 percent
Gross national income per capita: US$31 460

FIGURE 15.5. The "jack" in the Union Jack is a "jack" only when it's on a ship. The more appropriate term is *Union Flag* when it's on a pole. Union refers to the several parts of the United Kingdom. It is quite a complicated flag, consisting of three crosses: the cross of St. George, patron saint of England, which is a red cross on a white background; the cross of St. Andrew, patron saint of Scotland, which is a diagonal white cross on a blue background; and the cross of St. Patrick, patron saint of Ireland, which is a diagonal red cross on a white background. The Welsh dragon does not appear on the Union Jack because Wales was united with England when the first Union Flag was created in 1606.

Aunt Margaret is really nice. We went to Kings Cross Station, and I got a sign with Platform 9 3/4 on it. But there is way more to London than Harry Potter. The Tower of London was built in 1100 CE! I've never seen a building that old! And Buckingham Palace is unbelievable. I really liked the many museums and art galleries, and I couldn't believe I was at the Globe Theatre. It's not Shakespeare's original theatre, but they've remade it to look exactly like it did in his day. Dad will be so happy I saw The Tempest there; that's his favourite play. I can't believe I've been almost a week in London . . . tomorrow we start to the coast. I'm looking forward to getting out of the city, actually. There are over seven million people in just the main part of London, and that doesn't include the suburbs, which make it, about, 13 million. That's a lot of people! It's crowded and busy all the time, and I feel okay on the underground now. I wonder if I'm picking up a British accent from Aunt Margaret . . .

## London

London is the capital city of the United Kingdom and is one of the major cities of the world. Continuously occupied since at least 40 CE, the initial settlement was located along the Thames River. The city grew rapidly during the Industrial Revolution, and many bridges were built across the river during this time. Much of the gently rolling land of the flood plain, which is prime agricultural land, has now been converted to urban use.

 Plan your own trip to London. In these sites you will find ideas for planning your trip. Visit <www.theworldtoday.ca> and follow "Links" to <www.historicroyalpalaces.org>, <www.museumoflondon.org.uk/>, and <http://na.visitlondon.com/index.html>. For all the UK, try <www.visitbritain.com>.

FIGURE 15.6. Tower Bridge across the River Thames in London was completed in 1894. The middle of the bridge can be raised to permit large vessels to pass underneath.

POST CARD

Hi Keri! First thing I did after I landed was find my aunt. Second thing? Buy this postcard for you. Tomorrow we're going to Kings Cross Station (of course) and I want to buy some kind of authentic Harry Potter souvenir.

Love, Me

P.S. I'm trying to talk my aunt into going to Bath, which is a city about 150 km west of London. I don't think we're going to have time, though. Our plans are to travel east, not west.

## Scandinavia: Visiting Denmark

Denmark comprises the peninsula of Jutland and 405 islands, of which 82 are inhabited. Many of the islands are connected by bridges. The largest, Zealand, is home to Copenhagen, Denmark's capital city. Denmark is the farthest south and most temperate of the Scandinavian countries, is mostly flat, and it has mild winters and cool summers.

Denmark used to be associated with the fierce Vikings. It remained neutral during the First World War and attempted to remain neutral during the Second World War, but Germany invaded it in 1940, and the country was occupied for the duration of the war.

**Denmark**

FIGURE 15.7. Denmark is a small country. About 65 percent of the land is farmland that produces mainly dairy products.

From London we travelled to a port city called Harwich. It's pretty close to London. We are now on a ferry to Esbjerg in Denmark. The ferry is amazing. The sea is beautiful. There's a strong breeze and it smells like salt. I was just reading the tour brochure about Copenhagen. They have free bikes! You pay a deposit like we do at home for a grocery cart, and the wheels have smiley faces on them.

## FAST FACTS
### about Denmark

Area: 43 094 km² (less than 7 percent of the size of Manitoba)

Population: 5.4 million

Crude birth rate: 12 per 1 000

Crude death rate: 10 per 1 000

Rate of natural increase: 0.2 percent

Capital city: Copenhagen

Life expectancy: 77 years

Population density: 125 people per km²

Language: Danish (also Faroese and Greenlandic)

Religion: Christianity (Lutheran)

Urbanization: 72 percent urban

Government: constitutional monarchy

Literacy rate: 100 percent

Gross national income per capita: US$31 550

FIGURE 15.8. The famous Little Mermaid statue in Copenhagen Harbour is a national symbol.

## Copenhagen

Copenhagen is recognized as one of the world's most pedestrian-friendly cities. Pioneering planning has gradually made the city more suited to walking and biking than to automobile travel. Streets have been converted into pedestrian walkways and parking lots into public squares.

More than 7 000 residents live in the centre of the city. Because they live and work in the area that they live in, they do not need cars. Many people bike to work, which is made easy because of the availability of free rental bikes and safe, designated bike lanes.

The buildings in Copenhagen are built low to reduce wind tunnelling and to allow breezes to pass over the buildings, which makes the city seem milder in winter. Many historic buildings have been preserved, and stoops, awnings, and doorways are designed to provide places for people to stop and talk.

### POST CARD

Hi Mom and Dad! We're in Copenhagen, and I just saw the little mermaid statue. Poor little mermaid! Did you know that people keep trying to cut her up? She's lost her head twice, her arm once, has had red paint thrown on her, and she was blown off her rock by dynamite once. And she really is little! Just over 1 metre high. Copenhagen is amazing, and Denmark is beautiful. The sea is everywhere. I can't keep it all straight—the Baltic Sea, the North Sea, harbours, rivers. It's like one big fishing village. After a bit more touring around Denmark, we're going to take the train down to Germany, stop in Hamburg, and go on to Berlin. Miss you!

Me

P.S. Aunt Margaret is as nice as you said she would be.

 Plan your own visit to Denmark or another Scandinavian country using this official tourism site. Visit <www.theworldtoday.ca> and follow "Links" to <www.visitdenmark.com>.

## Central Europe: Visiting Germany

Much of northern Germany, located close to the North Sea and the Baltic Sea, is lowland. Inland, the land begins to slope higher in altitude, reaching its highest point at the Alps in the south. Because of the sea, the climate is temperate in the northwest and north, with rain all year round, mild winters, and cool summers. In the east, the climate is more continental, like that of our prairies, where winters are very cold for long periods and summers are very warm. In the centre and the south, there is a transitional climate that may be predominantly oceanic or continental, depending on the proximity to the sea. The River Rhine is one of the great transportation routes in the world, linking important industrial areas, such as the Ruhr area north of Cologne, with the North Sea.

## FAST FACTS
### about Germany

Area: 357 022 km² (about 55 percent of the size of Manitoba)

Population: 82.5 million

Crude birth rate: 9 per 1 000

Crude death rate: 10 per 1 000

Rate of natural increase: -0.1 percent

Capital city: Berlin

Life expectancy: 79 years

Population density: 231 people per km²

Language: German

Religion: Christianity (Protestant, Catholic)

Urbanization: 88 percent urban

Government: federal republic

Literacy rate: 99 percent

Gross national income per capita: US$27 950

### Germany

FIGURE 15.9. Germany stretches from the North Sea and Baltic Sea in the north to the Alps in the south. It has more people than any other European country and is an important industrial and agricultural country.

### Berlin

Berlin became Germany's capital in 1871, and it quickly rose to prominence as an industrial and commercial centre. Its canal system and railways made it a transportation hub. Berlin survived war and depression and remained a European cultural centre right up until the Second World War. When 70 percent of Berlin was destroyed in Allied bombing raids, plans were made to rebuild the city.

After the war, the Soviets, who occupied East Berlin, further demolished beautiful historic buildings, including the Berlin City Palace, which was built in 1443 and had survived the war.

The Berlin Wall was built in 1961 to prevent people from communist East Germany escaping into democratic West Germany. The building of the wall almost resulted in another war, but West Germans were allowed to visit their East-German relatives on the other side of the wall. After the collapse of the Soviet Union in 1991, the wall came down, though over a kilometre remains as a tourist attraction and outdoor art exhibit.

 Find out more about and discover the attractions of Germany. Visit <www.theworldtoday.com> and follow "Links": <www.wikipedia.org/wiki/Ludwig_II_of_Bavaria> and <www.germany-tourism.de>.

FIGURE 15.10. The Brandenburg Gate is a well-known landmark in Berlin. Designed to represent peace, it was constructed in the late-18th century.

Somehow, our being in Germany makes the Second World War seem a lot more real. We visited a concentration camp and went to a memorial for the Holocaust. What a terrible time that must have been. Later, in Berlin, we walked along streets that used to hold watchtowers when Germany was two separate countries from 1945 until 1990 (East Germany and West Germany). East German guards were in the watchtowers and shot anyone they saw trying to escape into West Germany. Being here makes it all seem so recent. On a happier note, I loved the Saturday markets, and the castles are incredible, especially those built for Mad King Ludwig II. I can't write about it all—there's too much stuff, but I'll certainly look him up when I get home! A fairy-tale castle at Neuschwanstein in Bavaria (southern Germany), including lovers, intrigue, and an unsolved mystery surrounding his death. It doesn't get much better than that!

POST CARD

Hi Keri! We're in Berlin—the capital city of Germany. Next to London, it's got more people living in it than any other city in Europe. Over three million people. I don't know why I always imagined Paris was as big as London!

My aunt and I have done most of the touristy things. We've gone to several art gallerys and museums. There are hundreds of art gallerys here and lots of museums. I'm having a hard time keeping track of everything we've seen! We're on our way to the zoo. The brochure says this has a greater variety of animal species than any other zoo in the world. I'll take lots of pictures!

Tomorrow we're taking a boat trip to Potsdam, a city about 25 km from Berlin. It's famous for its castles, especially one called Sanssouci. It was built in the mid-18th century as the summer palace of Frederick the Great of Prussia.

Love, Me

## Eastern Europe: Visiting Ukraine

Ukraine consists of gently rolling, fertile plains (like our prairies, but called *steppes*) and plateaus, with many rivers that flow south to the Black Sea and the Sea of Azov. The Danube delta is on the southeastern border, and the only mountains are the Carpathians, which are located in the west; there are parts of the Crimean peninsula, however, that are quite hilly. Along the Black Sea coast, the climate is temperate, almost Mediterranean; the winters are mild and summers warm. The inland region has a more continental climate; the summers are hot and the winters cold. The west and north get a lot of rainfall, while the east and southeast are drier.

Ukraine has spent much of its history in political turmoil. It was an important centre for eastern Slavic culture until the 15th century. Since then, it has been divided among many different powers over hundreds of years: Russia, Poland, Lithuania, and the Turkish Empire. After the Russian Revolution in 1917, Ukraine enjoyed a brief period of independence that ended when it was absorbed into the communist rule of the Soviet Union. When the Soviet Union fell in 1991, Ukraine became independent once more and has held democratic elections since then.

**Ukraine**

FIGURE 15.11. Ukraine is the largest country in Europe. Most of the country occupies part of the extensive plains that stretch from the Baltic Sea to the Black Sea.

## FAST FACTS
### about Ukraine

Area: 603 700 km² (about 93 percent of the size of Manitoba)

Population: 47.1 million

Crude birth rate: 9 per 1 000

Crude death rate: 16 per 1 000

Rate of natural increase: -0.7 percent

Capital city: Kiev

Life expectancy: 68 years

Population density: 79 people per km²

Language: Ukrainian, Russian

Religion: Christianity (Ukrainian Orthodox)

Urbanization: 68 percent urban

Government: republic

Literacy rate: 99 percent

Gross national income per capita: US$6 250

### Kiev

Kiev, the capital of Ukraine, is another city founded on the banks of a river: the Dnieper. It officially became a city in the 5th century, though archaeological digs show that there were inhabitants there perhaps 20 000 years ago. Kiev is one of the oldest cities in the region and continues to be one of the most important. It is a very green city; many trees and gardens are found within the city limits. Today, the population of Kiev is about three million.

FIGURE 15.12. The interior of St. Sophia Cathedral in Kiev. Constructed in the 11th century, the cathedral is widely regarded as a masterpiece of monumental art and is elaborately decorated with frescoes (wall paintings; the paint is applied to wet plaster and the colour sets as the plaster dries).

 Plan your own trip to Kiev. Visit <www.theworldtoday.ca> and follow "Links" to <www.kiev.info/culture/index.htm> or <www.countriesandcities.com/countries/ua/>.

I'm glad we flew from Berlin to Kiev. It would have been a long train ride—over 1 200 kilometres—and Aunt Margaret said she didn't know what the border crossings or roads would be like. We're going to do a seven-day tour of Kiev. That should be okay, but I think it's usually old people who go on those sorts of things. Lots of interesting stuff to see, at any rate. What keeps surprising me is how old all the buildings are here in Europe. People in Canada think my house is old, and it's just over 100 years! Buildings here aren't really old unless they're 300 or 400 years old, but there are even some that are almost 1 000 years old. Makes me feel strange to look at them. The people who built them—would they have been really different from me, or the same? Did they worry about friends, did they fight with their parents, and did they go places with their relatives? Who knows? Imagine— they wouldn't have even known that North America existed, and they had never used cotton, and they thought the world was flat.

POST CARD

Hi Everybody! Hope you're doing okay. I heard that the weather there has been bad.

Tomorrow we start on our tour of Kiev. Aunt Margaret says she doesn't know the first thing about Ukrainian or Russian history, so she thought a tour would be best. So far it looks amazing. There are tons of chestnut trees! And so many old buildings—you wouldn't believe it. We're going to a circus and the zoo, too! You can look at our tour online if you go to www.ukrainianexpress.com. It's the seven-day tour! I miss you!

Love, Me

## Southeast Europe: Visiting Greece

Greece is often called the cradle of Western civilization and the birthplace of democracy. Few places around the world have so much visible human history. Surrounded by the Mediterranean and Aegean seas, Greece's climate has mild, rainy winters and hot, dry summers. Around 80 percent of Greece is mountainous or hilly, and its few rivers are not major transportation routes. Much of the land is dry and rocky, though western Greece has lakes and wetlands. The Peloponnesus Peninsula is linked to the mainland by the Isthmus of Corinth. Greece has thousands of islands. Its forests are home to some of the last brown bears in Europe.

For many years, small Greek cities functioned as city-states, each with its own small kingdom. The city-states united in the 5th century BCE when the Delian League was formed. Greek culture was a primary influence when the Roman Empire was built, and, indeed, it affected much of Europe. Greek civilization has influenced our language, politics, education, philosophy, art, and architecture. Some famous historic Greeks include Herodotus (geographer and historian), Hippocrates (the father of modern medicine), Alexander the Great (who conquered much of western Asia and also Egypt in north Africa), Socrates, and Plato (famous Greek philosophers whose teachings still affect western thinking). And, of course, don't forget Eratosthenes (mentioned in the introduction of this book).

 Herodotus (484–ca. 425 BCE) was probably the first scholar to argue that all history must be treated geographically and that all geography must be treated historically. Do you agree? Why or why not? Discuss.

### Greece

FIGURE 15.13. Much of Greece is mountainous and rocky, and most of the people live in coastal locations or close to rivers. The Greek islands make up about 20 percent of the area of the country.

- —— International boundary
- —— River
- ● Capital city
- ○ Other major city

## FAST FACTS
### about Greece

Area: 131 957 km² (about 20 percent of the size of Manitoba)

Population: 11.1 million

Crude birth rate: 9 per 1 000

Crude death rate: 10 per 1 000

Rate of natural increase: -0.1 percent

Capital city: Athens

Life expectancy: 79 years

Population density: 83 people per km²

Language: Greek

Religion: Christianity (Greek Orthodox)

Urbanization: 60 percent urban

Government: parliamentary republic

Literacy rate: 98 percent

Gross national income per capita: US$22 000

## Athens

Athens, the capital of Greece, has a population of just over 700 000; however, when the surrounding area is included, the population numbers closer to four million. Initially, at the time of first settlement, Athens was located on the summit of the Acropolis and protected on all sides but the west by steep slopes. It was the artistic and cultural centre of the Western world in 500 BCE. Wars and other rivalries caused its decline, however. It was chosen as the capital of modern Greece in the 19th century, mostly for historic and sentimental reasons, as it was no longer a major centre. It then grew rapidly and experienced many of the problems that come along with rapid urbanization. The air quality declined, and pollution began to damage the ancient buildings. Steps have now been taken to remedy Athens's environmental challenges, but there is much still to be done.

Plan your own trip to Greece. Visit < www.theworld today.ca > and follow "Links" to <www.cretetravel.com> or <www.athensguide.org>.

FIGURE 15.14. The marble columns of the Temple of Poseidon, south of Athens. The Temple was built in the 5th century BCE.

Great trip! We took the train to Odessa, and then we took a ferry across the Black Sea from Odessa to Istanbul. Istanbul is right at the tip of two continents! We spent a few days there and then took the train to Greece. Aunt Margaret wanted to rent a car in Greece so we could be in charge of our own schedule this time. So far, Greece has been fantastic—it's even older than the other cities we've visited. Greece is kind of overwhelming—one of the most amazing places I'll ever see. I love the islands and the small villages with the whitewashed houses. I was told that the white reflects the sunlight and helps keep the houses cool inside. And the water! It's so blue! Aunt Margaret made me eat some strange seafood. She said you couldn't be in Greece and not eat squid. It was okay, but I'm not used to that at all. We pretty much just eat pickerel at home. Home. I think I'm a little homesick today.

POST CARD

Hi Keri. Greece is beautiful and lovely and dirty and ancient and amazing all in one. It's really overwhelming. I think the ancientness of it starts to get to you. I don't know how to explain it. I love it here.

Love, Me

## Southern Europe: Visiting Italy

Italy is shaped like a boot, with the Apennine mountain range running down the centre and joining the Alps in the northwest. The climate is Mediterranean, with dry, hot summers and mild, wet winters. Northern Italy comprises a large plain, watered by rivers running down from the Alps. It is the wealthiest part of the country, and home to the best farmland and the major industrial cities of Turin and Milan. Vatican City and San Marino are small sovereign states entirely surrounded by Italy. The two major cities in the south are Rome and Naples. At the tip of the "boot" lies Sicily, and further west is Sardinia; both of these islands are part of Italy. Another large island off the coast of Italy, Corsica (just north of Sardinia), is part of France.

FIGURE 15.15. Italy is a large peninsula in the Mediterranean Sea. The shape of the country is often described as being like a boot that is kicking the island of Sicily into the sea. The two large islands of Sicily and Sardinia are part of Italy.

## FAST FACTS
### about Italy

Area: 301 318 km² (almost half the size of Manitoba)

Population: 58.7 million

Crude birth rate: 9 per 1 000

Crude death rate: 10 per 1 000

Rate of natural increase: -0.1 percent

Capital city: Rome

Life expectancy: 80 years

Population density: 192 people per km²

Language: Italian (also German, French, Slovene)

Religion: Christianity (Catholic)

Urbanization: 90 percent urban

Government: republic

Literacy rate: 99 percent

Gross national income per capita: US$27 860

Like Greece, Italy has a long history and has greatly influenced the cultural and social development of the modern Mediterranean area. Italy was particularly influential during the Roman Empire and, later, the Holy Roman Empire, which was a political grouping of much of Central Europe from about 800 CE until about 1800. Italy became a country in 1861, when King Victor Emmanuel II united the many small states in the area.

## Rome

Rome is built on seven hills, and there are fertile fields and forests close to the city. Rome was first developed along the banks of the Tiber River. There are many ancient buildings, especially in the city centre. After the unification of Italy in 1871, Rome became the capital, and rapid growth followed. Today the population is almost three million. Many people live on the outskirts of Rome, and up to one million people commute into Rome for work each day. This causes air pollution, which can damage the historic architecture. The sprawl of the city has used up some of Italy's prime agricultural land.

 Plan your own trip to Italy. Visit <www.theworldtoday.ca> and follow "Links" to <www.forbeginners.info/rome>, <www.italiantourism.com/>, and <www.underome.com>.

FIGURE 15.16. The ruins of the Colosseum in Rome are a powerful symbol of the Roman Empire. Built in the 1st century CE, it was the most impressive of all Roman buildings, and the remaining structure is an impressive sight even today. It was here that the Romans killed thousands of people (some of whom they saw as criminals, while others were professional fighters, or gladiators) and large numbers of animals.

It seems like if you want to get anywhere in Europe, you better take a ferry or fly. The roads are so busy, and everyone drives too fast. The flight from Athens to Rome took just over an hour, and Aunt Margaret said that it was cheap. She sure doesn't seem to worry about money too much! I can't imagine taking this trip with my whole family—we'd be paying for years. I feel really lucky that Aunt Margaret asked me to travel with her this summer. It's too bad we had to choose between Rome and Venice. I really wanted to see both, but this way, we're going to take the train all the way along the coast from Rome to Monaco and Nice, and then to Paris. I can't wait to see the Eiffel Tower!

**San Marino** Probably the oldest country you've never heard of, San Marino is located entirely within Italy and was declared an independent nation in 301 CE. Its population is just under 30 000, and all its people live in an area of 61 square kilometres. If you're into Formula One car racing, you're probably aware that the San Marino Grand Prix is named after the country of San Marino. But the race doesn't happen there; it takes place about 100 kilometres to the northwest.

POST CARD

Mmmm . . . gelato. You can find gelato everywhere here! Aunt Margaret prefers the iced cappuccinos, but I can't get enough of the gelato. So many flavours, so little time! It almost makes me miss Slurpees a little less. One of my favourite tours was of the Roman underground— catacombs, tunnels, ancient aqueducts. But what's with the dogs? There are stray cats and dogs everywhere! They're not getting my gelato!!

Love, Me

## Western Europe: Visiting France

France is shaped like an irregular hexagon, with mountains or seas on five of the six sides: in the south, the Mediterranean Sea and the Pyrenees mountains form two of the sides; in the west, there is the Atlantic Ocean (the Bay of Biscay); in the north is the English Channel; and in the east are a series of mountain ranges, including the Alps, Jura, and Vosges. Only the sixth side is low-lying land; this is the northeast, where France borders with Belgium and Luxembourg. Within France there are rolling hills, gentle sloping river valleys, and plains in the north and west. The south-central area is the mountainous Massif Central.

The climate of most of France is temperate, with cool winters and mild summers, though the south of France is Mediterranean with hot and dry summers, and mild winters. Agriculture is very important to the French economy, more so than to the economies of most of the other of the more-developed countries. The most important crops are grapes (for wine) and wheat. France is also a leading industrial and trading country.

France has been occupied by humans for thousands of years. About 10 000 years ago, France was a Celtic territory known as Gaul. The name *France* comes from the Latin word *Francia*, which means "country of the Franks." The Franks were of Germanic origin, and they conquered the area in about 400 CE, when the western Roman Empire was falling. France became a separate country in the 9th century.

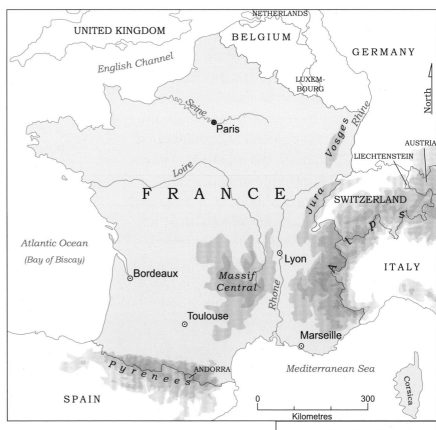

**France**

**FIGURE 15.17. France is the second-largest country in Europe (after Ukraine). Much of the land area is hilly or mountainous, but France is also an important industrial and agricultural country.**

— International boundary
— River
● Capital city
○ Other major city

## FAST FACTS
### about France

Area: 551 500 km² (about 85 percent of the size of Manitoba)

Population: 60.7 million

Crude birth rate: 13 per 1 000

Crude death rate: 8 per 1 000

Rate of natural increase: 0.5 percent

Capital city: Paris

Life expectancy: 80 years

Population density: 109 people per km²

Language: French

Religion: Christianity (Catholic)

Urbanization: 76 percent urban

Government: republic

Literacy rate: 99 percent

Gross national income per capita: US$29 320

## Paris

Paris was founded about 200 BCE by the Parisii (a Celtic tribe) as a fishing village on an island in the River Seine. The location was selected for defensive reasons; it is hard to sneak up on someone who is on an island. You can still visit mediaeval buildings on the Ile de la Cité. The metropolitan population of Paris is over 11 million, and, of Western cities, only Manhattan is more densely populated. The high population density puts intense pressure on the river, and by 1960 the Seine was heavily polluted. Initiatives to restore the Seine and other rivers have been only somewhat successful in spite of the restoration of wetlands, better farming practices, and sewer upgrades.

FIGURE 15.18. The Eiffel Tower was built for the Paris International Exhibition of 1889, which commemorated the centenary of the French Revolution. The tower is named after its designer, Gustave Eiffel. It is 300 m high and was the tallest building in the world until 1931, when the Empire State Building in New York City was completed.

 Plan your own trip to France. Visit <www.theworldtoday.ca> and follow "Links" to <www.culture.gouv.fr/culture/arcnat/lascaux/en/ www.fodors.com/> and <www.v1.paris.fr/en/>.

What an amazing trip. Of course we stopped for a look at the leaning tower when we went through Pisa, and we stopped in Genoa, where Columbus was born. Monaco and Nice were amazing. Mostly we just lay around on the beaches. After all that ancient stuff and sightseeing, I was ready to work on my tan and read a book. We saw part of the Loire Valley on the train to Paris—purposely didn't take the high-speed train and travelled in the daytime so we could see the sights. Was that ever beautiful. Everything is so green, and there are fields of lavender and vineyards, and I never imagined anything like it. We stopped at a lavender farm—friends of Aunt Margaret own it—so we stayed in a real French farmhouse. I need to work on my French! Good thing Aunt Margaret speaks it. Rome to Paris is only about 1 000 km, but we took eight days to do it because we stopped at so many places.

## POST CARD

Mom and Dad: Yum, roasted chestnuts at Montmartre. What a fun place—artists everywhere—Aunt Margaret and I got our portrait painted together so we'd always remember our time in Europe. Sacre Coeur is built on the highest hill in Paris and is such an amazing place. If you climb to the top (Montmartre,) you get the most amazing view of Paris. And the stone they used to make it, somehow, on humid days, it soaks up the moisture in the air and it looks like it glows. It's so beautiful. I think it's one of the most beautiful buildings of the whole trip. Oh, but there have been so many! I can't believe I'll be home in 2 days. On the one hand, I can't wait. On the other, everything will seem so ordinary!

Love, Me

# PEOPLES AND PLACES OF THE AMERICAS

16

## Guiding Questions

1. What are some of the distinguishing characteristics of the geography of the Americas?

2. Why are the countries of North America among the most developed and most powerful in the world, whereas the countries of Central and South America are less developed?

We go on another whirlwind trip in this chapter. This time, it is around the Americas. Watch for excerpts from a travel journal and for postcards home to get a young English person's perspective about some of the peoples and places of the Americas.

## Introducing the Americas

The Americas have high mountains in the west and lower mountains in the east. The Western Cordillera is a continuous sequence of mountain ranges that run from northern Alaska, through British Columbia, and on to California. They continue through Central America and are called the Andes in South America. The Yaghan Indians (disussed in chapter 11) lived at the southern end of these mountains, in Tierra del Fuego. The lower, eastern mountains are called the Appalachians in North America and the Brazilian Highlands in South America.

West of the Western Cordillera in central North America are the fertile Great Plains. In the southern part of North America, these plains are desert-like, while in the north there are the forests, lakes, rocks, and rivers of the Canadian Shield. In the far north there is tundra. East of the plains and south of the Canadian Shield are central lowlands, an area of rivers and lakes, and an area of rolling hills that used to be forest but now is agricultural and urbanized. In South America, the largest area between the western and eastern mountains is the extensive Amazon River Basin.

Dad is a travel writer. As part of the research for his new book, he decided that he had to visit Canada, the United States, and some of the countries in Central and South America this summer. Lucky me—I'm going along with him. As I thought about the trip, I realized he must be mad—Canada alone is about the size of all of Europe! However, Dad says that we must visit what he laughingly calls the "colonies," and see what they're about. Mum won't come. She hates to leave her garden and doesn't like travel, but she wishes us well. I hope that Dad remembers to drive on the wrong side of the road!

## Satellite Image of North America

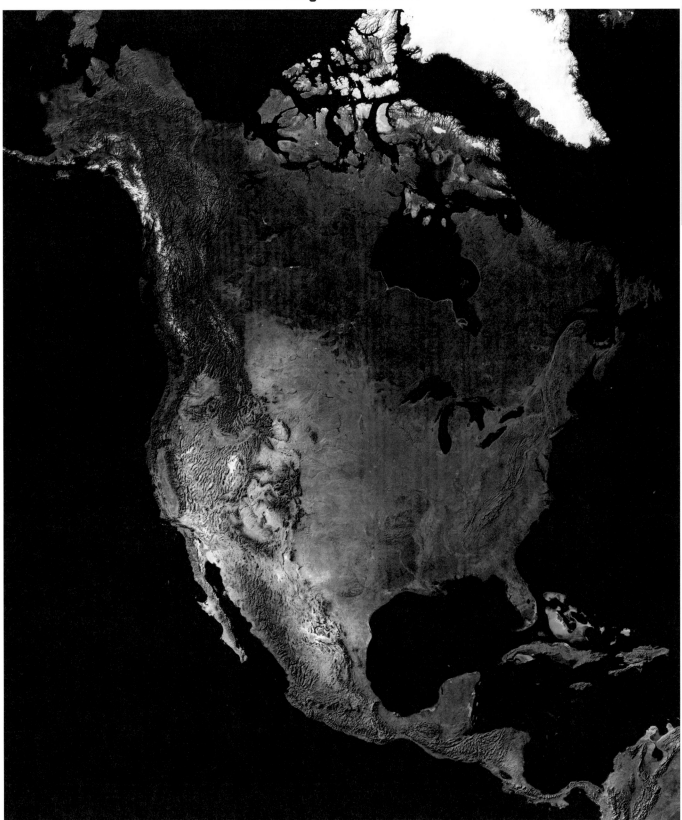

FIGURE 16.1. This satellite image of North America shows the true colours of the continent as seen from space. White areas are either glaciers in mountain regions or ice sheets. Dark green areas are either agricultural crops or forest. Light green and brown areas are either agricultural crops or drier grasslands and plains. Lightest brown and yellow areas are deserts. Black or dark blue areas are oceans; light blue or turquoise areas indicate very shallow water.

## Comparing Europe and the Americas

The trip from Europe to the Americas is one that has been made by millions of people since the first Europeans began to travel west searching for new ocean routes to Asia and other new lands. Of course, the land of the Americas was new only to them; indigenous peoples had been living in North, Central, and South America for thousands of years.

Different understandings of land ownership, intelligence, social norms, and cultural practices caused most Europeans to misunderstand the inhabitants of the Americas as backward and even sub-human.

The Americas developed in relative isolation from the rest of the world. Cultures developed here for thousands of years; languages and religions went unchallenged by other groups. Because of the huge ocean expanses separating the Americas from other parts of the world, there was little or no interaction with others. People in the Americas did not benefit from the advances in science and math and weaponry that took place in China and Europe. Their views of the world were tied to their religious beliefs, which were based on their understandings of the physical world.

The Americas had less suitable land to work with than Europe did, and there were no horses or oxen to use as working animals. South Americans used the llama and alpaca as pack animals, but these were unsuitable for ploughing. North Americans had no large animals suitable for domestication, so their agricultural practices were more dependent upon human labour than those of the Europeans. The key crops throughout most of North America were corn, beans, and squash. Some groups were mainly foragers, collecting their food from wild sources. In chapter 3, we noted that the Americas do not spread a great distance latitudinally (that is, east-west) and that this limited the spread of agricultural.

When the Europeans arrived, the clash between cultures was particularly destructive to the indigenous peoples. Indigenous peoples knew nothing about the European way of waging war; the Europeans played by a different set of rules and had different weaponry. Also critical was the fact that the peoples in the Americas had had no exposure to many of the diseases that Europeans inadvertently brought with them and to which Europeans had built up a natural resistance.

Europe and North America are similar to but different from each other. Both continental regions are parts of the more-developed world, although it is the United States that is a major political and economic force in the world today. One big difference between Europe and North America is that North America is made up of just two countries (Canada and the United States), whereas Europe includes more than 40 countries.

Central and South America are both part of the less-developed world and are both divided into many countries. They share the problem of low economic development, but both regions might be described today as awakening giants.

 Talk about some of the places where you have travelled within North America. What were they like? Did you find the people there very different in outlook, or were they quite similar to you? Name three other places you would like to go in the Americas, and say why you want to go there.

## Satellite Image of South America

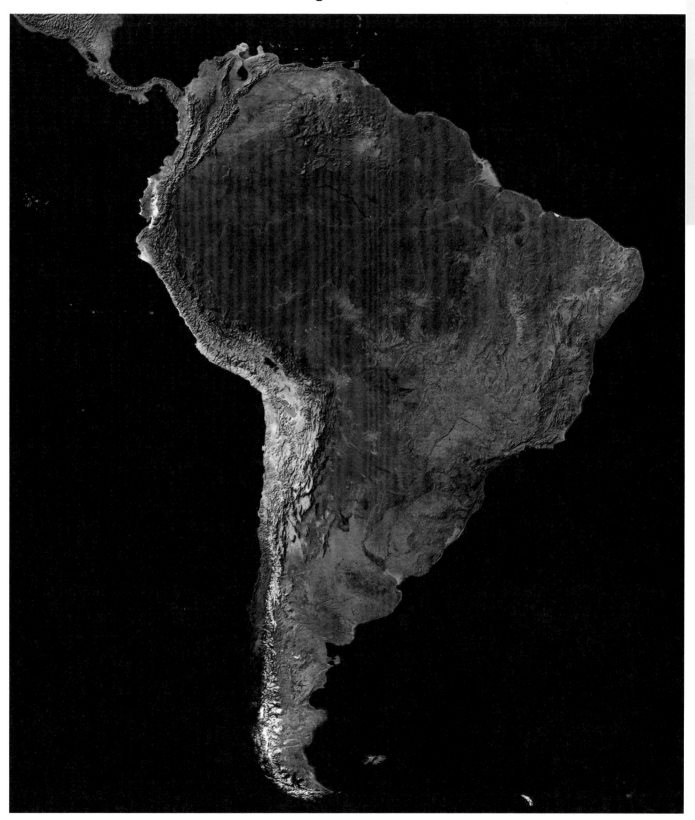

FIGURE 16.2. This satellite image of South America shows the true colours of the continent as seen from space. White areas are either glaciers in mountain regions or ice sheets. Dark green areas are either agricultural crops or forest. Light green and brown areas are either agricultural crops or drier grasslands and plains. Lightest browns and yellows are deserts. Black or dark blue areas are oceans. Light blue or turquoise areas indicate very shallow water.

## Canada

Canada is the second largest country in the world in terms of area and has more coastline than any other country in the world; its population, though, is quite small. Most of its people live in a narrow strip along the Canada-United States border, which is also known as the *49th parallel* in western Canada. Areas in the north are almost uninhabited, and there are thousands of square kilometres that have no road access.

A look around your school will probably tell you that Canada does not have a **homogenous** culture. Canadians come from many different countries and cultures. Canada celebrates this cultural diversity and makes multiculturalism a policy that recognizes Canada as a "cultural mosaic"; Canadians celebrate different places of birth, different languages, and different religious practices and beliefs. This is in contrast to the United States, which also includes members of many different cultural groups but has a policy of assimilation, often called the "melting-pot" approach.

Today, about 40 percent of Canadians are of British descent and about 27 percent are of French descent. Another 20 percent are from other European backgrounds, 10 percent are of Asian origin, and 3 percent are from First Peoples and Métis (mixed First Peoples and European) backgrounds.

**Canada**

FIGURE 16.3. This map, like several of the other maps of large areas in this book, includes a graticule—that is, a set of intersecting lines of latitude and longitude; each line of longitude indicates north and all lines converge at the North Pole.

— International boundary
------- Provincial boundary
— River
● Capital city
○ Other major city

## FAST FACTS
### about Canada

Area: 9 984 670 km²

Population: 32.2 million

Crude birth rate: 10 per 1 000

Crude death rate: 7 per 1 000

Rate of natural increase: 0.3 percent

Capital city: Ottawa

Life expectancy: 80 years

Population density: 3.2 people per km²

Language: English, French

Religion: Christianity (Protestant, Catholic), but increasingly diverse

Urbanization: 79 percent urban

Government: confederation with parliamentary democracy

Literacy rate: 97 percent

Gross national income per capita: US$30 660

## Travelling through Canada

Canada's capital city, Ottawa, is much younger and smaller than many European capital cities. Ottawa has a population of just over 800 000 within its city limits, and just over one million when the outlying areas (where people live and commute to work in the city) are included. Ottawa was settled by Algonquian people but by 1759 was under British rule. Queen Victoria named it the capital of Canada in 1855. In 1936, Prime Minister Mackenzie King decided that Canada's capital city should have a large number of parks and green spaces, and today it is a beautiful city.

 For a variety of images of Canada, visit <www.theworldtoday.ca> and follow "Links" to <www.imagescanada.ca>. Plan your own trip across Canada: follow "Links" to <www.freshtracks.ca/> or <www.gc.ca/othergov/prov_e.html>.

FIGURE 16.4. Inside Yoho National Park in the western slopes region of the Rocky Mountains. Yoho is one of 41 national parks in Canada. It is home to rock walls, spectacular waterfalls, soaring peaks, and varied animal and plant species.

To recap: 17 days and over 6 000 km across Canada, and we scarcely saw it! We spent an afternoon at Peggy's Cove, two nights in Montreal, another in Ottawa, two nights in Toronto, a day at Niagara Falls, then doubled back to Toronto before travelling right through northern Ontario (two days!), stopped for a few hours in Winnipeg, made it to Banff and Jasper for several nights, and then on to Vancouver. It was cold in the mountains! I needed to wear my jumper every night. Dad's planning to hire a car now, to take us down the west coast and into America.

POST CARD

Hallo Mum! We were really tired by the time we deplaned in Halifax, found a cab, and got to the railway station. Dad wants to travel by train all the way across Canada, but this is not always possible, so we will be hiring a car or taking a "bus" sometimes. There was no queue at all! I wonder who takes the train here? Not many Canadians, certainly.

Roald

P.S. The tea here is terrible. They dip little bags into cups, and the water scarcely boils. You'd laugh, Mum, some of the very fanciest restaurants serve a "British High Tea." It's quaint.

**homogenous** Formed from parts that are all of the same kind. For example, a homogenous culture has all of the people speaking the same language and practising the same religion.

## The United States of America

The United States is more densely populated than Canada is. It has a slightly smaller land area and a population almost 10 times that of Canada. The United States has a varied geography. The north experiences cold winters and hot summers. Farther south, the winters are mild and the summers are very hot, especially in the southwest, where there is a large desert area. The southeastern coast has regular hurricanes and other tropical storms, and the southwest coast experiences earthquakes. Generally, the east is more populated than the west, although there are several large west-coast cities. The major industrial region is southeast of the Great Lakes.

## The United States

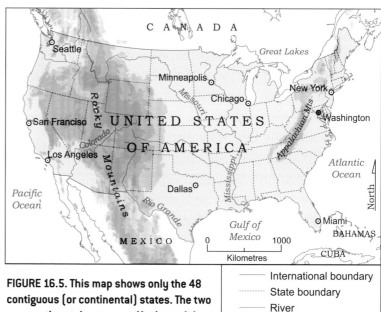

FIGURE 16.5. This map shows only the 48 contiguous (or continental) states. The two non-continental states are Alaska and the Hawaiian islands.

International boundary
State boundary
River
● Capital city
○ Other major city

## FAST FACTS
### about the United States

Area: 9 629 091 km²

Population: 296.5 million

Crude birth rate: 14 per 1 000

Crude death rate: 8 per 1 000

Rate of natural increase: 0.6 percent

Capital city: Washington, D.C.

Life expectancy: 78 years

Population density: 30 people per km²

Language: English (also Spanish)

Religion: Christianity (Protestant, Catholic)

Urbanization: 80 percent urban

Government: constitution-based
    federal republic

Literacy rate: 97 percent

Gross national income per capita: US$39 710

## Climate and Population in North America

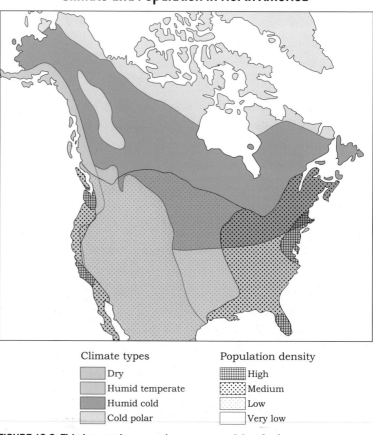

Climate types
- Dry
- Humid temperate
- Humid cold
- Cold polar

Population density
- High
- Medium
- Low
- Very low

FIGURE 16.6. This interesting map shows a general, but far from exact, relationship between climate type and population density. What are some other factors that help explain why we live where we do?

## Travelling through the United States

The first president of the United States, George Washington (1732–1799), chose Washington, D.C., as the new site for the capital city (D.C. stands for District of Columbia). Rumours abound to explain this choice. Was it the natural beauty? Or was it the geographic situation near the centre of the newly formed country? Or was it the potential of the geographic site on the navigable Potomac River? Or was it because he thought it would increase the value of his considerable land holdings in the area?

Washington did not grow much until the Civil War, when thousands of union soldiers came to the area to protect it from the southern American forces, and also to administer the war. Strict regulations have governed building in Washington. The basic city plan was modelled on Paris, many of the building are low, and the Capitol Building can be seen from almost every vantage point within the city.

Plan your own trip to the United States of America. Visit < www.theworldtoday.ca > and follow "Links" to <www.usatourist.com> or <www.usatourism.ca>.

Dad likes to drive these big North American cars. We've rented a "minivan" for the trip. They call it a minivan! It's practically a lorry!! It uses a lot more petrol than our car back home, but Dad doesn't seem to care, because petrol is a lot cheaper here. He's happy to be driving something so big, and he's remembering the traffic rules, mostly. I'm amazed by how large everything is here. But there is so much distance. We are not seeing much of the country, but I would have been back and forth to Spain from England 20 times by now. I wonder what the rest looks like? Our schedule did not allow us to explore the states east of the Rockies. Checking out the Gulf of Mexico and the heavily populated and industrial northeast cities such as New York, Boston, and Philadelphia will have to wait for another trip. Southward we go. By the way, I think I like the Pacific Ocean better than the Atlantic—it's bluer and warmer and more welcoming, somehow. I think the Caribbean will be even nicer, though.

FIGURE 16.7. Inside Olympic National Park in Washington state. This park includes glacier-capped mountains, wild Pacific coastal areas, and extensive areas of old-growth forests, including temperate rainforests.

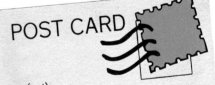
POST CARD

Hi! (that's how they say hallo in America!)
We are driving along the west coast. It is beautiful. Sometimes the cliffs seem to drop right into the sea, and the seaside is not half bad. Lovely, in fact. I was disappointed by Hollywood. I thought it would be great, but as soon as you're away from the famous theatre and Rodeo Drive there was a lot of poverty. We did see a movie set, though. That was nice.

Roald

## Central America (Mexico)

Mexico makes up the bulk of Central America, stretching over 3 000 kilometres from north to south, with terrain that ranges from hot and dry deserts in the north to tropical rainforests in the south. Central Mexico is mostly plateau; there are mountain chains in the east and west, and there are lowlands leading to the sea.

Central America was first inhabited by foragers and then were home to the agricultural civilizations of the Maya (300 CE to 1440) and the Aztec (1200 to 1521). The Spanish ruled most of the area after colonization, but what is now Mexico revolted in 1810 and finally gained independence in 1821. Geographers often define all of the Americas except for Canada and the United States as Latin America because of the colonial influence of Spain and Portugal and the domination of the Catholic religion.

The other countries making up Central America are Guatemala, Belize, El Salvador, Nicaragua, Costa Rica, and Panama. The Caribbean Islands stretch out across the Gulf of Mexico and the Caribbean Sea. Their natural beauty makes them a popular winter destination for many North American and European people who want to escape the cold winter weather of the north.

The countries of Central America are considered less-developed countries, but there is evidence of economic development in many places. Industry is growing, and so, too, is tourism. As well, there are signs that these countries are becoming more democratic. The Panama Canal was constructed in the early 20th century and is a very important trade route.

**Mexico**

Figure 16.8. Mexico comprises several different geographic regions; the most notable distinctions are among the semi-arid north, the central-core region that includes Mexico City, and the relatively remote mountainous south.

## FAST FACTS
### about Mexico

Area: 1 958 201 km²

Population: 107.0 million

Crude birth rate: 23 per 1 000

Crude death rate: 5 per 1 000

Rate of natural increase: 1.8 percent

Capital city: Mexico City

Life expectancy: 75 years

Population density: 54 people per km²

Language: Spanish

Religion: Christianity (Catholic)

Urbanization: 75 percent urban

Government: federal republic

Literacy Rate: 92 percent

Gross national income per capita: US$9 590

 You are sailing through the Panama Canal from the Pacific Ocean to the Atlantic Ocean. While in the canal, are you heading east or west? Use an atlas to check your answer.

## Travelling through Central America

Mexico City is huge, with a population of about 19 million. Historically, it was located on an island in Lake Texcoco and was the capital of the Aztec Empire. The Spanish destroyed the entire city when they invaded in the 1520s and built on the ruins of what they had destroyed. Most of Lake Texcoco has been drained to make room for development.

 Plan your own trip to Mexico. Visit < theworldtoday.ca > and follow "Links" to < www.go2mexico.com/ > or < www.visitmexico.com >.

What a region! Such a variety of peoples and places. It's so warm compared to England. When it rains, it's quick and then over. We found the Aztec ruins very interesting and have made several trips to different ones. Dad was amazed that such advanced civilizations lived here—they never taught him that in school, he says. I also liked snorkelling. I'd never done that before but the underwater sights were just as amazing as anything I've seen on land! Unfortunately, we will not go to any of the Caribbean countries or the rest of Central America. There's no time, and we must see the Andes, the rainforest, and the great Amazon River.

 Discover more about Lake Texcoco. What, if any of it, is left? What environmental ramifications did draining the lake have on the area?

FIGURE 16.9. Uxmal, in the Yucatan Peninsula, was a major Maya city that flourished from about 600 CE to about 900 CE and had a maximum population of about 25 000. Shown here is part of the Nunnery Quadrangle, a collection of 4 buildings.

## POST CARD

Hallo Mum! We crossed the border on a coach (they call it a bus, here), and I noticed two things. One was the "people crossing" signs on the motorway into Mexico when we were still in America. The sign is a mum and dad and child with a suitcase. I found out that people cross the border from Mexico into the United States to find work, but they need to run across a highway that is full of cars and 10 or 12 lanes wide. So they tell the drivers to watch out so the people don't get run over. The other thing was how easy it was to get into Mexico. They didn't check passports, and our coach didn't even stop since we got a "green light" at the border! All those around us said getting back in to the United States is harder. I miss you.

Roald

## South America

South America may be generally divided into two geographic regions: the Andean region, which includes Venezuela, Colombia, Ecuador, Peru, Bolivia, and Chile; the Basin region, which is mostly lowlands and includes the countries of Guyana, Suriname, French Guiana, Paraguay, Uruguay, Argentina, and Brazil.

### Visiting the Andean Region (Venezuela)

Venezuela is the most northerly of the South American countries. The name means "little Venice"; an early European explorer named it when he saw villages built on stilts along the water. Venezuela is home to Angel Falls (the world's highest waterfall), fertile plains, rainforest, and the Andes. Caracas, the capital city, has a population of over five million people. It is located in a valley, and the temperature is constantly spring-like. Venezuela has large oil reserves and is the fourth largest producer of oil in the world. However, corrupt governments over the years have squandered the money made from this rich resource.

The Andes run along the entire west coast of South America, from Venezuela westward and then southward. They divide in some parts into east and west ranges, with valleys and plateaus in between. Lake Titicaca, on the border of Bolivia and Peru, is the world's highest large lake, at 3 810 metres above sea level. The lake provides a moderating influence on the climate around it, and this allows for crops to be grown at these high altitudes.

 Plan your own trip to the Andes. Visit < www.theworldtoday.ca > and follow "Links" to < www.visit-chile.org >, < www.isram.com/latournew/index.htm >, or < www.peru.org.pe.>. You will find on these sites interactive maps and information about various countries in South America.

**Venezuela**

**FIGURE 16.10. Located in northeastern South America, Venezuela includes lowland regions and high mountains with wide valleys. Most of the people live in the valleys.**

## FAST FACTS
### about Venezuela

Area: 912 050 km² (almost as large as British Columbia)

Population: 26.7 million

Crude birth rate: 23 per 1 000

Crude death rate: 5 per 1 000

Rate of natural increase: 1.8 percent

Capital city: Caracas

Life expectancy: 73 years

Population density: 29 people per km²

Language: Spanish (also Italian and Portuguese)

Religion: Christianity (Catholic)

Urbanization: 87 percent urban

Government: federal republic

Literacy rate: 93 percent

Gross national income per capita: US$5 760

*Travelling through the Andean Region*

In the north, the climate is tropical in the low-lying regions and cool in higher regions. Farther south, most of Chile is temperate, with marked seasonal differences. Many of the highest peaks are snow-capped year-round. As in California, the valleys of Chile are particularly suited to growing both table grapes and grapes for wine production, and soft fruits like peaches and plums. Its location in the southern hemisphere means that Chile is able to produce fruit during the European and North American winter and can export these at a premium. If you travel to the far south of Chile during July or August, you can expect cold, rainy, and even snowy, weather.

We took a cruise and stopped at many ports along the way—in Colombia, Ecuador, and Peru. We also saw the Galapagos Islands. It was expensive, Dad said, but worth it. It was Charles Darwin who made the Galapagos Islands famous. He began to develop his theory of evolution after he saw the flora and fauna of these isolated islands. I wish I could have seen these islands 100 or 200 years ago.

 The Atacama Desert is in Chile and is the driest place on earth. Protected on all sides by high mountain ranges, it receives practically no rainfall and is home to little plant or animal life. It was once mined for sodium nitrate, a fertilizer, but demand fell when synthetic fertilizers were made after the Second World War.

POST CARD

Hi Mum! We are in Caracas, Venezuela. After a long cruise, we were ready for some land. After Caracas we are going to fly to Brazil for our last hurrah, an eco-tour of the Amazon Basin and the famous rainforest. I'm a little worried because they say it rains almost every day there. Will it rain all the time? Still, one shouldn't miss the chance to see this if we are so close. And I guess it's called "rainforest" for a reason. Well, at least we have our anoraks.

Roald

FIGURE 16.11. A cable car ascends Mt. Avila National Park with downtown Caracas, the capital of Venezuela, below. Mount Avila (2 400 m high) is located between the Atlantic Ocean coast and the city.

*Visiting the Basin Region (Brazil)*

The Amazon River Basin is the location of the world's largest tropical rainforest. The Amazon is the world's second longest river, after the Nile. Many species of plants and animals have been discovered in the rainforest, and many more are yet to be discovered. Some indigenous peoples have lived here for centuries, maybe millennia, and it is possible that there are tribes living here who still have not had contact with the rest of the world.

Since 1978, over 530 000 square kilometres of Brazilian rainforest have been destroyed. This is happening for several reasons, including clearing for logging, pasturing cattle, growing crops for subsistence, growing crops for selling, and developing infrastructure such as roads and reservoirs for hydroelectricity. Soybeans are becoming one of Brazil's largest cash crops, and they are grown on land that was once rainforest. Despite worldwide pressure to preserve the rainforest, there are few signs that the destruction is stopping.

**Brazil**

**FIGURE 16.12. Brazil, the largest country in South America, shares a boundary with all South American countries except Chile and Ecuador.**

## FAST FACTS
### about Brazil

Area: 8 511 965 km² (about 85 percent of the size of Canada)

Population: 184.2 million

Crude birth rate: 21 per 1 000

Crude death rate: 7 per 1 000

Rate of natural increase: 1.4 percent

Capital city: Brasilia

Life expectancy: 71 years

Population density: 21 people per km²

Language: Portuguese

Religion: Christian (Catholic)

Urbanization: 81 percent urban

Government: democracy, federal republic

Literacy rate: 86.4 percent

Gross national income per capita: US$8 020

Dad's in a bad temper this morning. I knew he shouldn't have tried the Caipirinha (quite the exotic drink!). Or maybe it's because of all the trucks we passed on the road as we were going to pick up our tour. After you see the rainforest, you can't imagine why people would want to destroy it to grow something as boring as soybeans. So much is being cut down or burned! It's mind-boggling. Dad says they've talked about saving rainforests since he was at school, and what has happened? Not much, he says. I think for the rest of my life I will ensure that I do not buy furniture that is made of rainforest woods like teak, mahogany, and cherry.

## Travelling through the Basin Region

Originally designed for about 500 000 people, Brasilia, the capital of Brazil, now has over two million people. It was located in a sparsely populated interior area to encourage settlement away from the coastal region. It was designed in the 1950s and completed in 1960, and is grand in scale and focus. It was designed with the car in mind; pedestrian traffic was not taken into account. Shaped like an airplane (or a butterfly, depending upon who you talk to) Brasilia replaced Rio de Janeiro as Brazil's capital city. Large parks and green spaces make it less densely populated than Brazil's other large cities and allow the population to enjoy wildlife inside the city.

South of Brazil are three other countries in the Basin: Argentina, Uruguay, and Paraguay. They are different from Brazil geographically because they are mid-latitude, not low-latitude, countries. Because European colonists did not establish plantation agriculture here, slaves were not imported, and most of the population is European. Paraguay has a majority **Mestizo** population. Uruguay and Argentina, especially, are important producers of meat and other animal products. The least developed of these countries is Paraguay, possibly because it is landlocked and therefore relatively isolated.

**Mestizo**  People of mixed European and Indian ancestry.

Plan your own trip to the Amazon rainforest. Visit < www.theworldtoday.ca > and follow "Links" to < www.safaribrazil.com/> or < www.brol.com/index.asp > .

**Brasilia**  Where it is said that the people are born with wheels instead of feet.

FIGURE 16.13. A toco toucan in Iguaçu Falls National Park, close to the border with Argentina. The toco toucan is the largest of the toucan family and eats small fruit, bird eggs, rodents, and insects. The Iguaçu Falls are one of the most impressive falls in the world, about 4 km across and with a vertical drop of more than 80 m.

POST CARD

Hallo Mum. Probably my last postcard to you before we make our way back to America before coming home. This has been the best holiday I ever could hope to have. Canada and the north seem like such a long time ago, and England is like a dream. We spent 8 days in the wilderness of the Amazon jungle and never saw any other tourists except those in our group. We were from all over the world, which made it very interesting. The Australian in our group was very afraid of any kind of lizard or crocodile, so don't believe what you see on the telly about Aussie crocodile hunters. We'll be home in a fortnight! I've got loads of snaps to show you.

Love, Roald

P.S. I'm sure your garden looks nice, but you really should have come.

What an unbelievable trip. I'm glad I have snaps, or my mates wouldn't believe the things I've seen and done. Motoring through America, taking the train through Canada, and spending the last few weeks in South America have changed my life. I never knew so many wild and beautiful places still existed. It will be good to get back to England, though. I shall never forget this trip.

I wonder where Dad will take me next summer? I did take a peek at the travel diary that he is keeping and he wrote an amazing poem about this trip. Maybe I can use that in my geography class next term. I couldn't have put it better myself!

# INFLUENCES OF THE PAST

1. How do events of the past influence the world today?

2. When were the Americas first peopled?

3. How has the Age of Collision affected the Americas?

4. How has the Industrial Revolution changed the human geographies of Europe and North America?

In this chapter, we consider three historical circumstances that help us understand the present-day human geographies of the Americas and Europe:

1. the settling of the Americas by First Peoples and, much later, by Europeans

2. the Age of Collision and European colonial activity

3. the Industrial Revolution of the 18th and 19th centuries

## Populating the Americas

Many First Peoples' stories relate the idea that they have "always been here," or that they "sprang from the land." This aspect of the stories is important, as it stresses the close relationship between peoples and the places where they live.

### Many Places, Many Peoples

There is still much to be learned about human movement into the Americas. It seems likely that people moved into northern North America not long after they developed the technologies needed to occupy northern Eurasia. Aboriginal people—called First Peoples in Canada—likely entered the Americas by crossing a land bridge from Asia to Alaska. The date is uncertain; some scientists think it was as early as 40 000 years ago; others think it was about 15 000 years ago. The land bridge was in place because the earth was much cooler at that time. There was more ice on the earth, and sea levels were probably as much as 300 metres lower than they are today. One reason people moved through these northern areas was that they followed game, including the woolly mammoth, an animal that was extinct by about 8 000 years ago.

The first people to move into the Americas had already adapted to the cold Arctic climate of northern Eurasia. Movement east and south through the Americas was a long process, involving adaptations to many different natural environments, including temperate, sub-tropical, and tropical lands. By about 8 000 years ago, people had migrated to all areas of the Americas, and, by about 5 000 years ago, some groups were practising agriculture.

As new areas were settled, distinct societies and ways of life formed. The Americas developed over several thousands of years as a complex of many different societies with different lifestyles, different languages, religions, and technologies. In some cases, groups of people cooperated with neighbouring groups; in other cases, there was conflict.

In general, people lived intimately with the natural environment that they occupied. Although we know few details, it seems likely that people lived comfortably. They were free from the diseases that Europeans suffered from; birth rates were generally low, and so was infant mortality.

Some groups lived by, off, and with the sea. The west-coast Haida of the Queen Charlotte Islands, British Columbia, depended on the riches of the northern Pacific, including sea otter and salmon. The Makah people, farther south on the Olympic peninsula of northwest Washington, hunted whales, which provided meat and oil for food, sinew for harpoon bindings, and bones for war clubs.

The plains Indians, who lived in the prairie region of Canada and the central plains of the United States, were semi-nomadic hunters and foragers who used bison as their main source of food, shelter, and clothing.

The woodlands peoples in the east, such as the Iroquois who lived around Lake Ontario, were primarily farmers and grew corn, squash, and beans.

The societies that developed in some parts of Central and South America were especially complex. Both the Maya of Central America and the Incas of South America practised

FIGURE 17.1. An Iroquois native American stands in the doorway of a reconstructed longhouse as he prepares to take part in a traditional ceremony.

agriculture and built large cities with huge temples and public buildings that could hold over 2 000 people, "without crowding," as one early European invader noted. Their main crops were corn, beans, and squash.

**Alfonso Ortiz**, a Tewa Indian who lives in the Rio Grande Valley of New Mexico, put it this way: "A Tewa is interested in our own story of our origin, for it holds all that we need to know about our people, and how one should live as a human. The story defines our society. It tells me who I am, where I came from, the boundaries of my world, what kind of order exists within it; how suffering, evil, and death came into this world; and what is likely to happen to me when I die.

"Let me tell you that story: Yonder in the north, there is singing on the lake. Cloud maidens dance on the shore. There we take our being. Yonder in the north, cloud beings rise. They ascend onto cloud blossoms. There we take our being. Yonder in the north, rain stands over the land.... Yonder in the north stands forth at twilight the arc of a rainbow. There we have our being."

# Europe before the Age of Collision

Because Europe is linked to Africa by land through western Asia, the peopling of Europe occurred earlier than it did in the Americas. Foraging peoples occupied most regions from the Mediterranean to the north of Europe probably about 40 000 years ago. Agriculture spread across much of the continent, beginning about 8 000 years ago. A large area of Europe was unified under Rome until the 5th century CE, and then the Huns raided from the east. Later, in the 9th century, Vikings raided from the north.

In chapter 1, we noted that the 1 000-year period from the 5th century to the 15th century is known in Europe as the Middle Ages. The Middle Ages were not a pleasant time for most Europeans. The **feudal system** was in full swing. Rich people had all the power, and the poor had few opportunities. The church was powerful and wealthy. Life expectancy was probably lower in Europe than it was in most of the regions around the world that Europe eventually "civilized," and the average person died of disease in his or her fifties.

Before European overseas expansion began in the 15th century, there were several powerful societies that had developed complex organizational structures, profound artistic expression, and advanced technologies in other parts of the world. These included China and India in Asia (see chapter 10), several areas in Africa (see chapter 13), and Central America. Despite the undoubted successes of these societies, it was Europe in the 15th century that moved overseas and dramatically changed the peoples and places of the world. The relative ease that came with the **Renaissance** and the **Age of Collision** followed the tough life of the Middle Ages.

**Age of Collision** The period from about 1450 until about 1800, which involved European overseas voyages to Africa, Asia, the Americas, and Australasia (Australia, New Zealand and other islands in the Pacific). These voyages resulted in numerous meetings, or collisions, between Europeans and the inhabitants of these areas.

**feudal system** A class system that gave the king all the power and all the land. He allowed nobles to use land. Knights served the nobles so that they could get land of their own, and the peasants, or serfs, farmed the land and did the hard labour. For all their hard work, peasants received protection from attack and very little else.

**Renaissance** The period of European history that followed the Middle Ages. It began in the late-14th century and lasted until about the mid-17th century. Literally a "rebirth," it included a series of European explorations and settlements overseas.

### TABLE 17.1. Selected Timeline for European Overseas Movement

| Date | Movement |
|------|----------|
| 1486–1487 | Bartolomeu Dias (Portugal) sails around southern Africa |
| 1492 | Christopher Columbus (Italian but sailing for Spain) arrives in the Caribbean |
| 1497–1498 | Vasco da Gama (Portugal) rounds southern Africa and reaches India |
| 1497 | John Cabot (Italian, but sailing for England) sights "new found land" while searching for a route across the top of North America to the riches of the east |
| 1519–1522 | Ferdinand Magellan (Portuguese, but sailing for Spain) voyages around the world |
| 1534 | Jacques Cartier (France) travels up the St. Lawrence River |
| 1768–1779 | James Cook (England) makes three voyages |

# The Age of Collision

As the Middle Ages gave way to the Renaissance, Europe turned its attention beyond Europe to what was, for them, the unknown world. Some European countries—especially Spain, Portugal, England, the Netherlands, and France—took advantage of the many inventions imported from China. As well, they began to learn more about the prevailing winds and ocean currents, developed new navigational technologies including an accurate calculation of latitude, and set out to explore other peoples and places. Often known as the *Age of Discovery*, this period is better termed the *Age of Collision*.

The European countries were encouraged in their explorations by the Three Gs:

1. Greed, a search for wealth, especially gold

2. Glory, personal and national ambition

3. God, a perceived need to spread Christianity

The specific desire to find a new passage to Asia that did not involve a long and dangerous trip around southern Africa fuelled exploration west across the Atlantic. This eventually led Europeans to the riches of the Americas. As Europeans encountered what were for them new places, and as they craved the gold and other wealth that these new places might provide, their centuries-old wars and rivalries were renewed.

 Why is the *Age of Collision* a more appropriate term than the *Age of Discovery*? What was it that "collided" during the Age of Collision? Discuss.

**European Movement Overseas**

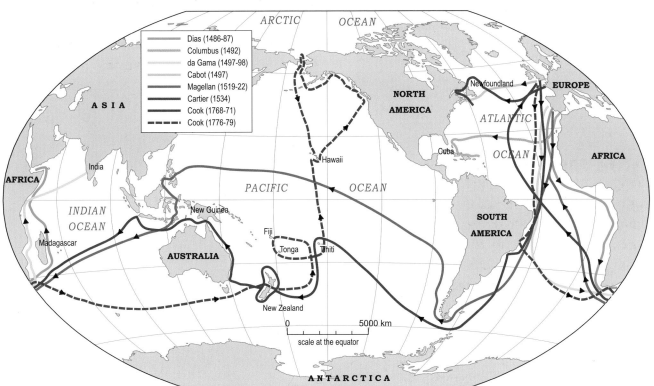

FIGURE 17.2. Only the first and third of the 3 voyages of Cook are included here.

## An Unequal Meeting

It is now clear that the European newcomers who came to the Americas beginning in the late 15th century were arrogant in their dealings with First Peoples. When they arrived in the Americas, Europeans ignored the rights of the indigenous peoples, simply assuming that the land was available for them to occupy. The Europeans who came to the Americas from Spain, Portugal, England, the Netherlands, and France were more technologically advanced than were the First Peoples. They had gunpowder and iron weapons, such as swords, pikes, and muskets. This technological superiority meant that they were able to dominate the First Peoples in military encounters, sending them away from their traditional areas if they chose to, and imposing new languages and new religions on them.

Sometimes historians would have us believe that the Europeans were benevolent, enlightened, and educated. In reality, however, their conduct was often hurtful.

**Where Have All the People Gone?** The most dramatic consequence of contact between newcomers and First Peoples—that is, the loss of population—was largely accidental. Before European contact, the number of indigenous people living in the Americas (what Europeans called the New World) is estimated to have been about 54 million people. This population decreased by about 90 percent between 1492 and 1650. How did this happen? While incoming Europeans killed large numbers of people at various times, the most important reason was that they inadvertently brought diseases that were not known in the Americas. It was these diseases, especially smallpox, that caused the enormous loss of life. This is perhaps the greatest tragedy of the Age of Collision, and it is a tragedy that occurred in many places.

There was then no sickness;
They had then no aching bones;
They had then no high fever;
They had then no smallpox;
They had then no burning chest
They had then no consumption
At that time the course of humanity was orderly.
The foreigners made it otherwise when they arrived here.

From a 16th century Maya book.

**FIGURE 17.3. Smallpox was one of several diseases introduced into the Americas by Europeans. This depiction of a person dying from smallpox in Peru dates from about 1700.**

The peoples and places of the Americas changed as Europeans travelled here. They moved in large numbers and brought with them their ideas about agriculture, including plants, such as wheat, and animals, such as horses. But it was not only the people and places of the Americas that changed. European peoples and places changed, too, when plants such as potatoes, corn, and tobacco were taken back to Europe. What might be called the *Columbian exchange* worked in both directions.

 Why do we hear so little about the coming of Europeans to the Americas from the perspective of the indigenous peoples? The romantic story of sea travel, exploration, and a new world filled with gold and other natural resources becomes a horror story of invasion, conquest, sickness, cruelty, and death. Think about this, and then head to the library and pick a number of books about the history of a country that experienced colonization. Glance through the first chapter of each book and answer the following questions:

- From whose perspective is the story written?

- Who is the target audience of the book?

- Would the explorers mentioned in the book feel pleased with the way they are portrayed?

- Would the indigenous peoples in the book feel pleased with the way they are portrayed?

- How often do the authors use the word *discovery*? Should they use this word?

**Where Did the Name *Indian* Come From?**
Christopher Columbus genuinely thought he had navigated his way to Asia and, therefore, assumed he was seeing the people of India. Even when Europeans realized that the Americas and Asia were separate continents, the name stuck.

 In October 1999, Christopher Columbus (ca. 1451–1506) topped a British Broadcasting Corporation (BBC) news online poll as the greatest explorer of the millennium. The Genoa-born explorer won the vote at the last minute, pushing Captain James Cook (1728–1779), who had been in the lead for most of the month, into second place. Columbus ranks as a great explorer for his bravery in sailing into the unknown. Those who voted for him in the poll did not seem concerned at Columbus's error in thinking that he had reached Asia. One participant said: "True, there were people already living in the Americas, and Christopher Columbus may have landed in the New World by accident, but that does not change the fact that his discovery changed human history immeasurably." Discuss the following statements:

- Do you think Christopher Columbus should be credited with discovering the Americas?

- Was he a "great" man?

**One of These Men Is Not Like the Other** The United States honours only two men with federal holidays bearing their names: Dr. Martin Luther King Jr. and Christopher Columbus (incidentally, Christopher Columbus never set foot in North America). One of them was responsible for opening up the Atlantic slave trade, and the other struggled to end the racial prejudice and hatred that was the legacy of the slave trade.

## The Industrial Revolution

The European movement overseas that resulted in the establishment of colonies throughout much of the Americas, Asia, and Africa is one of the two major changes that occurred in the world in the past 500 years. The second major change is the Industrial Revolution. Both changes dramatically reshaped the world.

*Revolution* is a very powerful word. People use it when referring to major political changes, such as those that occurred in France and in the British-American colonies in the late 18th century. People also use the word when referring to major social changes, such as the way people function in the world and view their world. For example, there was a scientific revolution in 17th-century Europe when new understandings of the relationship between the earth and the sun were developed. *Revolution* is a term that suggests massive, and essentially unexpected, change in the established order.

Was the Industrial Revolution really a revolution? On the one hand, yes, it was; take a look at table 17.2, which notes just a few of the many technological advances that occurred within quite a short time period of less than 100 years. On the other hand, perhaps it was not quite so revolutionary; there were some important changes in European agricultural technologies that preceded the Industrial Revolution and helped it happen. For example, animal breeding practices were improved and more effective crop rotations were developed that helped maintain soil fertility. Such changes resulted in significant increases in food production, which in turn created surpluses that fed more people. These changes also freed up some agricultural labourers, who began working in other occupations.

### From Hands to Machines

Essentially, the Industrial Revolution involved the application of power-driven machinery to **manufacturing**. Instead of making things by hand, people used machines. The Industrial Revolution started in England and spread quickly through Europe and North America, both of which were transformed from

### TABLE 17.2. Seven Key Events of the Industrial Revolution

| Date | Key Events |
|------|-----------|
| 1709 | Abraham Darby (ca. 1678–1717) uses coke to smelt iron ore, replacing increasingly scarce wood and charcoal as fuel (coke is coal that has been heated to remove gases). |
| 1712 | Thomas Newcomen (ca. 1664–1729) builds the first commercially successful steam engine. |
| 1733 | John Kay (1704–1780) invents the flying shuttle, an improvement to looms that enabled weavers to weave faster. |
| 1764 | James Hargreaves (1720–1778) invents the spinning jenny, the first machine to improve upon the spinning wheel. |
| 1769 | Richard Arkwright (1732–1792) patents the water frame, the first powered textile machine. |
| 1775 | James Watt (1736–1819) invents the steam engine, a much more efficient engine than Newcomen's engine. |
| 1792 | Eli Whitney (1765–1825) invents the cotton gin, a device to clean raw cotton. |

**manufacturing** The word *manufacturing* is derived from the Latin *manu factus*, meaning "made by hand." Manufacturing is the process of making a raw material into a finished product either by hand or, more usual today, by machine. For example, iron ore is used to make steel. Manufacturing today requires people either to do the work directly or to run the machines. It also requires capital—that is, money to pay workers and to buy machines. Today, most manufactured goods are intended for sale to others.

essentially agricultural into industrial societies.

There are eight key events associated with the Industrial Revolution:

1. Coal became the key source of power. Before the Industrial Revolution, charcoal was used, but it had become scarce and expensive (charcoal is made by heating wood).

2. People moved from rural areas to the industrial towns that developed near coalfields. Here they worked in factories that produced goods inexpensively.

FIGURE 17.4. A small factory town in the 19th century. This is Pella, in Iowa. Note the belching smoke and the workers' homes in the background.

3. New inventions, such as power looms, made spinning cloth more efficient, which in turn led to an abundance of inexpensive cotton goods. People who had previously had to wear wool clothing next to their skin could now afford more comfortable, cotton, underwear. Colonial activity supported the new industrial activities by providing many new raw materials; for example, England grew cotton in Egypt and India.

4. A new method of iron smelting, using coal (the blast method), was developed, and the iron-and-steel industry flourished. Metal goods, including knives, forks, scissors, and weapons, became readily available.

5. Horse-drawn travel gave way to rail travel. The first passenger railway opened in England in 1825, and, within 30 years, over 16 000 kilometres of track were laid in Europe. The railroad had a huge effect on Canada; some provinces joined confederation mainly because of the promise of a railroad.

6. The steam engine was invented and used increasingly to transport such items as fresh fruits and vegetables over many kilometres.

7. Personal transportation possibilities increased, which allowed for an increase in social interaction. Chapter 7 introduced two terms related to this change: *time-space convergence* and *shrinking planet*. Both terms refer to the fact that the peoples and places of the world are increasingly interconnected.

8. New farm machines, such as steam tractors and steel ploughs, were invented, resulting in increased crop yields and decreased labour needs.

## Capitalism

The Industrial Revolution was about much more than industry. An essential component of the changes that occurred during the Industrial Revolution was the development of a new social and economic system known as **capitalism**.

Before the Industrial Revolution, agricultural labourers worked for their social and political masters, and the masters—or barons—were responsible for the welfare of their labourers. People lived in self-sufficient communities and consumed only what they produced. But the introduction of steam power disrupted the balance in these agricultural societies.

As people moved from farms to cities in order to work in the new factories, the old feudal social system changed. The new relationship between workers and employers was defined in terms of cash, one of the most important features of capitalism.

**Trade Unions** The Industrial Revolution paved the way for people to become rich, but it also saw continued human rights abuses: men, women, and children had to work long hours in dangerous conditions, and they were punished if they complained. Slowly, by working together, people began to gain rights in their workplaces, and trade unions evolved. Trade unions became legal in Britain in 1871 and in Canada in 1872.

**capitalism** Began in 18th-century Britain when industrialists began to employ workers, displacing feudal landowners in political, economic, and social importance. Capitalism involves the production of goods through private ownership. It also involves banking and borrowing money.

FIGURE 17.5. Anasazi hand prints on a sandstone wall. The Anasazi live in the desert landscape of the American southwest.

 Local geographies changed dramatically in many areas as factories were built, towns grew rapidly, and railways were added to the landscape. Large numbers of people moved from agricultural areas into new industrial areas to live and work. Discuss three reasons showing that the changes caused by the Industrial Revolution were an advantage; discuss three reasons showing that they were a disadvantage.

## The Importance of the Past

Chapter 13 began with the suggestion that the past is prologue. This chapter has provided additional support for this statement. The world today cannot be understood without an appreciation of what happened in the past. Looking back and sorting out what was important and what was not important is far from easy. This chapter has focused particularly on three important periods in the past that have contributed much to the way the world is organized today:

1. The peopling of the Americas was the final phase in the expansion of *Homo sapiens sapiens* around the world. People moved from northern Asia during a period when the earth was much cooler than it is today; they then gradually moved south and east through the Americas, reaching the southern tip of South America about 8 000 years ago. For many thousands of years, the earth was settled by groups of people who had only limited contacts with other groups. Each group developed its own distinctive lifestyle, which included its own language, religion, and general way of life.

2. The Age of Collision effectively ended the long phase of human history when different groups of people were essentially separate from each other. The consequences of the European "discovery" of new groups of people were usually devastating to those groups. Throughout much of the Americas, as well as throughout Australasia, Asia, and Africa, long-established ways of life were dramatically transformed. But it was in the Americas that another, unintended, transformation occurred: because of disease, indigenous groups suffered huge population losses. (Because indigenous populations in other parts of the world were not as susceptible to the diseases brought by Europeans, they did not suffer similar losses.) The Age of Collision resulted in changes to European geographies as well, as farmers in Europe started growing some American crops.

3. The Industrial Revolution transformed the ways of life of people living in Europe and North America. New technologies, combined with the new social and economic system of capitalism, resulted in new landscapes and new ways of life. In some respects, these transformations are continuing today.

# MOVING TO THE CITIES

**18**

## Guiding Questions

1. What are some things that city dwellers enjoy?

2. What are some things that city dwellers would change if they could?

3. What are some common problems faced by people in large cites in Europe and the Americas?

4. What would happen in the future if people continued to flock to cities?

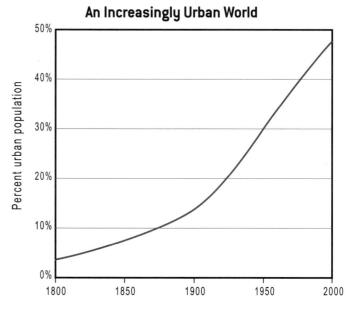

FIGURE 18.1. The percentage of the world population living in urban centres has increased since 1800 and continues to increase.

Whether you live in the city or in the country, you know there are advantages and disadvantages to living in each place. Often, people living in one place or the other daydream about moving and, if they do move, find that neither place is perfect.

What do most people in the world think? Based on what is happening today, the answer is clearly that people prefer cities. Around the world, people are flocking to cities, or what we call urban areas. More and more people are living in cities, and the number of large cities has increased significantly in recent years. In 1900, there were 12 cities with more than one million people; in 1950, there were 83; and, in 2000, there were 411.

Today, about half of the world population lives in urban areas, and this percentage is increasing. There are two big differences between the situations in more-developed countries and in less-developed countries:

1. In more-developed countries, about 76 percent of people live in cities, and this percentage is increasing relatively slowly.

2. In less-developed countries, about 41 percent of people live in cities, and this percentage is increasing relatively quickly.

Cities in the more-developed world often grow outward, in the form of suburban expansion, often onto prime agricultural land. Much of this **exurban growth** was encouraged by the development of transportation networks, first of railway lines and, later, of roads. More recently, urban expansion has been characterized by **sprawl**—that is, when people move from both inside the city and rural areas into new housing developments that are close to an existing city.

Of course, living in a city does not necessarily mean a better quality of life. In 2004, approximately 30 percent of urban dwellers in the less-developed world lived in poverty. Many of these poor people live on the outskirts of the city, in slums, or **shanty towns.**

 Your family is moving to a new province, and your parents ask you where you would like to live, in the country or in a large city. List five reasons explaining why you would like to live in the country. List five reasons explaining why you would like to live in a large city. Think about these lists and then decide where you would like to live. Discuss your reasons and your decision with classmates. Does everyone in the class feel the same way?

**exurban growth** The development of residential subdivisions in the countryside outside a city, often taking a bead-like form because of development along railway lines or roads.

**shanty towns** In the less-developed world, these are urban areas of low-quality, often temporary, housing at city margins. They are often located on difficult ground such as steep slopes or land likely to flood and lack water, sewage services, and electricity. There are many local names: they are called *barriades* in Peru, *favelas* in Brazil, and *villas miseries* in Argentina.

**sprawl** The development of new housing in areas close to a city. Private developers select new housing sites based on the cost of land, suitability for construction, and transportation access to the city. Sprawl often results in a patchwork-quilt type of landscape, with housing and farming areas scattered across a landscape. Sprawl also reflects the fact that many people want to own a large area of land, and this is not usually possible inside the city.

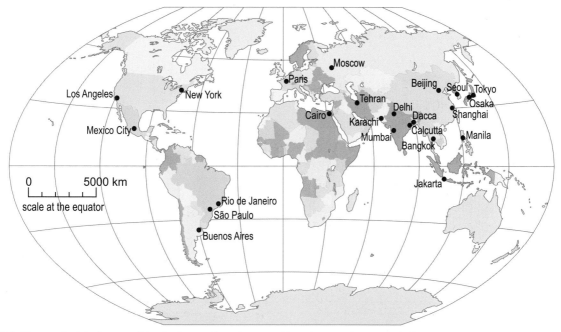

**Cities with Populations Greater than 10 Million**

FIGURE 18.2. Almost all of the largest cities in the world are in coastal locations, and most are in less-developed countries (see figure 3.1 to locate the less-developed countries).

# What Is a City?

There is not an accepted universal definition of how many people are needed to make a place urban. In Canada, the definition of urban is: "cities, towns, and villages of 1 000 population or more." In the United States, the minimum is set at 2 500; in some other countries, the minimum is set as high as 20 000.

Canada is a highly urbanized country: 79 percent urban in 2004 (and rising). But our population is relatively small, and we do not have many very large cities. Our three largest are Toronto, Montreal, and Vancouver.

Argentina has more people than Canada (Argentina about 38 million; Canada about 32 million) and is even more urbanized than Canada; 89 percent of the population of Argentina is defined as urban. Much of the urban population of Argentina lives in one large city, Buenos Aries, which has a population of about 13 million people.

## Some Useful Terms

### Census Metropolitan Area
In Canada a census metropolitan area (CMA) has at least 100 000 people. There are 25 CMAs in Canada. Winnipeg is the only CMA in Manitoba. There are two in Saskatchewan: Regina and Saskatoon.

### Conurbation
Conurbation is formed when several settlements that are close together expand so that they become one continuous urban area, for example, Toronto, Canada.

### Global Cities
Global cities are not really defined by their size—although they are big—but rather by the fact that their influence extends throughout the world. They are the cities at the centre of economic and cultural globalization (see chapter 7). There are three global cities today: New York, London, and Tokyo.

### Megacity
The term *megacity* is sometimes used to refer to an exceptionally large city, usually more than 10 million people, for example, Mexico City, Mexico; Calcutta, India; São Paulo, Brazil.

### Megalopolis
The term *megalopolis* applies when several already large cities have expanded to form an exceptionally large urban area. The term was first applied to the area from Boston through New York to Washington in the United States.

### Metropolis, Metropolitan Area, and Urban Agglomeration
The terms *metropolis, metropolitan area* and *urban agglomeration* are all loosely applied to any large city.

 For statistical data on the size and population of Canadian urban centres, visit <www.theworldtoday.ca> and follow "Links" to <www12.statcan.ca/english/census01/home/index.cfm>. How many people are in Toronto, Montreal, and Vancouver? How many people are living in the urban centre nearest to you?

 Using an atlas, find five of the world's largest cities. What are some unique features of the geography of each? In what kind of physical geographic region is each located? (See chapter 2 for help with this.)

# Cities Are Growing

Two factors contribute to a city's growth: the natural increase of the city population that results from the difference between births and deaths; and rural-to-urban migration. Urbanization in the more-developed world went hand-in-hand with the Industrial Revolution. After about 1750, urbanization occurred because of the new job opportunities in cities when the rural poor were losing their land or their labouring jobs. As migrants moved to cities, they provided cheap labour for factories. However, life in cities during the Industrial Revolution was disease-filled and dangerous; people had to endure poor sanitation and crowded living conditions. Death rates were higher than birth rates; most urban growth resulted from rural-to-urban movement.

Migration is the key factor in the growth of cities in the less-developed world now, but the rate of natural increase is also very high. The slums and townships that cluster around the edges of cities are poorly planned, crowded, and disease-ridden, but there is greater access to health services now than there was in Europe and North America during the Industrial Revolution. Vaccinations, health education, and birth control all contribute to a healthier and longer-lived population.

See table 18.1 for a list of the 15 largest cities in the world, and the population of

FIGURE 18.3. This image, which dates from 1880, shows a cross-section of a slum apartment dwelling in New York City with graphic images of poverty circumstances.

each. (Keep in mind that different sources give different populations, because they use different definitions of the urban area.)

## TABLE 18.1. The Fifteen Largest Cities in the World

| Rank | City | Country | Population in millions |
|------|------|---------|------------------------|
| 1. | Tokyo | Japan | 35.3 |
| 2. | Mexico City | Mexico | 19.0 |
| 3. | New York | United States of America | 18.5 |
| 4. | Mumbai (Bombay) | India | 18.3 |
| 5. | São Paulo | Brazil | 18.3 |
| 6. | Delhi | India | 15.3 |
| 7. | Calcutta | India | 14.3 |
| 8. | Buenos Aries | Argentina | 13.3 |
| 9. | Jakarta | Indonesia | 13.2 |
| 10. | Shanghai | China | 12.7 |
| 11. | Dhaka | Bangladesh | 12.6 |
| 12. | Los Angeles | United States of America | 12.1 |
| 13. | Karachi | Pakistan | 11.8 |
| 14. | Rio de Janeiro | Brazil | 11.5 |
| 15. | Osaka-Kobe | Japan | 11.3 |

Source: Population Division of the Department of Economic and Social Affairs of the United Nations Secretariat, 2004. *World Urbanization Prospects: The 2003 Revision.*

## Problems of Urban Growth

Life in a big city anywhere in the world can be very difficult for poor people. For example, all large North American and European cities suffer serious problems of poverty and homelessness. But the problems are much greater in the shanty towns of cities in less-developed countries. Most of these shanty towns have developed because poor people have abandoned their rural life and moved to the city with few, if any, possessions and without jobs.

There are 8 problem areas typically found in shanty towns and other poor areas of large cities in the less-developed world:

1. There are no sewers, no sewage-treatment plants, and there is no garbage pickup.

2. Clean, safe water is not usually available. (Think about how water gets to your home. Cities in the more-developed world pipe treated water directly to your house.)

3. Medical clinics and hospitals are few and far between.

4. When people set up homes in shanty towns, they do so without the guidelines of city planning; basically, they just find the materials they need and set up homes wherever there is space.

5. People do not own the land on which their houses are located. Large corporations can (and do) buy the land and remove the people living there.

6. People are sometimes not even able to find materials with which to build a shack for themselves and end up living on the street. Some rapidly growing urban areas in less-developed countries have large populations of children who are abandoned, orphaned, or otherwise separated from their parents (they are known as *street children*).

FIGURE 18.4. There are poor people in all cities. Top: a man digs a sewage ditch next to his house in a slum district of Nairobi, Kenya. Bottom: a homeless man begs for money; the location is New York City, but the scene could be in any large city in the world.

7. Because shanty towns are often located downwind of heavy industrial areas, air pollution is heavy. This is a concern in both more- and less-developed countries, but it is potentially worse in less-developed countries because these countries are less likely to have laws in place to control pollution.

8. There are few schools to educate the many young children.

## Push Factors and Pull Factors

Why would someone choose to move from a rural area to a city in the less-developed world? The reasons are identified as "push" factors and "pull" factors.

Push factors refer to the reasons that people leave a place. Four of the most important push factors are weather; war and unrest; shortage of land; and HIV/AIDS.

### Weather

Rural economies are very weather-dependent, and weather fluctuations may make the difference between a family having enough food and going hungry. In the early 21st century, droughts in the African countries of Niger, Chad, Mauritania, and Sudan prompted many rural poor people to move to cities.

### War and Unrest

Life in rural areas is especially unsafe during times of war and unrest. If people are forced off their land or out of their homes by enemies, they tend to seek the safety of numbers and travel to nearby cities.

### Shortage of Land

Land usually passes from parents to children in less-developed countries. Land that supported perhaps five people one or two generations ago may now need to support 30, so some choose to move away.

### HIV/AIDS

In many rural areas, a person faces shunning if the community discovers that she or he has HIV/AIDS. Life in a city offers more anonymity, and some people choose to move rather than face the rejection of their friends and family.

Pull factors refer to the reasons people move to a place. Four of the most important pull factors are better income; perceived social equality; more freedom for women; more opportunities for children.

**Working Children** During the Industrial Revolution, many children from poor families worked long hours, six days a week, to help provide for their families. Some people recognized the need for these children to learn and began what they called *Sunday School*, which was, quite simply, school that took place on Sunday, the only day that these children didn't go to work.

### Better Income

The main reason people move to urban centres is to earn an income. The work may be low-paying, back-breaking, exhausting, and demanding, but people want to find work. Some people work as domestic servants. Others find work as labourers, gardeners, and garbage collectors.

### Perceived Social Equality

Social differences do not stand out as much in cities as they do in villages, where understanding is based on centuries'-old traditions.

### More Freedom for Women

In cities, women tend to enjoy more freedom, more opportunities for education, and are usually able to find paid work outside the home. They are less likely to have to depend on a male relative for economic support so have more control over their own lives.

### More Opportunities for Children

People will often move to cities in the hope that their children will have more and better opportunities.

 For an interesting website designed to guide thinking about cities, visit < www.the worldtoday.ca > and follow "Links" to < www.newcolonist.com >.

## A Tale of Three Cities

We now explore three very different cities, and three very different peoples and places: Amsterdam in the Netherlands, São Paulo in Brazil, and Chicago in the United States. As you read about these cities, think about a city in Europe or the Americas that you would like to find out more about and prepare to do a study of your own.

As you explore Amsterdam, São Paulo, and Chicago, ask the following five questions about each one:

1. Where is it? Why is it there? Why should I care? (In answering these questions, we are exploring the key geographic facts and issues of the city.)

2. How has this city changed over time? (In answering this question, we are exploring its changing geography.)

3. How do people make their livings in this city? (In answering this question, we are exploring the geography of its economy.)

4. What are some challenges this city faces? (In answering this question, we are exploring current geographic issues.)

5. Why would I want to visit this city? (In answering this question, we are exploring its distinctive geographic features.)

a.

b.

c.

e.

f.

d.

FIGURE 18.5. The photos on this and the facing page show scenes of Amsterdam, São Paulo, and Chicago. Can you tell which is which? What do these photos tell you about the cities, their geographies, and the people who live there?

ANSWERS
a) Chicago
b) Amsterdam
c) São Paulo
d) Amsterdam
e) São Paulo
f) Chicago area

## Amsterdam

Amsterdam is located in the Netherlands, a country known for its protective dikes, tulips, banking, and canals.

### Key Geographic Facts

Amsterdam proper has a population of just over 700 000, but, including the larger metropolitan area, it is more than one million. It is situated on 14 polders (land areas reclaimed from the sea), which are kept dry by 84 pumping stations. Almost one quarter of Amsterdam is made up of canals and rivers. While parts of the old city are 60 centimetres above sea level, other, more recently created, parts are six metres below sea level. There is a complex network of dikes and canals that keep the land dry, but periodic flooding is commonplace.

Amsterdam has a temperate marine climate. Although its latitude is similar to that of Winnipeg, temperatures are moderated by the North Sea, so it is cooler in summer (highs about 25°C) and warmer in winter (lows about 0°C) than Winnipeg. In this respect, it is similar to Vancouver, where the climate is moderated by the Pacific Ocean.

The Amstel River and its canals rarely freeze, but, when they do, many residents take to the ice on long speed-skating blades. The city is laid out in a series of concentric circles. The oldest parts of the city are in the centre, and generally the city is "younger" the farther out it spreads.

### Changing Geography

The first recorded event in Amsterdam's history was the 1204 building of a bridge across the Amstel River. Doors on the bridge dammed the river and an inlet formed, thus creating a small harbour.

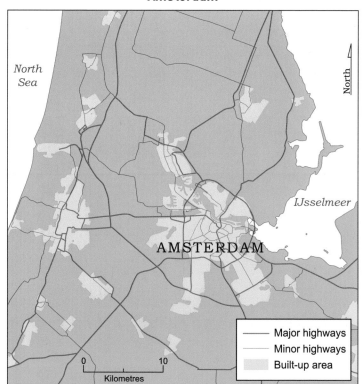

FIGURE 18.6. This map shows the location of Amsterdam, the network of major roads in and around the city, and other nearby built-up areas. It is located between the North Sea and the IJsselmeer, which is a shallow, freshwater lake.

People who lived there (the Amstelledammers) began to demand tolls from the traders of beer and herring who passed through the area. The town got its first charter in about 1300.

FIGURE 18.7. An aerial view of the streets and canals of Amsterdam. Note the regular layout and the many trees.

FIGURE 18.8. Germany invaded the Netherlands in May 1940, and this 1940 photo shows German troops driving along a main street in Amsterdam.

## Geography of the Economy

In the 17th century, when its ships sailed to North America, Indonesia, Brazil, and Africa, the Netherlands entered what is known as the *Golden Age*. Wealthy Dutch merchants financed exploration and trade all over the world. Amsterdam expanded its canal system, and it was during this time that the "ring" shape was developed. The city became a leading financial centre in the world, and an important port and cultural centre. It grew rapidly during the Industrial Revolution. Like many other places in Europe, Amsterdam suffered great losses during the Second World War, including most of its Jewish population (these dark days are documented in *The Diary of Anne Frank*. [Trans. by B.M. Mooijaart-Doubleday. London: Heron Books, 1973.] During the "hunger winter" of 1944–1945, almost all the trees were cut down for firewood, and many people died of starvation.

Amsterdam was home to the world's first stock exchange, and finance is still an important economic activity; just over 8 percent of the workforce is employed in the financial sector. During the Golden Age, many diamond cutters came to Amsterdam, and diamond-cutting is still a leading industry. Amsterdam continues to be an important port city, exporting agricultural products such as sugar beets and livestock, but its most famous agricultural export is tulip bulbs. Heineken Breweries is internationally known for its beer, which is exported to approximately 120 countries around the world. Recently, Amsterdam has focused on new technologies, such as computers, telecommunications, and biotechnology. Some multinational companies (e.g., Sony, Canon, and IBM) have their European headquarters in Amsterdam. Tourism is also a key industry, and the city is generally regarded as one of the top five to visit in Europe.

FIGURE 18.9. Taken in 1944, toward the end of the Second World War, this photo shows a small boy outside a bombed-out house.

## Current Geographic Issues

The Zandvoort Beach is a beautiful long beach located very close to Amsterdam. Many tourists and residents of the city enjoy going there on hot summer days. Parking is free, but the parking area usually fills quickly. And it can take over two hours to travel the 35 kilometres by public transit from Amsterdam's central train station to the beach.

## Distinctive Geographic Features

Amsterdam is a beautiful old-world city, and many parts date back to the Middle Ages. There are narrow cobblestone streets and crowded markets. If you were to visit, you would be amazed at the number of bikes on the streets and parked outside bus and train

terminals. People in the Netherlands are very energy conscious, and if they can bike, walk, or take public transit, they do. Public transit is very well planned and convenient. Some of the most interesting places to visit include the beach, the castles, the museums (Amsterdam has more museums per person than any other European city), and the house of Anne Frank.

 How would you deal with the congestion at Zandvoort Beach if you were:

- a tourist?
- a public transit officer?
- a member of city council?
- a hotel operator serving the tourist industry?

Give reasons for your answer.

 For an interesting site that shows historic maps and buildings of Amsterdam, visit < www.the worldtoday.ca > and follow "Links" to < www.bmz.amsterdam.nl >. For beaches, < www.infozandvoort.nl/ >; for castles, < http://home.tiscali.nl/friederichs/kastelen.html >; for museums, < www.rijksmuseum.nl/index.jsp >. For a site devoted to the memory of Anne Frank (1929–1945), < www.annefrank.org/ >. There is a good site about bikes in Amsterdam at < http://flee.com/amsterdam/index.html >. For more, follow "Links" to < www.travel forkids.com/Funtodo/Netherlands/amsterdam. htm >. By the way, you may not able to read all these sites, but the pictures are amazing.

FIGURE 18.10. The beach at Zandvoort, one of the busiest in Europe.

## São Paulo

São Paulo is located in Brazil, a country known for its long, sandy beaches, the Amazon rainforest, coffee, and soccer.

### Key Geographic Facts

New York, New York, is not the only place with a double name. São Paulo, Brazil's largest city, is located in São Paulo, Brazil's most populous state. São Paulo, with a population of over 10 million people, makes Amsterdam look like a small town. The larger metropolitan area, of which São Paulo is the centre, swells the number of people living there to more than 18 million people. That is more than half of Canada's population! Perhaps the most notable feature of São Paulo is its ongoing rapid growth. As recently as 1960, the population of the metropolitan area was under four million. Can you imagine the urban problems that arise from an increase in population of more than four times in just over 40 years?

Unlike most other colonial cities in Brazil, São Paulo is not on the coast, although it is close. Located on the Serra do Mar cliffs close to the port city of Santos, São Paulo enjoys a tropical climate. However, the altitude makes for slightly temperate weather. Built along the Tiete River, it has direct access to the natural harbour of Santos, allowing São Paulo to develop as a major transportation and shipping hub. Ethnically diverse, São Paulo continues to develop as a commercial and industrial centre, and much of the population growth is associated with ongoing industrialization. It is interesting to note that Brazil and Canada are major competitors in the manufacture of commercial aircraft.

### Changing Geography

Portugal became interested in Brazil after one of its fleets, which was sailing south and intending to round Africa, sailed much too far west and reached the coast of South America.

São Paulo

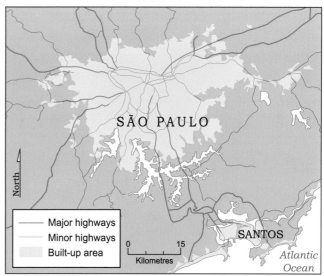

FIGURE 18.11. This map shows the location of São Paulo and the network of major roads in and around the city. Note the links to the port city of Santos.

Indigenous Tupi-Guarani Indians had settled at the site of São Paulo long before Europeans arrived. Portuguese Jesuit colonists, known as *Paulistas*, established a settlement here during the colonial era in 1554. From this location, Jesuits moved inland, and the growing city became the control centre for much of the Portuguese colony. Officially incorporated as a city in 1711, it became a chief exporter of Brazil's agricultural commodities, particularly coffee.

Immigrants started to arrive from all over the world in the mid-1800s, beginning with settlers from Italy, who came to work in the nearby coffee plantations. The area settled by the Italians began as a shanty town. Now it is one of the trendy districts of São Paulo. A national law school was founded in 1827, which helped São Paulo develop into a well-respected urban centre.

 For a site with information and photographs of São Paulo, visit < www.theworldtoday.ca > and follow "Links" to < http://members.aol.com/ pochetti5/sampa-brazil.html >.

## Geography of the Economy

São Paulo is a major industrial city. More automobiles are assembled there than in any other place in Brazil. Textiles, processed food, pharmaceuticals, furniture, and computers are all key to the urban economy. São Paulo has abundant hydroelectric power from local sources. In addition to the law school, São Paulo has many important schools and universities as well as a world-renowned art museum. Because of rapid urbanization, pollution is heavy. Some of the concern over air quality is being alleviated by the use of ethanol to fuel automobiles. Ethanol is produced from sugar cane, and sugar cane is one of Brazil's major crops. Ethanol reduces toxic emissions and allows Brazil to be less dependent on oil-producing countries.

FIGURE 18.12. An aerial view of São Paulo. Note the very large apartment building in the left of the photo.

## Current Geographic Issues

As in many other cities in the less-developed world, too many people are moving into São Paulo too quickly. It is impossible to provide the necessary urban services: roads, a water supply, and electricity, for example, which most of us take for granted. One especially tragic situation is the conditions under which street children live. In São Paulo, about 20 percent of all children live on the streets. Few of these children live beyond the age of 25, and estimates suggest a suicide rate as high as 60 percent. Street children are often abused, exploited, and even murdered.

## Distinctive Geographic Features

São Paulo is one of the most diverse and interesting cities in South America. The weather is great, and there are many fascinating places to explore, including the beaches, the museums, and the nearby Amazon rainforest.

 How would you help street kids in São Paulo if you were:

- a city or social-services planner?
- a foreign-aid worker?
- a community or religious leader?
- a junior-high-school student in Canada?

Give reasons for your answer.

 For more information on visiting São Paulo, go to <www.the worldtoday.ca> and link to <www.fodors.com/miniguides/mgresults.cfm?destination = sao_paulo@142&cur_section = fea&feature = 30011>. Sometimes the information is available only in Portuguese, so understanding this website could be a challenge!

FIGURE 18.13. The port city of Santos is a major industrial centre. Men are shown here repairing the hull of a large ship.

 For more information about street kids and how to protect and help them, visit <www.theworldtoday.ca> and follow "Links" to <www.streetchildren.org.uk> and <www.homelessworld.org.>.

## Chicago

Chicago is located in the United States, a country known for its role as a world leader, and its powerful military, democratic institutions, and influential popular culture.

*Key Geographic Facts*

Chicago is situated at the southwestern corner of Lake Michigan. It is strategically located—that is, between the industrial heartland of the United States to the east and the agricultural heartland to the south and west. The original city site was at the mouth of the Chicago River, and much of the land was swampy and had to be drained before building could take place. Today, the city has a population of almost three million in an area of approximately 500 square kilometres. When the surrounding continuous urban area, sometimes called *Chicagoland*, is included, there are about 10 million people in about 10 000 square kilometres (that is 100 km x 100 km). Chicago's central location and its accessibility to a great variety of transportation modes made it a popular hub for transporting items that had to be moved quickly, such as grain and meat. Today, Chicago is an important industrial and transportation centre and home to the headquarters of many large companies.

### Chicago

**FIGURE 18.14. This map shows the built-up area and the network of major roads in and around the city. Chicago stretches along the edge of Lake Michigan.**

American poet Carl Sandburg (1978–1967) provided a powerful picture of Chicago in the opening lines of his poem entitled "Chicago" [In *Chicago Poems*. New York: Dover Publications, 1994.]:

> *Hog Butcher for the World,*
> *Tool Maker, Stacker of Wheat,*
> *Player with Railroads and the Nation's*
> *Freight Handler;*
> *Stormy, husky, brawling,*
> *City of the Big Shoulders*

How would you describe a city you know in a few lines of poetry? Discuss with classmates, and together write about the city of your choice.

**FIGURE 18.15. One of Chicago's famous elevated railway trains crossing over La Salle Street. Note the many very tall buildings.**

## Changing Geography

For thousands of years before the Europeans arrived, indigenous peoples travelled through and occupied the region where Chicago now exists. The area's first European settler was Jean Baptiste Point du Sable, who arrived in the 1770s. Chicago was nearly destroyed in 1871 by fire. After the fire, the city was rebuilt, and industrial growth resumed. By the early 20th century, Chicago was important for meat-packing, furniture-manufacturing, and printing and publishing. Suburban development increased in direct relation to that of transportation, and the city spread outward, first with steam trains, then with an electrical railway, and, by the 1930s, with parkways.

## Geography of the Economy

Chicago is home to many large companies, including Boeing, Sara Lee, Rubbermaid, Kraft, Sears, and McDonald's. Chicago's stock exchange is also important to the city, and modern commodities trading was pioneered here.

**Water Treatment** The Chicago River flows into Lake Michigan, and most of Chicago's sewer systems used to drain into the Chicago River. As the river became more polluted, people started becoming sick with cholera. A doctor discovered the association between the illness and the contaminated water, which in turn caused a flurry of action. For instance, the flow of the Chicago River was reversed so that it emptied into the Illinois and Mississippi rivers via the Sanitary and Ship Canal rather than Lake Michigan. Today, Chicago treats its waste water before dumping it back into the river system.

FIGURE 18.16. The world headquarters of McDonald's are located just outside Chicago. McDonald's Plaza is an office complex. Close by is Hamburger University, McDonald's worldwide management training centre.

## Current Geographic Issues

One challenge facing Chicago is that, as it continues to spread outward into Chicagoland, prime agricultural land is being eaten up by commercial and residential development.

## Distinctive Geographic Features

Chicago is not as intimidating as New York, and it is less smoggy than Los Angeles; it is a fun place to visit. Just about every place you would want to go is easily reached by foot or public transit. Should you get there, you can visit:

- some of the worlds' tallest office buildings

- Graceland (a cemetery and a tourist attraction; just about every famous person ever buried in Chicago can be found here)

- the Magnificent Mile (shop 'til you drop)

- uptown (if you love live music, or maybe just want to expand your horizons; it is hard not to appreciate jazz and the blues after visiting Chicago)

- museums (there are lots of great museums in Chicago, and many of them have free-admission days)

**Chicago's Flood of 1992** In 1899, a series of interconnecting tunnels was built 40 metres beneath street level. The tunnels housed railroad tracks that were used to haul coal to and remove ashes from the office buildings in the downtown area. This system served Chicago well, right up until the 1940s, when other power sources replaced coal. On 13 April 1992, workers were placing support pillars into the Chicago River bottom. One pillar punctured a tunnel and formed a hole the size of a car. River water poured into the tunnels and flooded office basements in the entire city-centre area. A state of emergency was declared, and the area was evacuated. The hole was eventually plugged, but the flooding caused close to $2 billion worth of damage.

FIGURE 18.17. This hayfield near Lockport, Illinois, is being harvested for the final time in July 2002. The land has been sold for new residential development. Note the new houses in the background. Lockport is about 50 km southwest of Chicago.

 How would you respond to the urban spread into agricultural land if you were:

- a farmer?

- a person wanting a home in the suburbs?

- a city planner?

- an environmental scientist?

Give reasons for your answer.

 For a great website, visit < www.theworldtoday.ca > and follow "Links" to < www.pbs.org/wgbh/amex/chicago/maps/index.html >; for a teenage take on Chicago, < www.teenchicago.org/ >; for information on Al Capone (1899–1947), an infamous American gangster, and other seedy aspects of Chicago's history, < www.chicagohistory.org/history/index.html >; for Graceland, < www.graveyards.com/graceland/ > . For Chicago neighbourhood tours, go to < www.chgocitytours.com >. For museums, < http://cgov.cityofchicago.org/ > and search "museums." There's much more at < www.877chicago.com/ >.

## Cities around the World: Different but Similar

As you explored Amsterdam, São Paulo, and Chicago, did you notice any similarities among them? There are many:

- The three cities are located close to major bodies of water and have easy access to shipping routes.

- The three cities experienced growth during the Industrial Revolution. During times of intense urbanization, housing is a huge challenge for the many impoverished people who move to the city. São Paulo is the only one of the three that is continuing to experience intense urbanization.

- The three cities are important railroad centres.

- The three cities have high-rise office towers and apartment buildings.

- The three cities are centres of culture and learning.

- The three cities are supported by nearby areas of rich agricultural activity.

- The histories of all three cities suggest that natural disasters, wars, disease, and other challenges slowed growth for a time but that people always regrouped and rebuilt.

One thing you might have thought of as you read this chapter is the ability that humans have to survive and even thrive in difficult circumstances. People in the most difficult slum areas build homes from items that we would take to the dump; children create toys out of tin cans and bits of old tires and soccer balls out of tightly bound rags.

Generally, when people live close together, they consume fewer resources, use less land, and enjoy improved social and economic standards. They tend to band together to tackle problems such as bad sanitation and disease.

 In the introduction to this book, we suggested that many differences among far-flung places in the world are gradually being erased as Western influences spread. Our study of three cities confirms this suggestion. An English-speaking visitor would find it easy to be understood in all three cities. A visitor to each of these cities would be able to find an American fast-food outlet such as McDonald's for lunch and stay overnight in a chain hotel such as the Holiday Inn. Are the world's cities beginning to look the same? Discuss this question.

 Select a large city in Europe or the Americas that you do not know well. Using library and Internet sources, research the following five questions. Include maps and diagrams with your answers.

1. Where is this city? Why is it there? Why should I care? (In answering these questions, you are exploring key geographic facts and issues.)

2. How has this city changed over time? (In answering this question, you are exploring changing geography.)

3. How do people make their living in this city? (In answering this question, you are exploring the geography of economy.)

4. What are some challenges that this city faces? (In answering this question, you are exploring current geographic issues.)

5. Why would I want to visit this city? (In answering this question, you are exploring distinctive geographic features.)

# TOWARD A SUSTAINABLE WORLD

**19**

## Guiding Questions

1. How can we ensure that continued economic growth and a satisfactory quality of life will be possible for future generations?

2. How is consumerism in more-developed countries affecting the environment?

Wetlands are amazing. They are natural water purifiers and a key part of the process of cleaning our environment. Wetlands are an important part of a complex food chain, the bottom of which includes microbes and bacteria. Wetlands typically absorb harmful bacteria and convert them to food for insects and other small organisms, which in turn are eaten by larger organisms that are higher up on the food chain.

You have probably heard about "agricultural runoff": the water that drains into lakes and rivers from farm fields that have been treated with fertilizer (phosphorus and nitrogen). Wetlands can clean up to 92 percent of all phosphorus and 95 percent of all nitrogen that enters from the watershed area draining into a wetland. Phosphorus and nitrogen in rivers and lakes can cause explosions in the growth of algae (algae bloom) and other plants, which can be harmful to an ecosystem.

Think back to chapter 18. What did the people of Amsterdam do with their wetlands? They drained and filled them. What did the people of Chicago do? They drained and filled them. What have the people of Winnipeg done? They have drained and filled them. What do most cities located near wetlands do? They drain and fill them to make more land available for people: for agriculture, suburbs, shopping centres, and industrial parks.

Wet and swampy land looks unproductive because crops cannot be grown, nor can houses or factories be built on it. Yet the environmental benefits of wetlands are so great that some cities in Europe have begun developing artificial wetlands to clean their sewage waste. Some cities in Canada are planning this kind of waste-treatement system.

**Wetlands Act Like Sponges** They absorb water when the ground is very wet in spring or during rainy seasons and slowly release water during dry times. They reduce flooding because of their water-holding capacity, and they decrease the effects of drought. A wetland area is an example of an ecosystem. Recall from chapter 2 that an ecosystem is the total environment of a community of plants and animals.

 For more information about wetlands, visit < www.theworldtoday.ca > and follow "Links" to < www.ducks.ca >.

FIGURE 19.1. The Okavango Delta wetland in Botswana, Southern Africa, is the largest inland delta in the world. It spreads in a maze of channels, lakes, and lagoons over about 15 000 km$^2$ of the arid Kalahari region. The area is home to many bird, animal, and plant species.

## How Human Activities Affect Natural Environments

As we have seen throughout this book, humans adapt to natural environments. For example, historically, we have chosen to settle in areas that allow us to practise agriculture, and we favour areas that allow us access to water for transport of people and goods. We not only adapt to natural environments, but we also change natural environments.

Many of the changes we make are intentional—for example in the domestication of plants and animals, the cutting down of forests to provide land for agriculture, and the mining of coal to provide power for industries. However, many of our changes have unintended, but negative, consequences that far outweigh the positive ones. The changes to wetlands are an example of such an imbalance.

Three key forces that drive what we do to our natural environments:

1. the number of people living on earth

2. our technologies: how we are able to change natural environments

3. the lifestyle we wish to follow: how we want (not just need) to live

To understand the way we affect our natural environments, it is critical to know how these three driving forces have developed. All three are more intense now than they were in the past. Twelve thousand years ago, when there were only about four million humans on earth—who lived a foraging lifestyle of hunting, fishing, and scavenging—very few changes to the natural environment were made. Furthermore, the changes that humans did make were likely short-lived. For thousands of years, humans lived lives focused mainly on survival: finding food and shelter.

Today, it is very different:

- there are many more of us (about 6.5 billion in 2006)

- we have developed numerous technologies—notably agricultural and industrial—that result in our changing natural environments, both intentionally and accidentally

- especially in the more-developed world, we do much more than merely seek to survive; as discussed in chapter 4, we seek to satisfy an ever-increasing list of wants.

In 50 years' time, when you are still likely to be alive, there will be even more of us (the current prediction for 2050 is 9.3 billion). Humans will have developed even more new technologies, and we will likely have added even more to our list of wants. This means that we will have an even greater effect on our natural environment.

 Discuss the following:

1. It is not possible for us to stop affecting our natural environment. We have to live, build shelters, and feed ourselves.

2. We need to think not only of ourselves but also of those who follow us: our children and their children. But how are we to do this? How can we live our lives so that we leave a world in which our children and their children can live healthy lives?

## Sustainable Development

We need to practise **sustainable development**. In the past, we did not consider the effect our actions had on the quality of life for future generations. We did not act responsibly. For example, we drained wetlands, cut down forests, and caused the extinction of entire animal species. One reason for this irresponsibility was that our planet Earth seemed so bountiful.

We humans are the dominant species on earth, and we have affected all of its ecosystems. Many ecosystems have been damaged or destroyed, especially through the conversion of natural habitats to agricultural or urban use. One notable consequence of our changes to ecosystems is a loss of **biodiversity**. Generally, temperate mid-latitude areas have been the most affected, while tundra, Arctic areas, and deserts have been least affected. However, as oil and other natural resources become scarcer around the globe, human activities will alter these regions as well.

Perhaps we need to do more than practise sustainable development. Perhaps we need some radical rethinking of our place in the world. Instead of thinking of ourselves as separate from other species and the natural environment, it might be better to think of ourselves as but one part of the earth's ecosystem. This means that we need to move away from an **anthropocentric** view of the world toward an **ecocentric** view.

**Who Benefits? Who Suffers?** Remember how Chicago solved one of the problems it faced? (See chapter 18.) Chicagoans must have been thrilled when the flow of the Chicago River was reversed and the drinking water became cleaner. This may have been development, but it was certainly not sustainable development. Sustainable development involves fixing a problem or satisfying a need in a way that does not harm others, either living or still to be born.

**anthropocentric** A view of the world that centres on humans as the dominant species on earth, seeing the welfare of this one species as of paramount importance. Other species are important only as they can benefit humans.

**biodiversity** A widely used abbreviation of biological diversity. Refers to the number and variety of organisms in a given region. An area with good biodiversity has many different organisms that are interrelated. It is estimated that there are between 5 and 10 million plant and animal species on earth, although only about 1.5 million have been catalogued and described so far.

**ecocentric** A view of the world that focuses on all of the natural environment, stressing that the interests of humans should not be placed above the interests of other species. This view stresses that the continued existence of humans is dependent on our seeing ourselves as but one part of the natural world and also on our treating the environment in a respectful way.

**sustainable development** Development that meets the needs of the present generation without compromising the ability of future generations to meet their own needs.

# Biodiversity

Biodiversity is related to latitude. On land, biodiversity is highest in tropical rainforests; marine biodiversity is highest in coral reefs. Generally speaking, the higher the biodiversity, the better our environment will be.

## Arguments for Biodiversity

Five arguments that support biodiversity as a good thing and that humans need to maintain have to do with:

1. Food: Because plants that are genetically similar could all be lost at once due to disease and pests, it is important that we have a genetically diverse pool of plants for our food supply. *Monoculture* is the term used to describe a dependence on plants that are genetically similar. Today, most of our food comes from about 20 plant and about 10 animal species.

2. Medicine: Many of our modern-day medicines are derived from plant sources—for example, heart stimulants, malaria treatments, anti-inflammatory medications, and cancer medications. As we reduce biodiversity, our chances of finding more of these helpful plants decreases.

3. Ecology: Many natural processes, such as soil formation and maintenance, and air and water purification, depend on biodiversity.

4. Beauty and interest: Imagine life if everything were the same colour, or if there were only one type of tree, flower, bird, or insect. It would be boring! Biodiversity keeps us interested and engaged in the world around us. It is, of course, very difficult to attach a monetary value to biodiversity.

5. Human rights: For many indigenous cultures, caring for the earth is a long-practised tradition. In order to preserve the human rights of minority cultures, we must also respect some of their beliefs about the earth and their total dependence on it.

**monoculture** The cultivation of a single crop on a farm or a region or a country.

**Types of Plants** Did you know that scientists have classified over 250 000 different types of plants and that there are more still to be discovered? We depend on only about 20 of these plant types for our food.

FIGURE 19.2. A golden coconut tree on a beach in Tahiti in the South Pacific.

## Arguments against Biodiversity

Some scholars argue that biodiversity is not crucial to the survival and well-being of the earth. Three arguments supporting the idea that biodiversity may not be a good thing are:

1. The economy would be restricted: If we put measures in place to keep biodiversity high, there would be too many restrictions on economic development. This argument highlights the obvious fact that humans reduce biodiversity as they engage in agricultural and industrial activities. Natural environments are changed into human-made environments, such as cities.

2. A few is enough: Who needs more than a few types of trees, animals, and plants? Why not keep the useful ones and not worry about the ones that are extinct or endangered?

3. Extinction is a natural process: Biodiversity has been fluctuating all along. Protection of biodiversity might have preserved the dinosaurs and the woolly mammoth.

Imagine what life would be like now if they had not become extinct! Extinction of a species is just part of the normal process of life. In fact, 99 percent of all life forms that have come before us are now extinct.

 List three reasons that show why biodiversity is important. List three reasons that show why biodiversity is not important. Should we adopt laws that protect biodiversity, or should we allow plants and animals threatened by extinction to die out? Make a decision and argue your case.

**Britain's Wildflowers**  In 2005, botanists completed a two-year study of Britain's wildflowers, concluding that 20 percent were critically endangered or facing extinction. Loss of habitat is a prime reason for the decline. Of concern to the scientists was the decline of plentiful flowers that are not yet endangered but have been reduced by as much as 50 to 80 percent.

FIGURE 19.3. Recently planted pine trees beside a mature pine forest on a hillside in the central region of North Island, New Zealand.

# Conserving Regions

One way to help preserve biodiversity is to try to conserve regions that have not yet been greatly affected by humans. Some of these regions are very large, and some are small (it is possible to find such regions within cities).

For instance, the Seine River Greenway in Winnipeg includes river-bottom forests, also known as *bois-des-esprits*. Although some of these are disturbed, there are approximately 32 hectares of pristine river-bottom forest still remaining. These areas are a sample of what the river and forest were like before the city of Winnipeg was built. They are the heart and lungs of the Greenway, an ecological jewel that merits conservation.

The undisturbed river-bottom forest has witnessed countless winters, floods, and droughts. It was constantly at risk from developers before a protection plan was approved. The plan was supported by the city and the province following appeals from citizens, including many students. Walking trails are included in the plan so that people who frequent the area can enjoy the forest without disturbing it. An interpretive centre is to be located nearby.

There are many examples of landscape **conservation** around the world. One is the European Ecological Network, which is working to ensure the protection and enhancement of the wetland functions and values of the Kopacki Rit and Beda-Karapancsa wetlands in eastern Europe. As well, it is working to protect and enhance the natural river dynamics of the portion of the Danube River that lies within the wetlands. Use an atlas, library sources, and the Internet to locate this region and learn more about it.

Another aspect of sustainable development is the restoration of regions to their former natural state that have been changed by humans. This **restoration ecology** is not

FIGURE 19.4. The Seine River Greenway in Winnipeg.

possible everywhere; for instance, Amsterdam can no longer be returned to its pre-urban state. But, in some places, restoration *is* possible.

The highest rate of tropical rainforest deforestation in Central America occurs in Costa Rica, and it is also here that there have been several successful attempts at restoration ecology. The Cloudbridge Project is a beautiful example of reforestation of a high-elevation rainforest that was damaged from fire and ranching.

**conservation** The management of an environmental region so that it will be maintained, restored, enhanced, and protected for a long time in such a way that it benefits humans and the environment.

**restoration ecology** Ideally, this is the complete return of an ecosystem disturbed by humans to its natural state, prior to human intervention.

 To find out more about the Seine River Greenway *bois-des-esprits* visit < www.theworldtoday.ca > and follow "Links" to < www.saveourseine.com >. Save our Seine is an organization dedicated to preserving the natural environment in Manitoba.

## Biosphere Reserves

Did you know that the United Nations, through its agency UNESCO, has designated Riding Mountain National Park as one of Canada's twelve biosphere reserves? (There are 356 biosphere reserves in 90 countries.) As defined by UNESCO, a biosphere reserve is a region that demonstrates a balanced relationship between humans and the **biosphere**. This means that people work cooperatively and in harmony with nature by conserving the ecosystem in which they live. It also means that there is some economic activity, often agriculture, and that the local economy is sustained within this healthy ecosystem.

### The Location of Biosphere Reserves in Canada

FIGURE 19.5. There are 13 biosphere reserves in Canada representing a variety of ecosystems; the first was established in 1978 at Mont St-Hilaire, Quebec. Each reserve is an ecosystem that offers ways to reconcile modern development with the conservation of biodiversity. Before UNESCO designates a biosphere reserve, it is necessary that local people demonstrate their commitment. Once a reserve is established, a community-based organization or committee coordinates the activities.

One of the oldest biosphere reserves in the world is found at Lobau, about 10 kilometres southeast of Vienna, Austria. This region is part of the famous Danube River **flood plain**. The area is a small sample of a landscape that once covered much of Europe. It is a river-forest system with many types of trees, grasslands, and wetlands, and it provides a home for many birds and other kinds of wildlife as well as several unique plant species.

Designated a biosphere reserve since 1977, Lobau is protected because it provides drinking water for the city of Vienna. Although there are no humans that live within this biosphere reserve, there are human activities, including agriculture, sport fishing, hiking, swimming, and some forestry.

**biosphere** This term has two related meanings. First, it refers to the totality of life on earth, literally everything that is alive. Second, it refers to the space occupied by living things. Sometimes the term *ecosphere* is used instead of *biosphere*.

**flood plain** A flat, broad river valley that floods regularly. Flood plains are valuable because the soil is rich as a result of the salt added during a flood. Certain plants and trees will germinate only with a flood/thaw cycle. Flood plains also protect other areas from flooding. Many people live in flood plains, and they are subject to flooding problems. Winnipeg is in the Red River flood plain.

# Two Stories: Chernobyl and Pisambilla

## Social and Economic Justice after Chernobyl

### The Background

Nuclear power is an alternative to other sources of power, such as coal, oil, gas, and hydroelectricity. Since the early 1990s, it has become a very important source. As of 2006, there are about 400 nuclear reactors in the world. The countries that rely heavily on nuclear power are all in Europe. Currently, few new nuclear power plants are being built. Those that are being built are very efficient and capable of producing much more power than conventional electric power plants. One significant problem with nuclear power is that it generates dangerous waste, but scientists are finding new ways to decrease this danger. Another significant problem is the possibility of a **nuclear accident**.

### The Problem

In 1986 the Ukrainian city of Chernobyl suffered a significant nuclear accident. A nuclear power plant that was built during the Soviet era released radioactive material due to human error, and the city is now abandoned. Surrounding agricultural and forest land was poisoned, and the economy was devastated. The fallout covered not only Ukraine but also Belarus, which neighbours Ukraine. It is estimated that the accident released 30 to 40 times the amount of radioactivity of the atomic bombs that were dropped on Nagasaki and Hiroshima at the end of the Second World War. Because it is not always possible to know what causes illness and death, it is impossible to be precise about the numbers affected, but many people died and many others have become ill because of the accident.

### The Location of Chernobyl

FIGURE 19.6. Chernobyl was a small town about 110 km north of Kiev and close to the present border with Belarus.

### The Solution

Little can be done to clean up the affected landscapes of Ukraine and Belarus. Only time will decrease the radioactivity at the site. But people continue to live in the contaminated areas because they have nowhere else to go. However, in 2003, a German organization began working with Belarusians to build homes away from the contaminated zones. As people move into these homes, they become attached to their new surroundings and build relationships with the people from the countries who are helping them.

**nuclear accident** The unintentional release of a substantial amount of radioactive material into the environment.

FIGURE 19.7. This officer is fixing a Forbidden Area sign on a fence marking the 30 km off-limit radius around Chernobyl.

## Respect and Care for the Community of Life in Pisambilla

### The Background

The community of Pisambilla, Ecuador, is accessible only by a narrow, winding gravel road that climbs from the town of Cayambe into the foothills of the Cayambe volcano. Located on the equator in the Andes mountains at an altitude of 3 500 metres above sea level, the climate is cold, and a strong east wind blows nearly all the time. In the dry season, the wind withers any plants that are exposed to it. The rainy season brings clouds and drizzle. When development workers with the Christian Reformed World Relief Committee (CRWRC), a partner agency of the Canadian International Development Agency (CIDA), arrived, they wondered why people chose to live there.

Inhabited primarily by indigenous people, the Pisambilla community was formed about 100 years ago by unruly workers in a **hacienda**, who were sent there as punishment. Today, this difficult beginning inspires a very strong community spirit, and the people are able to work together to overcome many of the challenges of this harsh environment.

### The Problem

It is difficult for families to make a living, feed everybody, and send the children to school in this harsh environment. Many people from communities like Pisambilla have moved to cities, hoping for a better life. Unfortunately, life in the city does not always work out, and people often end up either begging or working for very low pay.

### The Solution

Working together with indigenous leaders from the community, CRWRC development workers began a project that has transformed the

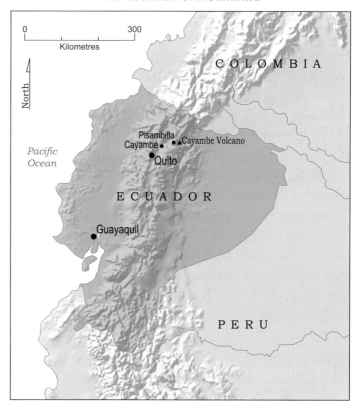

**The Location of Pisambilla**

FIGURE 19.8. Pisambilla is located in the Andean mountain region of northern Ecuador, close to the Cayambe volcano.

community. For example, the people are now growing vegetables in plots that are fenced in or that have natural windbreaks of small trees. The increased availability of nutritious food is only a tiny aspect of what makes the CRWRC work successful. It has given the people a model for cooperative change. They realize not only that positive change is possible but also that they themselves can bring about the changes.

**hacienda**  A Spanish term for a large agricultural estate. Similar to a ranch.

FIGURE 19.9. The agricultural landscape around Pisambilla.

# The Earth Charter

*The Earth Charter* is a statement that was developed during the Earth Summit, a United Nations Conference on the Environment and Development held in Rio de Janeiro in 1992. You can think of it as a kind of "rights of the earth" document. *The Earth Charter*, the document that came out of the summit, is a foundational statement agreed upon by most of the countries of the world. Even though agreement does not always result in action, *The Earth Charter* is an important document because it clearly highlights key ways to ensure that we live in a sustainable world. It includes the following 16 statements, organized under four headings:

## Respect and Care for the Community of Life

1. Respect the earth and all its diversity.

2. Care for the community of life—all life—with understanding, compassion, and love.

3. Build democratic societies that are just, participatory, sustainable, and peaceful.

4. Secure earth's bounty and beauty for present and future generations.

## Ecological Integrity

5. Protect and restore the integrity of earth's ecological systems, with special concern for biological diversity and the natural processes that sustain life.

6. Prevent harm as the best method of environmental protection and, when knowledge is limited, apply a precautionary approach.

7. Adopt patterns of production, consumption, and reproduction that safeguard the earth's regenerative capacities, human rights, and community well-being.

8. Advance the study of ecological sustainability and promote the open exchange and wide application of the knowledge acquired.

## Social and Economic Justice

9. Eradicate poverty as an ethical, social, and environmental imperative.

10. Ensure that economic activities and institutions at all levels promote human development in an equitable and sustainable manner.

11. Affirm gender equality and equity as prerequisites to sustainable development and ensure universal access to education, health care, and economic opportunity.

12. Uphold the right of all, without discrimination, to a natural and social environment supportive of human dignity, bodily health, and spiritual well-being, with special attention to the rights of indigenous peoples and minorities.

## Democracy, Non-Violence, and Peace

13. Strengthen democratic institutions at all levels, and provide transparency and accountability in governance, inclusive participation in decision-making, and access to justice.

14. Integrate into formal education and life-long learning the knowledge, values, and skills needed for a sustainable way of life.

15. Treat all living beings with respect and consideration.

16. Promote a culture of tolerance, nonviolence, and peace.

 *The Earth Charter* can be considered a "rights of the earth" document. How does this compare to the human-rights documents discussed in chapter 5?

# Eco-Footprints: How Big Are Yours?

Are you wearing sandals or big, steel-toed boots? How many worlds would it take to support the population if everyone used resources the way you do?

Your eco-footprint measures, in hectares, the amount of resources that you, as an individual, take up. At present, there are about 1.8 biologically productive hectares available per person in the world. North Americans tend to require the greatest amount of space for their needs and wants (the biggest footprint), most Europeans are somewhere in the middle, and most less-developed countries use the least amount of space. Bangladesh uses only 0.5 hectares per person. Canadians on average use 8.8 hectares per person; if everyone lived at the level of most Canadians, we would need approximately five planets like Earth to sustain us all. No wonder people daydream about colonizing Mars!

Canada still has an abundance of natural resources, including the most plentiful supply of fresh water in the world, clean air, and long distances between cities. We therefore imagine that a lot more of the earth is available for our use than there really is. We live in a cold climate and need to use more resources to keep us warm in the winter than people do in warmer climates, a fact that is taken into account when we calculate the eco-footprint of the average Canadian. If you live in a city, the calculation of your eco-footprint takes into account the roads and infrastructure of the city, even if you, as an individual, do not use a car.

Think about Canada: Why are the densely populated areas located where they are? One primary reason that cities develop where they do is that, historically, people chose to live where there was good agricultural land, easy transportation routes (usually rivers or lakes),

"If you are planning ahead for a year, sow rice;
For ten years, plant trees;
For a hundred years, educate the people"
(Chinese proverb).

and a habitable climate. In effect, we choose to grow houses instead of crops on good agricultural land (for one thing, it is inexpensive and easy to dig and install sewer lines and other underground services in areas that are good for agriculture). We need to be concerned about this trend.

Prime agricultural land continues to be consumed by new urban subdivisions. This is especially true around Toronto, in the Niagara Peninsula of Ontario, in the Okanagan Valley of British Columbia, and around Vancouver. Orchards, fields, and small forests have been replaced by strip malls or houses with big garages. In the Niagara Peninsula, people may commute over an hour just to get to work, putting a burden on transportation systems and polluting the air.

In some cases, the ever-increasing demand for houses has pushed development even onto unstable slopes, which in turn has deforested areas that used to harbour wildlife, prevent soil erosion, and provide areas of natural beauty.

The negative consequences of our energy-wasting ways are increasing as the population of the world increases. As more people populate the earth, the strain on the natural resources will grow. In chapter 20, we will examine some of these consequences and suggest some steps we can take to prevent further harm.

 Check out your eco-footprint before you continue reading. Visit < www.theworldtoday.ca > and follow "Links" to < http://ecofoot.org >.

# SHARING THE PLANET

Think way back to your kindergarten days. Remember the activity area that everyone always wanted to play in—the popular one? Chances are that the teacher had some method in place to make sure that everyone got a chance to play in the favoured activity centre. Your teacher did not allow only the strongest children, the quickest children, or the most aggressive children a chance to play in the popular activity centre; the teacher made sure that everyone got a turn, even the shy children.

Think of our planet as a kindergarten classroom arranged into various activity centres. Some centres have it all: lots of toys and opportunities to play, and all the milk and cookies a child could want. Other activity centres are less welcoming; the children who play there do not have much. They would like to play somewhere else, but they cannot,

because there is nobody to make sure that everyone has a turn in the popular activity centre.

If the planet were a kindergarten classroom, is your activity centre (where you live) one of those areas that has it all? We live on this planet without someone like a teacher making sure that everyone gets a turn in the centre that has it all. In the real world, it is the citizens themselves, of each and every country, who need to make sure everyone is playing fair.

Sharing the planet is a lot more complicated than sharing an activity centre in a kindergarten classroom. It involves the wise use of resources, a do-no-harm approach, an awareness of how much there is to be shared and how many people there are that need to share it. It also involves an awareness of how your actions affect this planet, the global village, and your neighbours around the earth.

 Discuss with your classmates the following questions: Do you remember your kindergarten class? What was the favourite activity centre? How did your teacher ensure that everyone got a chance to be in the favoured centre? How is our world like a kindergarten classroom? How is our world not like a kindergarten classroom? Give reasons for your answers.

# Natural Resources

Natural resources are the resources needed by humans that are produced by the earth's natural processes. They include air, soil, fossil fuels, minerals, plants, and animals. Some of these resources are renewable, which means that they are naturally restored as they deplete. For example, if we fish using appropriate quotas, then fish resources will always be available to us. Similarly, if we harvest forests in a way that allows new growth to occur, then forest resources will always be available to us. Others resources are not renewable. For example, the oil and gas that we mine from the ground are not replaced naturally (except over the very long period of geological time).

As you saw in chapter 19, Canadians, like people in many other more-developed countries, tend to use up lots of natural resources. We live in a country that "has it all." We continue to use up our resources very quickly, without always taking into account how it might affect some of our global neighbours. Consider this: the wealthiest 20 percent of the world's people (which includes Canada), consume 86 percent of its resources, while the poorest 20 percent consume only 1 percent. Chances are, in your kindergarten classroom, the teacher made sure you cleaned everything up at the end of the day. Here in the kindergarten classroom of earth, few measures are taken to ensure that we clean up at the end of the day. Hopefully, this chapter will encourage you to do your part.

Cleaning up after our human activities is not always possible. Sometimes our activities cause irreversible changes. For example, when we build a shopping centre or a new housing development on farmland, there is no possibility of returning the land to its earlier use.

FIGURE 20.1. Children playing in a kindergarten class.

 It is difficult today not to have heard of global warming. It features regularly in the media. Take this opportunity to look at recent issues of newspapers and news magazines, follow the news on radio and television, and perhaps use an Internet search engine to look up "global warming." Based on your review of the media, write down three facts about global warming that surprise you and three facts that you already knew.

**Question** Does sharing the planet mean that we need to ask ourselves whether our human choices and activities are contributing to some negative and irreversible changes to the natural environment?

**Answer** Yes. Human choices and activities lead to many negative changes. The most discussed negative change is global warming. (If the answer is yes, then we need to rethink and change our lifestyles.)

## The Natural Greenhouse Effect

We need the **natural greenhouse effect**. It is an important physical phenomenon that helps keep us, and all other living things on our planet, alive. Heat from the sun reaches us in the form of shortwave **radiation** and is able to pass easily through the atmosphere and warm the earth's surface. Some of this heat radiates back from the earth's warmed surface, but now it is in the form of longwave radiation, which is unable to pass easily through the atmosphere. Some naturally occurring gases in the earth's atmosphere absorb this long-wave radition, and these gases contribute additional warming to the earth. It is this additional warming that we call the natural greenhouse effect.

So, what difference does the natural greenhouse effect make to temperatures on the earth's surface? Consider this: without the natural greenhouse effect, the **average global temperature** would be about minus 15°C. Very few living things could develop and survive. But the natural greenhouse effect gives us an average global temperature of about plus 15°C. That is quite a difference!

Which gases in the atmosphere are responsible for this remarkable physical circumstance? The earth's atmosphere consists of two principal gases: nitrogen (78 percent) and oxygen (21 percent). That adds up to 99 percent. It is the other 1 percent that allows for the natural greenhouse effect. It includes carbon dioxide ($CO_2$), methane ($CH_4$), water vapour ($H_2O$), and ozone ($O_3$).

### Natural Climate Change

Climates change naturally, and the earth has gone through many climates. Much early movement of humans around the world occurred during periods of much colder temperatures (the ice ages). Although the causes of major climate changes are not fully understood, it is possible that they are caused by slight changes in the axial tilt of the earth and slight variation in the earth's orbit around the sun.

The most recent ice age ended about 10 000 years ago, but temperatures on the earth continue to change gradually anyway. Consider the past 1 000 years, for which relatively detailed documentation is available. The period from 1000 to 1200 was very warm, whereas the period from 1450 to 1850 was much cooler.

**average global temperature** A concept (generalization) rather than a fact, because there is not enough equipment to measure it precisely. In principle, it is calculated by measuring the temperature each day of the year at many locations all around the world and calculating an average temperature for each location. All of these averages are then added together, and a single grand average is calculated.

**natural greenhouse effect** Refers to the blanket-like effect of the atmosphere in retaining heat at the earth's surface.

**radiation** Transmission of energy in the form of electromagnetic waves.

**Short and Long Wavelengths** Why does the wavelength change when the sun's rays bounce off the earth's surface and head back toward the atmosphere? It is because wavelength depends on the heat of the object emitting the rays—the hotter the object, the shorter the wavelength; the cooler the object, the longer the wavelength. Of course, the sun is very hot, so it emits shortwave rays, whereas the earth is comparatively cool, so it emits longwave rays.

**Climate and Weather** We are talking about climate in this chapter, not about weather. Check back to chapter 2 if you are unsure about the difference between the two.

In summary, there are two very important facts about the greenhouse effect and global warming:

1. There is a natural greenhouse effect: the earth's atmosphere is like a blanket that keeps the earth's surface warm. This is crucial to the survival of life on earth.

2. Temperatures on the surface of the earth have been changing naturally for millions of years. These cycles of climate change proceeded for most of that time without any "help" from human beings. Scientists are not entirely certain about why these cyclical changes occur.

**Jean-Baptiste Fourier** The idea of the natural greenhouse effect can be traced back to Jean-Baptiste Fourier (1768–1830), a French scientist who suggested in 1827 that an "atmospheric effect" kept the earth warmer than it would be without atmospheric gases. Have you noticed that the temperature falls lower overnight if the sky is clear than if the sky is cloudy? This is because clouds work to retain heat that has built up over the day. In a desert area, where skies are usually clear, nighttime temperatures are often dramatically lower than daytime temperatures.

**Other Planets** Do other planets have a natural greenhouse effect? Some do, some don't. Venus is closer to the sun than is Earth, and its atmosphere is mostly $CO_2$, a greenhouse gas, so a lot of radiation from the sun is retained. The result is that the surface temperature of Venus is as high as 460℃. Mars is quite different. It is farther from the sun, and it has very little atmosphere, so there is hardly any greenhouse effect. The surface temperature is as low as minus 113℃. As Goldilocks might say, "Venus is too hot, Mars is too cold, but Earth is just right."

## The Atmospheric Greenhouse Effect

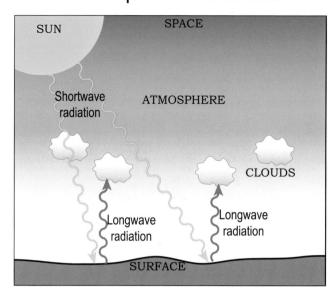

FIGURE 20.2. Shortwave radiation from the sun passes easily through the atmosphere. The returning longwave radiation from the surface of the earth is absorbed by the atmosphere or reflected back to the earth's surface.

## The Greenhouse Effect in a Parked Car

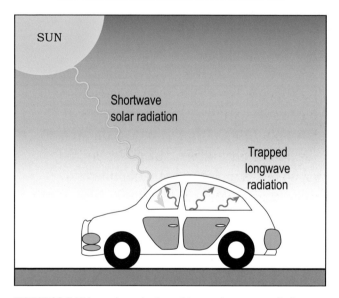

FIGURE 20.3. This car is parked outside on a hot summer's day on the prairie. Shortwave solar radiation passes through the car windows and heats the inside of the car. Some of this radiation bounces off the warmed surfaces inside the car as longwave radiation and tries to get out of the car. But the glass windows of the car prevent the longwave radiation from escaping and further warm the inside of the car (in the same way that the greenhouse gases prevent longwave radiation from escaping the earth). The result is that the air inside the car becomes much warmer than the air outside. Something similar happens in your tent when you are camping. Greenhouse gases in the atmosphere, the car windows, and the tent material all do the same thing: trap longwave radiation.

# Global Warming Caused by Humans

There is good reason to believe that something new began to happen about 1750 and is continuing today. A scientific consensus is emerging that, for the first time, it is humans who are causing **global warming**. As noted in chapter 18, there are three driving forces behind this:

1. There are now so many of us. Remember from chapter 3 that the number of people on earth increased very slowly for many thousands of years. This slow growth changed dramatically about 1750, and rapid growth has continued through to today and will continue until the middle of this century. The more of us there are on the earth, the more we change it to satisfy our needs and wants.

2. We are continually developing new technologies. Again, the key date is about 1750, when the Industrial Revolution began (as discussed in chapter 17). Probably the single most important industrial development was the mining and burning of coal to provide power for new machinery. Today, oil is a very important source of power. In general, the more things we do, the more we change our natural environments.

3. Not only are we able to do more and more, but also, more and more of us want more and more things. As discussed in chapter 4, for those of us in the more-developed world, our wants go far beyond merely satisfying our basic needs.

Why does it matter that humans are causing some global warming? Most scientists are certain of only two facts:

1. The global warming caused by humans is proceeding rapidly—more rapidly than changes would occur naturally.

2. The global warming caused by humans is unwelcome, for several reasons: it will lead to melting of the ice in the Arctic and Antarctic regions, which, in turn, will lead to a higher sea level and flooding in coastal areas (melting of the ice will mean that less sunshine will be reflected back into space and the absorbed heat will further warm the atmosphere); it will cause changes in global circulation, which will lead to unpredictable changes in precipitation (causing changes in such human activities as food production); it will lead to warmer (and thus expanded) oceans, which will lead to a higher sea level.

There are two things about global warming that scientists are much less certain about:

1. How to measure the temperature increase we are causing: Because temperatures change naturally anyway, it is very difficult to know how much of any change that occurs is related to what we are doing and how much is natural. It is possible that the increase in global temperatures that is caused by human activities is about 0.5°C and that there will be a further increase caused by humans of between 1.5°C and 3.5°C during this century. This may not sound like a lot, but consider that the average global temperature during the last ice age was only about 5°C less than it is today.

**global warming** The scientific fact that human activities, especially the burning of fossil fuels, are adding to the greenhouse gases that are naturally present in the atmosphere and causing a rise in temperatures on the earth's surface. Note that a small but vocal minority of scientists question the reality of global warming, and some others question the role we, as humans, play in global warming.

2. What should we be doing about temperature increase: How should we be responding to the fact that we are causing global warming?

## Three Important Gases

The three most important gases related to global warming caused by humans are carbon dioxide, methane, and chlorofluorocarbons.

### Carbon Dioxide

Carbon dioxide ($CO_2$) is used by plants in the process of photosynthesis. When plants take in $CO_2$, they store carbon (C) in the plant and release oxygen ($O_2$) into the air. (Interestingly, humans do it the other way round. We breathe in $O_2$ and breathe out $CO_2$.)

As we humans began to practise agriculture, we burned the natural plant vegetation to make way for cultivated crops. Burning vegetation releases the C stored in the plant material, adding $CO_2$ to the atmosphere. $CO_2$ is a powerful greenhouse gas. We have been doing this for a long time, but we have been doing it especially intensely over the last few hundred years.

Over millions of years, when plants die, the waste plant material becomes what we call *fossil fuel:* coal, oil, and natural gas, for example. Since about 1750, we have been discovering and removing these fossil fuels from just beneath the surface of the earth, where they are naturally stored. The use of fossil fuels requires burning them, and this releases the stored carbon, which adds $CO_2$ to the atmosphere.

When we burn fossil fuels, we are interfering with the natural cycle. We are releasing millennia-old sources of stored carbon into the atmosphere very quickly. Because we use fossil fuels to power many of our industrial activities, to heat our homes, to grow our crops, and to move from place to place in cars and airplanes,

we are today adding ever-increasing amounts of $CO_2$ into the atmosphere. Burning fossil fuels is the major way that we are adding to the natural greenhouse effect.

While it is immediately obvious to people that burning fossil fuels causes pollution, it has become clear only in the last few decades just how damaging this might be to the long-term health of our atmosphere and climate.

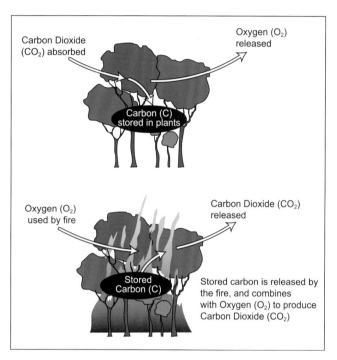

Carbon Dioxide ($CO_2$) absorbed

Oxygen ($O_2$) released

Carbon (C) stored in plants

Oxygen ($O_2$) used by fire

Carbon Dioxide ($CO_2$) released

Stored Carbon (C)

Stored carbon is released by the fire, and combines with Oxygen ($O_2$) to produce Carbon Dioxide ($CO_2$)

FIGURE 20.4. Carbon dioxide. When plants decompose or burn, the stored carbon is released into the air. It combines with oxygen and becomes $CO_2$. Think of it as a math equation something like this: $C + O_2 = CO_2$.

 It is helpful to pause and make sure that you understand the three driving forces behind temperature change. Discuss these in a small-group setting and prepare a brief group summary statement of each of the three. Report your summaries to the class and then prepare a class statement. This statement will help you as you work through the next few pages, on global warming, and will also help if you study other major human effects on natural environments.

## Methane

Methane is another greenhouse gas. There are several major sources of methane; rice paddies, swamps, and wetlands all produce methane when decomposition occurs underwater and carbon combines with hydrogen.

Cud chewers—sheep, goats, camels, and especially cattle—also produce methane. There are over one billion cattle around the world, and their "burps" are major sources of methane. Methane is a byproduct of the bacteria that aid the digestion process, and, because these animals are unable to absorb methane, it is released into the atmosphere. It is estimated that cud-chewing animals are responsible for about 15 percent of all methane production in the world.

## Chlorofluorocarbons

Chlorofluorocarbons (CFCs) are also potent greenhouse gases. They do not occur naturally. Rather, they were developed for use in refrigerators and air conditioners and as propellants in aerosol cans. In 1987, an international agreement, known as the the Montreal Protocol, called for a reduction in the use of CFCs and, by 1993, CFC pollution had dropped dramatically. Nevertheless, they remain in the atmosphere, and they will remain there for decades more.

FIGURE 20.5. Everyone loves a campfire. When you watch a campfire, you are watching the stored carbon reunite with oxygen and becoming carbon dioxide once again. What the wood stored, the fire releases.

**Question** What are we doing that causes global warming?

**Answer** Through our agricultural, forestry, and industrial activities, we are releasing gases into the atmosphere that are adding to the natural greenhouse effect.

Are you confused about what we ought to be doing about global warming? So are some scientists, governments, and many other people. Look back to your review of the media and at your responses (on page 289) about global warming. (1) Do your responses correspond with the information on this page? (2) Do the media provide accurate information about this very complex and very challenging topic? (3) What questions have been stimulated by the information in this chapter but have not been answered?

## Possible Consequences of Global Warming

Scientists agree that global warming caused by humans will likely be two to three times more pronounced in higher latitudes than in the tropics. It will also likely be greater in the Arctic than in the Antarctic.

Some of the possible consequences of global warming are:

- melting ice sheets and glaciers, which will, in turn, cause a rise in the sea level and possible flooding of low-lying coastal areas

- later snowfall and earlier snowmelt, according to season

- major redistribution of worldwide precipitation patterns

- intensification of extreme weather conditions (e.g., hurricanes, droughts)

- shifts in ecosystem boundaries, northward in the northern hemisphere and southward in the southern hemisphere

- melting of the permafrost

- later freezing and earlier break-up of ice on rivers and lakes

- lengthening of growing seasons

- relocation or dying-out of many wild plant and animal species

- spread of infectious diseases as warmer temperatures allow insect populations to spread over larger areas

**Methane** Most of our waste is disposed of in landfill sites. The decomposition of this waste is also a major source of methane emissions. For example, in 1999, of the estimated 535 million tons of methane emissions, 375 million tons were the result of human activities and 18 percent of those came from waste disposal. That's a whole lot of methane.

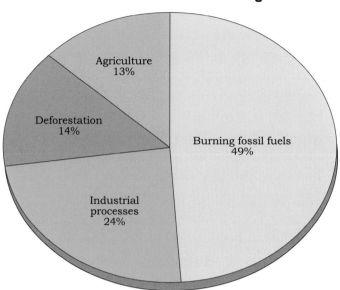

### Contributions of Various Types of Human Activities to Global Warming

FIGURE 20.6. Note the major role played by the burning of fossil fuels.

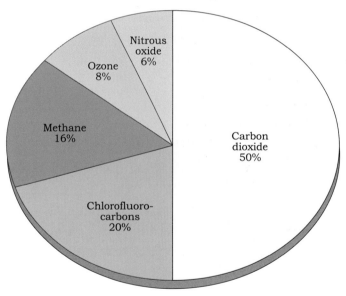

### Contributions of Various Gases to Global Warming

FIGURE 20.7. Note the major role played by $CO_2$. Also note that nitrous oxide comes from chemical fertilizers and from car emissions.

## Are You in the Smoking Section?

Restaurants, airplanes, and even movie theatres used to have areas set aside for customers who wanted to smoke. Imagine yourself in the non-smoking section of an airplane travelling to Europe during those times. There was no physical wall separating you from the smokers. Being in the non-smoking section made no difference, as the smoke infiltrated the air of the entire airplane and eventually got to where you were seated.

Our global village is a little like that airplane. The air we breathe makes its way around the globe in about 30 days. This means that one country cannot produce large amounts of greenhouse gas emissions without affecting all the other countries in the world. Canada may reduce energy consumption and switch to cleaner energy sources like wind power and hydroelectricity, but, unless the United States and other countries do the same thing, we will be affected by their smokestacks and exhaust systems as surely as the people who sat in the non-smoking section of an airplane were affected by the people smoking in the smoking section.

What can be done about global warming? The answer is simple: reduce greenhouse gas emissions. But agreeing to reduce emissions, then actually doing it, is not proving easy. The Kyoto Accord, agreed to in 1997 and to have been implemented by many countries in 2005, is one attempt by much of the world community to get everyone out of the smoking section. If we all agree to cut down on our emissions and take steps to reduce the amount of fossil fuels we burn, we will see positive results in our atmosphere. The main points of the Kyoto Accord include:

- enhance energy efficiency
- promote sustainable forest management, including reforestation
- promote sustainable agriculture
- research, promote, develop, and use new and renewable forms of energy
- reduce and phase out all government grants and other monies going to greenhouse-gas-emitting sectors of the economy
- encourage reforms in greenhouse-gas-emitting sectors of the economy and promote limiting and reducing emissions of greenhouse gases
- limit and reduce methane emissions through better waste management

 You are planning to interview three people: an elderly person, a person who "thinks green," and someone who does not believe that global warming is really happening. Brainstorm with your class about three questions you might ask each of these people relating to climate change, resource use, and any observations that they have made about weather. Do not forget the difference between climate and weather that was noted in chapter 2.

"Only when the last plant has died, the last river is poisoned, the last fish is caught will we realize that we cannot eat money" (Cree saying).

## Take a Walk, or Plant a Tree

Each of us can make a contribution to the health of our planet in many small ways. It is hard to imagine, but, every time you get into a car, you contribute to global warming. Since it is difficult for us to immediately see the results of our actions, we often forget that we really can make a difference if we decide to take action. Small steps are the key.

Very few people would stay on the Kyoto Accord "energy diet" if it meant that they would never be able to use a car again. Instead, they might think of small ways they could reduce personal emissions, perhaps by riding a bike instead of asking for a ride in a car. There are many good books and Internet sites that can help you find ways to use less energy. Search for them and make a list of things you could do to make a difference.

One of the more enjoyable ways to reduce your effect on the globe and your global village is to take a walk in an area of your community that is still in a natural state. Discovering the beauty of pristine places will help you realize what a treasure they are, and we tend to take care of those things that we treasure. Most students learn about nature from films instead of from nature itself; we are becoming less and less connected to our natural environment and its beauty. Enjoy watching nature shows on television, but go one step further: get out and get into nature. It is one small step.

Another enjoyable way to reduce your effect on the global village is to plant a tree. Nothing cleanses the air of carbon dioxide better than trees. Imagine the positive effect if you asked for a tree for your birthday, or if you led a tree-planting initiative in your school.

Take these facts into account: One tree produces about 150 kilograms of oxygen each year, and two trees can easily supply one person's oxygen needs. Each year, this same tree will clean 170 kilograms of carbon dioxide from the atmosphere by storing carbon in its wood and from cooling the environment around it. And each year, this tree will absorb almost five kilograms of other pollutants from the air around it.

Trees are an amazing source of clean air, not to mention shade, wildlife habitats, fruits and nuts, and rustling leaves. They are fun to climb. Find out more about trees, and you will not be able to resist planting one.

Reducing your emissions has a positive effect on your global neighbours. Smaller eco-footprints mean more wild areas, more biodiversity, and better health for our global village.

 In this chapter, we've mentioned how reducing emissions is like getting out of the smoking section, going on an energy diet, sharing the activity centre, and reducing your eco-footprint. Discuss some other analogies you can think of for reducing your energy consumption.

FIGURE 20.8. Misty forest around Lake Superior, in northern Ontario.

## What Might Be Our Global Future?

Global warming is just one of many negative effects on natural environments and on our lives that are caused by human activities. There are other major negative effects as well, most of which have been especially significant in recent years.

### Depletion of the Ozone Layer

Ozone is a form of oxygen that is created in the upper atmosphere. It is a good thing, because it protects us from the harmful ultraviolet rays that are part of solar radiation. It has been depleted, mainly because we have added CFCs to the atmosphere.

### Rainforest Removal

Once seemingly remote, tropical rainforests are now exploited and often even removed, to make way for livestock farming and soybean cultivation. The loss of rainforests means a huge reduction in biodiversity; many scientists believe that rainforests are home to about half of all plant, animal, and insect species. Removal of these forests also means the loss of the natural environments where indigenous peoples live. Not all rainforests are tropical, however. The west coast of Canada has temperate rainforest (and these, too, have been heavily affected by logging).

### Desertification

Desertification refers to the expansion of desert into areas that were previously grassland because of overgrazing of livestock. But desertification can occur elsewhere. For example, the "dustbowl" conditions that afflicted parts of the prairies and the plains farther south in the United States in the 1930s are an example of desertification; these conditions were caused mainly by lack of soil conservation during a natural drought cycle.

**Hydroelectricity** is a very clean source of power, as no fuel is burned. It is renewable and, once the dam itself and the associated buildings are completed, inexpensive. Unfortunately, however, dams on rivers affect river ecosystems, often killing some species of fish. As well, some large dam projects have forced people to relocate.

### Air Pollution

Industrial activities and high concentrations of population in cities are major causes of air pollution. Air pollution is often related to health problems, including lung disease and some cancers.

FIGURE 20.9. Two worlds. Top: the Amazon rainforest near Manaus in Brazil. Bottom: pollution pouring from the chimneys of a coal-powered power plant near Nottingham, in central England.

## Acid Rain

Industrial sulphur dioxide emissions are expelled into the air and then carried hundreds, perhaps thousands, of kilometres by wind. If they mix with moisture in the atmosphere, they may fall to the ground as acid rain. Acid rain causes respiratory problems for humans and does much damage to freshwater lakes, other environments, and even to buildings.

Judging by what we have discussed in this chapter, the future does not look too bright. There are lots of people living in the world, and our numbers are still increasing rapidly. We are always developing new technologies so that we can, for example, remove the forests more quickly. We are striving to satisfy the consumption wants of people in the more-developed world and also trying to improve the lifestyles of the many impoverished people in the less-developed world. We have more people, more and better technologies, and more needs and wants to be satisfied; and all this is occurring on the same small planet with the same mix of natural environments.

There are many reasons for concern. Global warming and other negative human effects are very clearly moving us into unknown territory. We are effectively conducting an experiment— changing the world we live in—without knowing what the result might be. It does not sound very sensible does it?

But, on the other hand, there are reasons for hope. The information in this chapter may dismay you, but it also ought to cheer you, because it shows that we are thinking seriously about what we are doing. We know about the problems we are causing, and we are doing something to solve them. Environmental issues are front and centre in the news, on government agendas, and in many large corporations.

FIGURE 20.10. Hope for the future of the planet is evident from these two photos. Top: garbage and recycling bins in Paris, France. Bottom: young people preparing a Greenpeace banner in Santiago, Chile. Greenpeace is an international organization focusing on environmental issues.

 Select any one of the negative human effects noted on this page and conduct research to understand more about why it is occurring today. Think about our discussion about global warming to help you conduct this research. In particular, remember the three driving forces noted on page 292 and try to decide if these are relevant.

# MAKING SENSE OF THE WORLD TODAY

## Putting It All Together

You have travelled a long way as you have worked with this book, weaving your way around the surface of the earth and journeying through time. Perhaps at the outset you were a little unsure about what it is that human geographers do and why they do what they do. But now you know a lot.

- You know that human geography is a social science concerned with the peoples and places of the world, with the way they are today, the way they were in the past, and, critically, with the way they might be in the future.

- You know that human geography is an especially useful social science because it has close links with the physical sciences, especially physical geography. You might say that human geography begins with the physical earth.

- You know that it is the integration of the human and physical worlds that geographers are interested in.

- You know that human geographers describe peoples and places and can, therefore, provide us with important facts that can help us decide how to take action.

- You know that human geographers try to explain why peoples are the way they are and where they are.

- You know that human geographers provide insights into how to improve places and the lives of people who live in those places.

- You know that human geographers think at both local and global scales, and about the links between the two.

- You know that the world today comprises two very different types of countries: less-developed countries and more-developed countries.

- You know that humans have steadily increased their technological competence, most notably through the domestication of plants and animals beginning about 10 000 years ago and, more recently, through industrial technologies beginning about 250 years ago.

- You know that the number of people in the world increased slowly for thousands of years, then began to increase much more rapidly about 250 years ago, and it might stabilize some time later in this century.

- You know the three driving forces—technology, the number of people, and consumption—that are behind the desire for humans to change the physical world today more than ever before.

You also know that the more you learn, the more questions you will have. In particular, knowing that the human geography of our world is changing all the time, you also want to know how it is changing and what it might be like in the future. There is so much more to know. Human geographies are changing everywhere for five reasons:

1. The many peoples and places of our world are becoming increasingly interconnected.

2. More and more countries are accepting democratic principles and acknowledging human rights.

3. People are continuing to move from rural to urban areas, often placing great stress on the rapidly growing cities.

4. The combination of many people, technological advances, and human wants is placing great stress on natural environments.

5. People in the more-developed world are becoming aware that it is morally necessary to work toward improving the quality of life in the less-developed world.

 Many people are deeply concerned about our world, but they do not necessarily agree about what our global future should or might be. Some people predict blue skies, others see cloudy skies. What do you see ahead? If you were asked to summarize the state of the world today in just one sentence, what would you say? Discuss this in class.

FIGURE C.1. Egyptian man uses a cell phone near the Pyramids of Giza—an example of Westernization.

## Doing Human Geography: Three Projects

### A Country Project

With the help of your teacher, select a country that has not been significantly discussed in this book. Now conduct basic geographic research using the following three steps:

*Step 1*
Write one paragraph on each of the following aspects of the physical geography of the selected country and prepare maps for two of them:

- climate

- landforms (mountains, plains, rivers)

- coastal features, if appropriate

- soils (suitability for agriculture)

- vegetation (forest, grassland, savannah, desert)

- natural resources

- natural tourist attractions

FIGURE C.3. Children orphaned by AIDS collect muddy water from a hole in Zambia.

*Step 2*
Write one paragraph on each of the following aspects of the human geography of the selected country and prepare maps for two of them:

- history

- population distribution and density

- culture (languages, religions)

- agriculture (types, crops, animals)

- urban centres (locations, size)

- industry (links to resources)

- trade

- transportation (roads, rail, river, air)

- tourist industry

(Consider other possible aspects: art, film, literature, famous people. And do not forget to add a bibliography and a title page suitably designed to reflect your country.)

*Step 3*
Prepare a 10 minute oral presentation that summarizes your project. Be ready to present it to the class.

FIGURE C.2. The geographic region of the prairies of Manitoba.

## Toward a More Equal World

It is next to impossible to predict the future. Most attempts are wrong. Still, it is important to attempt predictions, as it helps us to know where we want to go and what we need to do to get there. One thing that we clearly need to do is reduce the inequalities between the more-developed world and the less-developed world. Are we moving in that direction? You be the judge.

*Step 1*

Select one of the following examples of global inequality:

- the distribution of HIV/AIDS
- human development (as measured in chapter 4)
- the availability of sufficient nutritious food

*Step 2*

Check current issues of newspapers and news magazines for information about your selected topic. Find Internet sites hosted by agencies of the United Nations and other reputable groups and search for discussions of your topic.

*Step 3*

Summarize the results of your research under two general headings: blue skies and cloudy skies. Is there a consensus among the members of the class, or are there divergent views? What is your opinion on this topic? Are things getting better, or worse?

## An Environmental Project

As you know, humans are the only species on earth capable of making major changes to natural environments. Unfortunately, many of our actions have negative consequences. Also unfortunately, government and business leaders do not always know how to deal with these issues. We need to engage in critically constructive dialogue, and human geographers can and do play an important role in these

debates. As a beginning geographer, it is now your turn. Select one of the following environmental issues:

- global warming that is caused by humans
- rainforest removal
- loss of biodiversity
- desertification
- ozone depletion
- acid rain
- pollution

*Step 1*

Check current issues of newspapers and news magazines for information about your selected topic.

*Step 2*

Find Internet sites hosted by agencies of the United Nations and other reputable groups and search for discussions of your topic. In particular, look for predictions about whether the issue is becoming more or less significant.

*Step 3*

Summarize the results of your research under two general headings: blue skies and cloudy skies. Is there a consensus among the members of the class, or are there divergent views? What is your opinion on this topic?

**FIGURE C.4. Plundering the rainforest—a commercial logger cuts down a tree in Gabon, Central Africa.**

## Learning from the Past

### Easter Island

Easter Island, or Rapanui, is a place that has inspired much debate and speculation since it was "discovered" by Dutch explorer Jacob Roggeveen in 1722. Most scholars now agree that the original inhabitants came from Polynesia as long ago as 400 CE and developed an organized society that reached its zenith between 1400 and 1600.

What impressed the Dutch when they arrived were the huge stone statues, or *moai*. They were made of rock that was quarried in one area of the island. How did the people manage to move the massive rocks into place? The islanders traditionally believed that the statues walked to the sites. Over the years, wild theories began to surface, and some people still make outlandish claims—for example, that aliens placed the statues, that the island was part of the lost city of Atlantis, or that highly advanced people lived there at one time.

The answer is much more simple, however. When the first settlers arrived on the island, they found a natural environment full of palms, trees, and wildlife. They used the trees to make canoes, spears, and weapons, and, possibly, to move their massive *maoi* by laying them on poles and rolling the poles. They also cleared land for agricultural purposes by the slash-and-burn method. Their population reached its peak around 1500, and the island may have supported up to 10 000 people for a time, but their careless use of natural resources caused environmental change and cultural decline.

As deforestation continued, the soil was less able to support plant life, hold moisture, and withstand erosion. Native animal species became extinct. The people were no longer

FIGURE C.5. Some of the giant stone monoliths, known as *moai*, that dot the coastline of Easter Island.

able to fish at sea because they no longer had the materials to make canoes that could transport them over long distances. The rats that they had inadvertently brought with them on their first voyage ate the seeds and nuts of the trees, and this prevented further germination.

Gradually, the fertile environment became a sandy, grassy wasteland. The people domesticated chickens and rats, which became main sources of food, and eventually the people turned to cannibalism as their society declined into warring clans. People began to live in caves to hide from their enemies. By the time the Europeans landed, the population was only about 2 000 impoverished people, who lived off small sea snails, chickens, and poorly grown crops. Virtually all the native species of birds and animals had been hunted to extinction.

Rapanui was annexed by Chile in 1888, after many of the people had been sold as slaves or had died from diseases brought by Westerners. At the end of the nineteenth century, only 111 original islanders were left.

Early settlers called the island *Te Pito O Te Henua*, "Navel of the World." The history of Easter Island has a lot to teach us. In a relatively short time, an isolated island bursting with life and supporting a vast ecosystem of varied plants and animals was destroyed by a rising population that had little regard for preserving its environment. There was rampant deforestation and careless resource management. An entire people declined and virtually died out, their history and culture now only a source of speculation by archaeologists and scholars. In the same way that many indigenous groups were, and continue to be, environmental leaders who

taught and can still teach us about sustainable living, so there are others who can teach us about what happens when a society does not maintain a healthy environmental balance.

## The Location of Easter Island

FIGURE C.6. Easter Island is in the South Pacific Ocean. It is one of the most isolated locations in the world.

 Some people say we will either learn from the example of Easter Island or follow it. What do you think? Is there any more important question today?

 To learn more about Easter Island and other interesting places in the world, visit <www.theworldtoday.ca> and follow "Links" to <www.mysteriousplaces.com>.

## Hope for the Future

In 2004, the United Nations Children's Conference on the Environment was held in New London, Connecticut. There were 450 children aged between 10 and 13 from 50 countries.

The children at the Conference expressed commitment to:

- respect, support, share, and celebrate indigenous peoples' cultures and knowledge

- not harm any plants or animals, but especially endangered species

- establish or volunteer at a local shelter for animals, either for domestic animals or for endangered species

- raise awareness about the importance of biodiversity

- use our water, energy, and other resources wisely

- collect and re-use rainwater

- educate ourselves and others about the value of water and the problem of pollution

- participate in local stream or coastal clean-ups

- buy and use energy-efficient products and conserve energy whenever possible

- plant trees, native plants, and rare species in our home communities

- eat foods grown without polluting chemicals

- write letters and petitions to our governments and community leaders and compel them to take action

The children challenged world leaders to:

- treat indigenous peoples fairly and respect their rights, including them in decision-making and giving back artifacts that were taken from them

- protect cultures and assist indigenous peoples to conserve their traditions by celebrating festivals and holidays

- stop the appropriation of land from indigenous peoples and look for ways to fairly repay them for their land if it is not possible to give it back

- protect natural biodiversity in their regions and set up nature preserves in sensitive areas

- provide alternative sources of food and employment for the people who currently depend on exploiting endangered species

- treat water as a global resource and share the resource

- enforce laws that stop the dumping of waste into waterways

- educate the public, using the media, school curricula, and any other available methods; remind them to use water, energy, and other resources wisely

- support and invest in agricultural practices that don't use polluting chemicals

- invest in alternative energy sources, making green energy affordable to everyone

- support local environmental groups

How about you? Do you share these commitments, and are you willing to face these challenges?

 Discuss the following topic with a small group and report your opinions to the class: Why I want to study more human geography.

 To learn about the United Nations Children's Conference on the Environment, visit <www.theworldtoday.ca> and follow "Links" to <www.icc04.org/home.html>.

# INDEX

# ILLUSTRATION CREDITS

*The publisher has made every effort to acknowledge all sources of illustrations, photographs, and textual materials that have been used in this book, and would be grateful if any errors or omissions were pointed out so that they may be corrected. The following illustrations are identified by figure number or page reference and, when there are multiple images for one figure number, from left to right, top to bottom, or clockwise from top left. Any figures not listed on this page are courtesy Douglas Fast, cartographer, University of Manitoba.*